THE PROPHETS OF ISRAEL

From Ahijah to Hosea

THE PROPHETS OF ISRAEL

From Ahijah to Hosea

by

H. L. ELLISON, B.A., B.D.

THE PATERNOSTER PRESS

SBN: 85364 088 2
Copyright © 1969 The Paternoster Press

AUSTRALIA:
Emu Book Agencies Pty., Ltd.,
511, Kent Street, Sydney, N.S.W.

CANADA:
Home Evangel Books Ltd.,
25, Hobson Avenue, Toronto, 16

NEW ZEALAND:
G. W. Moore, Ltd.,
3 Campbell Road, P.O. Box 24053
Royal Oak, Auckland, 6

SOUTH AFRICA:
Oxford University Press,
P.O. Box 1141, Thibault House,
Thibault Square, Cape Town

Made and Printed in Great Britain for
The Paternoster Press Paternoster House
3 Mount Radford Crescent Exeter Devon
by Cox & Wyman Limited Fakenham

TO

ALL MY PUPILS

WHO IN THEIR ZEAL FOR LEARNING
ENCOURAGED ME TO CONTINUE
TEACHING AND STUDYING

CONTENTS

LIST OF ABBREVIATIONS

ANET   Pritchard (Ed.), *Ancient Near Eastern Texts.*
AV   Authorized or King James's Versions (1611).
Cam.B.   Cambridge Bible for Schools and Colleges.
Cen.B.   Century Bible (old edit. *c.* 1900).
DOTT   Winton Thomas (Ed.), *Documents from Old Testament Times.*
H.A.T.   *Handbuch zum Alten Testament.*
HDB   Hastings's Dictionary of the Bible – 5 vol. edit.
Heb.   Hebrew.
ICC   International Critical Commentary.
Int.B.   Interpreter's Bible.
JTS   Journal of Theological Studies.
K.A.T.   *Kommentar zum Alten Testament.*
LXX   Septuagint – the standard Greek translation of OT made between 200 and 50 B.C.
mg.   margin.
Moffat   Moffat, *A New Translation of the Bible* (1913–1926).
MT   Massoretic Text – the standard text of Heb. OT.
NBC   The New Bible Commentary (1953).
NBD   The New Bible Dictionary (1962).
NEB   New English Bible – NT only in 1961.
Peake   *Peake's Commentary on the Bible* (new edit. 1962).
Phillips   J. B. Phillips, *Four Prophets* (1963).
RSV   Revised Standard Version (NT 1946, OT 1952).
RV   Revised Version (NT 1881, OT 1885).
Syr.   The Syriac translation of OT, possibly as early as A.D. 200.
T.Com.   Torch Commentaries.
tx.   text.
V.T.   *Vetus Testamentum.*
Vulg.   Jerome's revision of the Old Latin translations of the Bible (A.D. 405).
WC   Westminster Commentaries.
Z.At.W.   *Zeitschrift für die Alttestamentliche Wissenschaft.*

For the rest standard literary abbreviations are used. Names of persons are in italics, when it is their book that is intended, e.g. *Hosea* = the Book of Hosea.

OT dates have been taken mainly from Thiele, *The Mysterious Numbers of the Hebrew Kings*, published by The Paternoster Press. Some may be disputed, but they are approximately correct.

PREFACE

In my teaching experience at Theological and Bible Colleges I soon discovered that it was easy enough to get my pupils through examinations, internal and external, but all too often they did not come to appreciate the prophets as living men. Above all the link of their message with the world of today seemed to be lacking.

Since, in the wisdom of our religious education experts, Amos and Hosea are often regarded as the most suitable introduction to the prophetic literature, I decided I would write on them. It soon became plain, however, that they could not really be made intelligible unless they were taken in their political and religious context. So this book has grown to cover all the recorded prophets whose work was done among the Northern tribes, though the chief emphasis has remained on Amos and Hosea. In the final chapter Jeremiah's prophecies to the broken remnants of Samaria are briefly considered.

Those for whom this book is primarily designed will have access to introductions to the Old Testament books, to histories of Israel, and to Bible dictionaries. I have, therefore, tried to keep such introductory and background information to a minimum. Where I have trodden what will seem to many to be a novel path or to have ignored too many other opinions, I have given references to other literature.

I deeply regret that my MS has been finished before the appearance of the Old Testament part of NEB for I should have been glad to use it. Since I did not want to carry on a continual discussion with RV and RSV, I have translated from the Heb., whenever it suited my purpose. When I came to *Hosea*, I discovered to my chagrin that there were many passages even in RSV which I did not understand as I should – and I had been expecting my pupils to do so! As a result I translated almost all of chs. 4–14 for myself. I must insist that my rendering claims no literary merits like Phillips's, and I should be very sorry if I heard that anyone was reading it in public. I have normally used the simple future, 'I shall, you will', instead of the coloured future, 'I will, you shall', because the latter introduces an emphasis which is not in Heb.

Perhaps the greatest weakness of RSV, so far as the Old Testament is concerned, is that it has no consistent policy with regard to textual emendations. I have gone on the principle that it is better to emend than to produce nonsense, or to force the Heb. to say what it obviously does not.

On the other hand, where the Heb. produces good sense, I have normally turned my back on attractive emendations, even where I have felt that they were probably correct. I owe a great deal to Rudolph's careful discussion of the text in his German commentary on *Hosea* (K.A.T., XIII, 1). Where I accept the same emendations as RSV, I normally leave it to my readers to trust its wisdom. Where I do otherwise, I have given nontechnical notes to show what is involved, but I have never given those who know no Heb. an excuse for showing off.

Much of the material appeared over a number of years in *The Hebrew Christian*, the Quarterly of the International Hebrew Christian Alliance, and most of the final chapter was part of a symposium issued by the same organization on *The New Covenant*.

In a book written over a long period of time it is impossible to iron out all the inconsistencies, and for these I apologize. I have, however, introduced one deliberately. Since I know that most of my readers will use Jehovah rather than Yahweh, I have used the former except in a few cases, where the latter seemed to sound better. I make no apologies for ignoring so much in modern Old Testament studies. Today so much new light has been thrown on the background and the by-ways of the Old Testament that there are few, if any, who would claim to have mastered it all. I have taught the Old Testament because I consider that it is a vital part of God's revelation to men, and that without it the revelation in Jesus the Messiah will not be fully understood. It is this vision I long that my readers should obtain. All that would becloud it, however true and interesting, I have tried to ignore.

H. L. ELLISON

CHAPTER I

HOW THE SPLIT BEGAN

As we read on from the Pentateuch through *Joshua* and *Judges*, we find the normal "children of Israel" increasingly paralleled by "the men of Israel," "Israel" and "all Israel." There seems in most cases to be no indication that any difference of meaning is meant. When we come to *I Samuel*, though the former term is found frequently enough in the Samuel chapters, it is clearly yielding pride of place to "Israel."

Suddenly, without the slightest warning, we find in 11:8 the contrast "children of Israel . . . men of Judah." The contrast, only not so marked, is repeated in 15:4. We finally meet its complete and unmistakable form in 18:16, "But all Israel and Judah loved David." It is not of importance that Judah receives special mention here; after all David was one of its sons. It is striking, however, that Israel should be considered a legitimate contrast to it.

It can only mean that even before David became "king over the house of Judah" (II Sam. 2:4) – note how in II Sam. 2:9 the other tribes can be called "all Israel" – there was a very real division between Judah and the rest of the tribes which seems to have showed itself particularly in matters military. How did this come about?

The serious Bible student has few more difficult tasks in the Old Testament than the reconciliation of Jdg. 1 with the story of the conquest in *Joshua*. It is interesting to note that most conservatives have come round (cf. Prof. F. F. Bruce's treatment of the subject in NBC on Jdg. 1) to recognize that the account of the death of Joshua (Jdg. 2:8 f.) stands in its chronologically correct position. In that case Jdg. 1 is a summary of the failures of the conquest, which were the seeds of the later tragedies of the period of the Judges, tragedies the full magnitude of which we have only recently come to realize. Then, *And it came to pass after the death of Joshua* (Jdg. 1:1) is the old superscription to, or title of the book, and not the beginning of ch. 1.

If this is so, and it is hard to doubt it, we may well, with a high degree of probability, associate the separation of Judah, together with Simeon as voluntary companion, from the other tribes with Achan's sin. Because the average reader of *Joshua* has never grasped how much about the conquest we are not told, he does not appreciate in what detail Achan's sin is brought before us. At the time it evidently shook Israel to the core. Even in the post-exilic genealogies in *Chronicles* the memory lives on, and we have Achan's name given as Achar to link him with the valley of Achor (I Chr. 2:7; Jos. 7:26). Jdg. 1:2 is not the first or the last case in the Bible where God's purpose and the result of human sin intertwine.

It is only in some such way that we can explain why Judah had its boundaries apportioned well before the bulk of the other tribes (cf. Jos. 15:1 with 18:1–3). If it be asked why this should apply to the house of Joseph as well (Jos. 16:1), it may well be that this is the earliest sign of that jealousy that will cross our pages again and again. They may have insisted on having equal rights with Judah, but see also p. 16.

Since we cannot identify either Bezek or Adoni-Bezek (Jdg. 1:4 f.), we are not in a position to get a clear picture of Judah's capture of Jerusalem. Did it sweep over the Jebusite town, destroying and burning, and then pass on, leaving the stunned survivors to come out of the holes where they had hidden to rebuild and refortify? Or was there a last desperate stand in the citadel, after the city had fallen, which the invaders could not be bothered to break? We cannot tell. All we know for certain is that a few years later the Benjamites were unable to dispossess the Jebusites (Jdg. 1:21).

The Jebusite fortress of Jerusalem occupied not merely a position of immense natural strength but one of the highest strategical importance. It effectively controlled the only feasible north-south road through the central hills of Palestine. In addition it sat astride the most important road from east to west linking the fords on the lower Jordan with the coastal plain. It is hardly credible that even nomads who had recently emerged from the wilderness would not have realized the importance of its position. In spite of that, Judah tamely allowed its prize to go back into the hands of its enemy.

I can find no other explanation for this than sheer indifference. Jerusalem belonged to the tribal portion of Benjamin. In addition, if the other tribes liked to remember Achan's troubling of Israel, Judah saw no reason why it should remove a thorn from Israel's flesh.

It would be easy to exaggerate the importance of Jebusite Jerusalem in the period of the Judges. The conquest had isolated it from other Canaanite towns, and there is no evidence that the Jebusites were bad neighbours. We need not doubt, however, that the story in Jdg. 19:10 ff may be looked on as typical. Jerusalem created a frontier, which was intensified in its effects by the nearness of the four-town Gibeonite league. These towns were under Israelite religious and civil control, but they remained a foreign body in Israel right down to the time of David (II Sam. 21:4).

The psychological effect of a frontier is very great, even when it can be crossed without let or hindrance. Bethlehem looked south to Hebron, while Gibeah and Ramah looked north to Shiloh and Shechem. The reality of this frontier is seen in Jdg. 5. Not only was Judah not represented in the victory of Deborah and Barak, but its presence was not even expected.

The effect of the frontier was the more serious because it coincided with a genuine geographical division in the hills. Though experts may quarrel as to where the natural frontier between Judea and Samaria should be drawn, no one who has seen the country has ever failed to remark on the obvious physical differences between the two provinces.

It might have seemed in the days of Samuel and Saul that the frontier was vanishing, even though unconquered Jerusalem stood as a constant reminder of it. Saul's writ ran from Dan to Beersheba, but there are ominous reminders, like the passages already quoted earlier in the chapter, that the old currents still ran strongly beneath the surface.

We know too little of conditions in the land after the defeat and death of Saul to know whether David was justified in accepting the crown of Judah alone (II Sam. 2:4). Little harm need have been done, and the North would probably have quickly accepted the implied invitation of David (II Sam. 2:7b), had it not been for the action of ambitious Abner. He probably hoped to make Esh-baal (cf. I Chr. 8:33; 9:39 with II Sam. 2:8) a stepping stone to the throne for himself. In any case Esh-baal was obviously a weak and ineffective man, possibly physically defective or mentally retarded, and Abner knew that he would be the effective power behind the throne. These dreams came to nothing with Abner's treachery and death and the foul murder of Esh-baal, so the northern tribes had no other resource than to turn to David.

Albrecht Alt has rightly recognized that in the ceremony described in II Sam. 5:1 ff. we do not have the restoration of the unity that was broken by the death of Saul and the events that followed.[1] To David's kingship over Judah was now added his kingship over the North, i.e. Israel. It was a dual monarchy united by having a common king. He soon set up his capital in Jerusalem, which was regarded as the king's private property, belonging to neither Judah nor Israel, because it had been captured by David's retainers ("his men", II Sam. 5:6). To this were then added the vassal states, which David conquered. They are never mentioned as part of Israel-Judah, whose limits still stretched from Dan to Beersheba; they were directly subject to the king. Note also how, even in the time of Isaiah, Jerusalem is constantly distinguished from Judah.

It is in terms of this situation and division that we can understand Absalom's rebellion better, with the North supporting Absalom, and the South remaining neutral – the fact that Absalom had himself crowned in Hebron hides this fact from the superficial reader. Here too we have the explanation of the strange duality in the story of Rehoboam, who as king yet comes to Shechem to be recognized as king. Judah had recognized

[1] *Essays on Old Testament History and Religion*, pp. 216–28.

him as king, but Israel had to do so too. It was one of the many cases where what was looked upon by the one party as little more than a legal fiction was regarded by the other as a living reality.

It is little likely that a man of the type of Rehoboam would have so readily listened to the voice of Shemaiah (1 Ki. 12:21–24), had he not realized that the North had acted within its legal rights. With the exception of II Chr. 13:4–12 there is no evidence anywhere that the Davidic kings regarded Israel as rebels, and even here far more emphasis is laid on the religious side than on the civil. That is why when Judah lay at the mercy of the North in the days of Jehoash (II Ki. 14:8–14) no attempt was made to incorporate it into the northern kingdom. They were sister states enjoying their separate existence in their own right.

This goes far to explain the ambiguous attitude of the prophets to Israel. Normally they regarded it as a state existing in its own right and by the action of God. There is no sign of that subversive action in favour of Judah which Edward Robertson thought he could observe.[1] There is no evidence of hostility to the dynasties of the North, dynasties which had in most cases known prophetic beginnings, except when the prophets conceived that they had stepped over the bounds of the permissible, and so the judgment of God had to be pronounced. On the other hand, they clearly foresaw the time when Israel as such would have to come to an end. Its very name proclaimed that fact.

Israel is the name of the Hebrew people in its relationship to God based on the Sinai covenant. It proclaims the oneness of the tribes in a unity of Jehovah's creation. Though the growing separation of Judah in the time of the Judges may have been mainly Judah's fault, the other tribes had no right to arrogate the name of Israel to themselves, for they were not Israel without Judah. The use of the name was even less justifiable when the North broke away under Jeroboam. They had the legal right to do it, but it was they who had broken away, and their use of the name Israel only underlined that they were not the whole, and that they could only become what they claimed to be by returning to the king who had God's promise of an abiding dynasty. So the prophets looked for the day when Israel would truly be Israel by its reacceptance of the Davidic dynasty, but there never was any pressure on the people to return. The separation was due to Israel's sin – and Judah's also – and union could come only when the sin had been dealt with.

This same principle underlies the prophets' attitude to the worship of the people. Solomon's temple in Jerusalem had taken the place of Shiloh as the visible sign of Israel's unity. With the unity gone, the central sanctuary had largely lost its meaning. It is our misunderstanding of *Deuteronomy* and of the development of the people's religion in practice that makes us think that God wished the worship of the people confined to one place and one

[1] *The Old Testament Problem*, pp. 21–28.

place only. Within the general worship of the people the central sanctuary played a role that no other holy place could. But once sin had destroyed unity, that role had largely vanished. The prophets were concerned not with the negative point that the people did not go to Jerusalem to worship, but with the positive and far more important question of the corruption of the worship that they did bring.

We may look on it in another way, if we wish. Under the monarchy as a whole the priest outweighs the prophet in Judah, but the prophet the priest in Israel. In Judah the people stood in formally correct relationship to God, but needed to be reminded that formality could never take the place of spiritual reality. In Israel the people stood in formal rebellion against God and so they had to submit their ways to God before there could be any question of any formal expression of renewed communion. In the south the stress in the story is on reformation, in the north on repentance and judgment.

CHAPTER II

THE ENVY OF EPHRAIM

EVEN WHEN WE HAVE GIVEN FULL WEIGHT TO THE FACTORS
mentioned in the previous chapter it should be clear that they are
insufficient to explain the lasting division between North and South
in Israel. To them must be added what is called in Isa. 11:13 "the envy of
Ephraim".

However the modern scholar may try to explain it, it is clear that the
Joseph tribes, Manasseh and Ephraim, occupy a position of special privilege
in the story of the conquest of *Joshua*. If we ignore the special case of the
division of Trans-Jordan by Moses, we find that Ephraim and half
Manasseh obtained their inheritance before any other of the tribes (Jos. 16,
17), except for the already mentioned instance of Judah. Moreover, it was
the heart-land of Canaan that became theirs. There is nothing in the census
lists of Num. 1 and 26 to explain such a priority, nor can we attribute it to
Joshua's having been an Ephraimite.

The reason is in fact suggested clearly enough in Scripture. I Chr. 5:1
only makes explicit what is implicit in Gen. 48:5, 15 f., that Jacob made
Joseph, the first-born of his second wife, his official first-born instead of
Reuben, who had forfeited the position by his immorality. This position is
reflected in the special blessing received by Joseph (Gen. 49:22–26).
Manasseh was the inheritor of Joseph's birthright, and this led to the tribe's
double portion of territory, but it soon became apparent that Jacob's
preference for (Ephraim Gen. 48:14) had been prophetic.

It is noteworthy that the first attempts at establishing a monarchy were
based on the Joseph tribes (Jdg. 8:22 f., 9:1 *seq.*). Though Gideon vigor-
ously refused the title of king, it should be clear enough that he enjoyed
virtually royal power and that his sons expected to follow him, cf.
Abimelech's remark (Jdg. 9:2). Gideon was of the tribe of Manasseh, and
it is in his time that we first meet with the "envy" of Ephraim, when they
turned on him for not giving them a sufficiently prominent position in his
campaign against the Midianites (Jdg. 8:1 ff.).

Ephraim's position must have been greatly strengthened by the fact that
the central or amphictyonic[1] sanctuary seems always to have been in their
territory until the capture of the ark and the destruction of Shiloh by the
Philistines, e.g. Shechem (Deut. 11:29, 27:12 f., Jos. 8:30–35, 24:1),
Bethel (Jdg. 20:18, 26 ff.) and Shiloh (I Sam. 1:3, etc.).

[1] Cf. J. Bright: *A History of Israel*, pp. 142–47.

It seems reasonable enough to suppose that a united monarchy would have been impossible except under an Ephraimite king – but would the other tribes have accepted this? The position was changed by two blows that humbled Ephraim for the time being. The former, their bloody defeat by Jephthah, followed a typical piece of insolent pride (Jdg. 12:1-6). The latter is only hinted at in Psa. 78:9, with which should be compared v. 67. It must remain a guess, but it does not seem unreasonable to link this Ephraimite cowardice with the two defeats at Eben-ezer (I Sam. 4:1-11).

As a result of these blows there was no overt Ephraimite opposition to the choice of Saul as king, though there may have been many from this tribe among the "sons of Belial" who refused to accept him at the first (I Sam. 10:27). The recognition of a Benjamite king was the easier because of the relative insignificance of the tribe (I Sam. 9:21), due to its almost complete annihilation earlier in the period of the Judges (Jdg. 20: 30–48). It is hardly pure coincidence that in the list of those who joined David before he became king (I Chr. 12:1-22) some of Manasseh are mentioned but none from Ephraim. There are, however, two in the list of David's mighty men who are probably Ephraimites, Benaiah the Pirathonite and Hiddai of the brooks of Gaash (II Sam. 23:30).

Some of the strongest supporters of Absalom's rebellion were Benjamites, impelled doubtless by other motives than love for David's worthless son. There is no evidence that Ephraimites played any prominent part in it; they were after all equally unconcerned with rivalries in the royal house or with the vain and outmoded hopes of Benjamin. Absalom's near approach to success must, however, have raised hopes in ambitious hearts. The older among them had seen one dynasty fall and now a second had tottered. Who knew? Ephraim's turn to provide a royal dynasty might be very near. So it was that when the time came to "chasten" Solomon and his dynasty "with the rod of men" (II Sam. 7:14) the scourge of God's anger was already prepared.

Already, when we considered the results of Achan's sin, we saw how God could use man's sin for His own purposes. This is shown even more clearly in the story of the birth of the Northern Kingdom. The naïve reader of *1 Kings* merely sees a man of God's choice swept into power by a spontaneous popular revolt. In fact, God's choice of the rod of His anger, like His choice of the Assyrian some centuries later (cf. Isa. 10:5-15), was the expression of His judgment on the instrument as well. Ephraim had never accepted God's act, which was later expressed by Asaph in the words:

Moreover He rejected the tent of Joseph,
and chose not the tribe of Ephraim;
but chose the tribe of Judah,
Mount Zion, which He loves. (Psa. 78:67 f.)

So God could use Ephraim, because Ephraim wanted to be used, but in His very choice the doom of Ephraim was implicit.

What a contrast there is between Ahijah the Shilonite's announcement to Jeroboam (I Ki. 11:29–39) and the anointing of David, or even of Saul. Jeroboam came from a family of no standing in Ephraim and was brought up in poverty by his widowed mother. He sacrificed his independence to become a royal retainer. In this service he proved himself so efficient ("the man Jeroboam was very able", RSV), that he was made an assistant of the hated Adoram and was put in charge of the forced labour of Ephraim and Manasseh.

One day when he was outside Jerusalem in his city finery he was met by Ahijah, a prophet who lived in the village that had grown up on the site of ruined Shiloh. He took him aside to a quiet spot and then suddenly snatched off his fine new mantle. Before Jeroboam had time to protest, he had torn it into twelve pieces, ten of which he ceremoniously handed back, telling him that even so God would rend the kingdom from his master and give him ten of the tribes. (The usual interpretation is that it was Ahijah's mantle that was torn, but the Hebrew permits and even suits the picture just given.)

There is nothing in all this to suggest that we are dealing with a man after God's own heart, and for that matter there is no anointing to express the Divine favour. The violence of the symbolism looked forward to the violence to come. Though God remains no man's debtor, and to His instrument there is due reward (I Ki. 11:37), yet in the following "if" there is far more the note of impending doom than a promise of blessing – note there is no such conditional promise at the anointing of Saul or David.

There was no waiting in faith for a man like Jeroboam. *Solomon sought therefore to kill Jeroboam* (I Ki. 11:40) – it is only in the luxuriant fancy of eastern legend that the birds of the air bring Solomon news of all that is happening! In the grim reality of a despotic reign he trusted to the much less romantic method of spies. There had been no one hidden behind the nearest thorn bush when Ahijah spoke to Jeroboam, but *he lifted up his hand against the king* (I Ki. 11:27). One version of the LXX actually gives us details of Jeroboam's revolt, but they are so incredible that we may dismiss the story as mere fancy. We need not read more into the words than that he started plotting, but a royal spy who had managed to join the conspirators will have carried his master word, and Jeroboam had to fly to Egypt for his life.

That exiled Jeroboam stayed in close touch with his Ephraimite friends is certain. He could never have reached Shechem in time, if he had been dependent on the ordinary sources of news, for such ceremonies were seldom long delayed.

As the representatives of Israel gathered, we can imagine the Ephraimite plotters passing the word around, "Let us ask for a reduction in taxation."

It is quite clear that the vast majority had no idea that they were being drawn into a plot against the monarchy. "Down with taxation!" was one thing, "Down with Rehoboam!" was quite another.

Under normal circumstances Rehoboam would doubtless have graciously slashed the taxes and reimposed them a year or two later. But Jeroboam had been recognized in the committee of grievances. The king and his younger councillors feared that the conspiracy had gone much farther than it really had and thought that the request for lower taxes was merely the thin end of the wedge. They maintained that the only possible policy in the face of this danger was a strong hand. The older men who still remembered Absalom's rebellion and David's wise withdrawal to Trans-Jordan counselled moderation, but this was not to the liking of Rehoboam, who had been born and bred in the purple.

So the fateful decision was taken. To all but a handful of the people Rehoboam's harsh answer must have come as an incredible shock. Indeed it may well have been only Jeroboam, with his personal knowledge of the pride and insolence of Solomon's court, who had anticipated it. As the king ceased his bluster a moment of indecision followed. Neither side had asked "What next?" Both sides had probably assumed there could be only one answer. Suddenly through the indecision and the murmuring cut a voice – an Ephraimite one? – to be taken up by man after man and tribe after tribe, *To your tents, O Israel*. In itself this meant no more than "Let's go home", but the last time it had rung out it had heralded Sheba's rebellion (II Sam. 20:1).

With a little understanding and yieldingness Rehoboam might still have saved his throne in the North, for the people had done no more than refuse to settle the formalities of recognition then and there. But as in his blazing anger he looked round his high officers of state his eye fell on the one who, more than any other, epitomized his father's autocracy and exactions, against which the people had protested.

"Adoram, round them up!" Adoram, or Adoniram (I Ki. 4:6), was the worst hated man in Israel. As a young man towards the end of David's reign he had been placed in charge of the forced labour (II Sam. 20:24), a position he had held throughout the reign of Solomon. Now, still strong and upright, though his hair was greying, and surrounded by his body-guard, armed to the teeth and with whips in their girdles as symbols of their office, he sallied out to see what the terror of his name would do. Amid the murmurs of hatred a stone suddenly struck him in the face – was it thrown by one of the plotters? Nothing more was needed. Before the king's incredulous eyes the master of the levy and his myrmidons disappeared under a hail of stones. His nerve cracked and he bolted for his chariot and made all haste for Jerusalem.

The representatives of Israel, who had intended no more than an orderly protest against high taxation and too much forced labour, now suddenly found themselves in open and unplanned revolt. We can easily understand why they unanimously hailed Jeroboam as their king, when he was presented to them by the exulting plotters of Ephraim.

It was one matter to seize the throne, another to hold it. But while Jeroboam desperately gathered whatever forces were available to him there came the incredible news that Rehoboam had tamely disbanded his army at the command of the prophet Shemaiah. It was now abundantly clear that it had not been the skill of the plotters but the working of the Divine will that had given Jeroboam the throne. Men of no faith are wont to tell us that if God were to do so and so, they would believe and trust. Jeroboam is only one of many examples which show us that no amount of Divine intervention will move a man to trust in God, if the will is lacking.

Jeroboam felt most insecure. He had no need to fear aggression from Judah, for Rehoboam had by his obedience to Shemaiah recognized the legal existence of the Northern Kingdom. But he feared the pull of Jerusalem, and he knew that he was a nobody compared with the members of the Davidic dynasty. Moreover, the force that had made him king could also hurl him from his throne.

In the thinking of the time a king was the representative of the gods, the head of religious as well as of civil affairs. Indeed, in Egypt the pharaoh was a god. The term "divine king" is commonly used to express the unique standing of these ancient kings. In Israel, however, the king had been denied the standing of high priest and indeed of prophet too. Both Saul (I Sam. 9:16, 10:1) and David (II Sam. 5:2) had been appointed *nagid*, which, whatever the English term we use to translate it, means the military and civil leader of the people. Similarly the term *nagid* is used, when God's judgment is pronounced on Jeroboam (I Ki. 14:7). Jeroboam, however, decided to strengthen his position by claiming powers denied him by God.

The writer to the Hebrews states as something self-evident, when writing about the high priesthood (5:4), he says, "One does not take the honour upon himself but he is called of God, just as Aaron was." As is made clear in Deut. 33:8 ff. the priest was far more than a sacrificer; he was also an expounder of God's will, and as such had to be appointed by God. When Jeroboam *made priests from among all the people, which were not of the sons of Levi* (I Ki. 12:31), it was equivalent to a claim that God had given him the authority to represent Him, and the same applies, of course, to his other religious changes.[1]

There is no need to doubt Albright's contention,[2] based on archaeological evidence, that Jeroboam's golden bulls (calves is a mistranslation) were not intended to represent Jehovah Himself, but rather the throne on

[1] Cf. NBC, p. 335b.
[2] *From the Stone Age to Christianity*, pp. 228ff.

which He stood. Certainly there was no thought that they represented any other god. But whereas in the Levitical economy Jehovah was conceived of as sitting enthroned upon the cherubim, heavenly beings, there in Bethel and Dan He was brought down to the level of the earthly. Doubtless Jeroboam was influenced by an appeal to Aaron's example before the details of the Levitical system had been promulgated in Israel. But since Aaron had not yet been consecrated as high priest, he possessed no authority at the time.

The same type of motive will have led to the choice of Bethel and Dan as his chief sanctuaries. Dan had been served by a priesthood that claimed descent from Moses (Jdg. 18:30, RV, RSV). On the other hand, Bethel awoke memories older than Moses himself. So Jeroboam tried to bolster his throne by every means that ingenuity could suggest.

Posterity, however, knows him as Jeroboam the son of Nebat, who made Israel to sin. As he went to the grave, his dynasty under the doom of God (I Ki. 14:7-16), he left his people with defiled sanctuaries, an invalid priesthood (in the developing story the northern priests are only mentioned incidentally) and a debased conception of their God, which was to show itself in a growing moral decline throughout the country.

Ephraim did not even find its dreams fulfilled. Baasha, who swept away the dynasty of Jeroboam, was of the tribe of Issachar. We are not told the tribal origin of Omri or Jehu, but we have no grounds for assuming they were Ephraimites. In addition, even under Jeroboam, the capital was soon moved from Shechem in Ephraimite territory to Penuel in Trans-Jordan, then to Tirzah in Manasseh, and from there again to Samaria within the same tribal boundaries.

CHAPTER III

JUDGMENT IN BETHEL

IF JEROBOAM BEN NEBAT LIVES ON FOR US AS THE MAN "WHO made Israel to sin," this is more than a mere condemnation of his sin. There are acts in the life of the individual, church or nation which are by their very nature irreversible. Such a one was Jeroboam's religious policy. He wrote it, as it were, into the basic constitution of Israel, and it was never really feasible for his successors to change it. For them to have done so would have meant the calling of the existence of the state in question. God, therefore, did not leave him without a warning – a call to repentance it hardly was, for things had gone too far for that – which was an implicit prophecy of the fall of the Northern Kingdom and all its ways.

That God used for this purpose an unnamed "man of God" from Judah (I Ki. 13:1) is no implicit condemnation either of Ahijah or of any other prophet who may have been living in Israel. Indeed the fact that Jeroboam was later to send his wife in disguise to Ahijah (I Ki. 14:2) strongly suggests that the old prophet had already given the king clear indications of how God viewed his policy. The argument from silence is seldom more dangerous than when applied to Scripture. The reason for the use of an "outsider" should be clear enough.

More often than we are apt to realize, the prophets, as they faced angry kings, carried their lives in their hands. It was not till the time of Elijah that the prophet acquired a certain immunity. It needed a miracle to preserve the one who challenged Jeroboam in the first flush of his "divine kingship" and in his royal sanctuary (cf. Amos 7:13). Since the message was purely one of judgment, God called on one who lived outside Jeroboam's jurisdiction and who would therefore need miraculous protection for as short a time as possible. The miraculous in Scripture occupies a far more restrained place than many care to realize. The completely apocryphal story of Rabba and Rabbi Zira (*Megillah* 7b) has in spite of its wild fantasy a true Biblical balance about it. The two rabbis celebrated Purim together, and the former became so drunk that he killed his companion. The next morning Rabba prayed for mercy and restored R. Zira to life. When Rabba invited him to share his next Purim feast, R. Zira declined, saying, "Miracles do not happen every day!" Even so God does not normally order a course of events that would involve continued miracle.

The story in I Ki. 13 has obviously been edited, probably by the compiler of the book, for the mention of Samaria (v. 32), which was not founded until the time of Omri (I Ki. 16:24), must be an adaptation of the prophet's words to later terminology, a practice we find more often in the Old Testament than is normally suspected. Since the men of Bethel recognized the fulfilment of the prophecy (II Ki. 23:17) but showed no recognition of the name, it seems likely that "Josiah by name" (v. 2) is also an editorial addition pointing forward to the fulfilment.

Jeroboam in his pride considered that he was inaugurating a new era, which he had marked by moving the New Year's festival (all evidence points to Tabernacles being so used at the time in Israel) a month later (I Ki. 12:32). Amid all the feeble pomp that could be mustered – how small compared with Solomon's Jerusalem! – he was preparing in all his glory as priest-king to offer up the inaugural burnt offering (this, and not incense, is the meaning of 13:1) when the man of God from Judah pushed his way through the startled attendants.

Denunciation of the proceedings was unnecessary; he merely foretold the coming of the house of David into its right again, and the abolition of all Jeroboam's religious arrangements. So far from his being, as he dreamt, the inaugurator of even greater glory than Solomon's, he was a mere parenthesis used by God for the chastisement of the true kings. Even the conditional promise of blessing (11:38) was now by implication annulled. Since we do not know whether the altar was made of unhewn stones or whether it was a casing of bronze filled for much of its height with earth, we cannot form a certain picture of how it was rent. But as the bold words rang out and the altar in reply collapsed in ruins at Jeroboam's feet, in blazing fury he pointed with outstretched hand and arm at the prophet: "Arrest him!"

Arrest, condemnation and execution would have followed hard on one another's heels had not the shocked king realized with horror that he could not lower his outstretched arm; it was paralysed. Doubtless Jeroboam, like so many of his kind before and after him, would have dismissed the rent altar with a shrug of his shoulders – mere coincidence. But the crippling touch of God's finger reduced him for a moment to abject humility. He, the "divine king", craved the prayers of the stranger from Judah, and when he was cured he was prepared to treat him as a most honoured guest.

The refusal to accept hospitality was blunt and categorical. No promises had been asked for before he prayed for the king, for he knew that they would be forgotten as soon as the memory of the fright had passed. He had been sent not to call Jeroboam to repentance, but to pronounce doom. The land was under God's sentence, accursed and unclean, and so he could not eat or drink while he was within its borders. He was even to return another way, lest those who had seen him passing towards Bethel should seek to detain him and offer him hospitality on his homeward way.

It is a common failing of ministers of the Word that though they believe it they do not take it seriously. This seems to have been the case with our prophet. He had demonstrated the impurity of Israel in the clearest possible way, but as soon as he had placed a hill between him and Bethel, instead of hurrying as fast as possible towards the frontier, he sat down under a terebinth to rest and think, and maybe to regret the festival meal and the reward he had had to forgo. If any think this a harsh judgment, let them bear in mind that it was only about six miles from Bethel to the frontier of Judah.

As he sat in the shade, an old man on a plump donkey came trotting along the road from Bethel. He stopped and called out, "Are you the man of God from Judah?" "Yes." The old man got off his donkey and hurried to him. "I am so glad I caught you in time. Please come home with me to Bethel and have a meal with me." The younger man apologetically declined, repeating the reasons he had already given Jeroboam.

"Ah!" said the old man. "That's all right. I am a prophet just as you are and an angel of God told me to go after you and bring you home for a meal."

The younger man gratefully accepted the new turn of events and went back with the old man. As they sat over a frugal meal – for the old prophet was not keeping Jeroboam's newfangled feast – the spirit of prophecy fell on the host and he pronounced doom on his guest for his disobedience. The meal ended in silence. Conscience-stricken, the old prophet hastened his guest on his way, even lending him his precious donkey to bring him the quicker over the boundary of Israel.

He was too late, and a few hours later wayfarers were filling the ears of Bethel with the news of a lion and a donkey standing guard over the dead body of a stranger on the road to Jerusalem. Sadly the old man went to collect the body of his guest, whom he had so shamefully deceived, and buried it in his own grave, where by his express command he was later himself buried. Bethel, profoundly shaken by the day's happenings, stored them up in its collective memory and waited for the fulfilment, which did not come until three centuries had rolled by.

Many find it hard to accept such a story. Quite apart from the miraculous element, they are revolted by the old man's ending his days in peace, while the man he had deceived was so suddenly cut off. Could this be the justice of God?

There is little point in asking why the old prophet of Bethel acted as he did. Whether his motives were good or bad, serious or trivial, the day of judgment will reveal. He stands for so many who base themselves on past service or reputation, but who have become enslaved by and conformed to the world around them. He was doubtless convinced that he was doing the right thing, but our convictions must never be allowed to displace God's commands.

For the man of God from Judah there is neither excuse nor extenuation. The very order to return by another road had been in implied warning. Had the old man lived in some village near the frontier of Judah we might be justified in finding some excuse for the younger man. But to go back to Bethel, to push through the crowd of holidaymakers thronging the gate, to set the place talking, "He's back!" He knew that he was not merely a voice, but also an example. He should have known that, while God wished the sinner to change, He would not change either His character or His message.

It is hard to believe that Jeroboam would have renounced his policy, of which he was doubtless very proud, and have placed his trust in God. So much is certain, however; when an excited courtier whispered into his ear that the prophet had returned and was having a meal at the old man's house, his heart told him that the warning he had heard was not to be taken too seriously. Not even the prophet's fate, stern, inexorable and not to be misunderstood, could re-establish the awe of that New Year's morning.

We need find no difficulty in the miraculous. In the Bible it is almost invariably found in moments of crisis, when the fate of the nation was at stake. Such a moment was Jeroboam's remodelling of religion to suit his purposes. The lion and donkey standing watch over the dead man were needed lest any should say with a shrug of his shoulders, "How dangerous the roads have become since Solomon's death," and dismiss the whole matter as an accident.

Israel had made its bed, and in it it had to sleep. The only prophetic message for the North in the next half-century, which has come down to us, is one of doom. Ahijah the Shilonite foretold that the sun of Jeroboam's dynasty would set in blood (I Ki. 14:16). When Baasha ben Ahijah for his own ends made himself God's executioner, in due course the word of doom came to his house too through Jehu ben Hanani (I Ki. 16:2-4).

Elah, Baasha's drunken son, duly fell at the hand of Zimri, a nobody, who had succeeded in becoming a successful chariot officer. Whether it was Zimri's lowly birth or the circumstances of the murder that revolted the people we do not know, but he was quickly eliminated. After only seven days on the throne he perished amid the flames of Jeroboam's palace, which he had set on fire above his head to serve as his funeral pyre.

For four years Israel devoured itself as two commoners, Omri and Tibni, faced one another in civil war, until the former triumphed. Israel had rejected a king by the grace of God, so now they had to know kingship by the grace of the sword, which rapidly swept them towards disaster, political and moral.

CHAPTER IV

THE TWILIGHT OF PROPHECY

THE PROPHET WAS GOD'S MOUTH, GOD'S SPOKESMAN (EX. 7:1 f., 4:15 f.). For as long as he was functioning in this way he was obviously outside human control; men had the right to question his claims to be a prophet (cf. Deut. 18:21 f.), but once this was granted they disobeyed his words at their peril (Deut. 18:19). It needs no stressing here that such an office would always be unwelcome to vested religious interests, to all who held their position by right of birth or the favour of the mighty and not because of their real spirituality.

We find this phenomenon in the early Church. There is today considerable controversy as to when the gifts of the Spirit dealt with in I Cor. 12–14 were withdrawn by God, if indeed they ever were. Personally I have little doubt that they began to become rare as soon as the elders of the local churches, which so rapidly became organized and stabilized, started imposing regulations on the prophets. We see a beginning of this in the *Didache*, now dated by most about the end of the first century. In the second century Montanist reaction to these regulations the error was made, as has since so often been the case, of laying more stress on how the alleged prophet spoke and less on what he said. The fact that the true prophet may on occasion be lost in an ecstasy is no proof that every ecstatic utterance is necessarily prophetic, or even of God.

Much the same happened in the Old Testament. In Samuel Israel had not merely the greatest of the Judges, but also the greatest prophet since Moses. In fact, he was the first and only man after Moses – until He whom they both prefigured came – to combine the offices of priest, prophet and king, for except that their office was not hereditary the Judges were essentially kings.[1] The people turned their back on God's raising up of leaders as occasion demanded in favour of the apparently stable régime of a man-controlled kingship.

Saul showed the new spirit in his effort to proclaim himself master of both priests (I Sam. 13:8–14) and prophets (I Sam. 15:3, 20–23), and his efforts lost him his throne.[2] It is hardly chance that Samuel had no real successor; Gad and Nathan are mere shadowy figures compared with him, and in the pomp of Solomon's court there was little room for the prophet. It is quite consistent with this that the twofold divine oracle of

[1] For more details see my *The Centrality of the Messianic Idea for the Old Testament*, pp. 15–18.
[2] Ibid, pp. 9–13.

blessing (I Ki. 3:5–15; 9:1–9) came in dreams and not through a prophet. We cannot be sure about the oracle of doom in I Ki. 11:9–13, but on the whole there seems no need to assume an unnamed prophet as its bearer.

We are not told how Zadok came to stand beside Abiathar in the high priesthood; the reference in I Chr. 12:28 might just possibly suggest that a political bargain was involved. It is more probable that David recognized that he was the legitimate high priest, for Abiathar was descended from Eli, who was of the house of Ithamar, and not of Eleazar and Phineas. Samaritan tradition may well be true that Eli had been able to obtain the office by sharp practice.[1]

Solomon's dismissal of Abiathar (I Ki. 2:26 f.), however, was a clear indication that he considered that the priesthood was under his control. Quite consistently with this, throughout the period of the Judean monarchy, we find religious initiative for good or evil in the hands of the king, while the priests merely obeyed his commands. The story of Uzziah (II Chr. 26 : 16–21) shows that it was the royal control of the priests and not usurpation of their functions that was normally involved.

It could hardly be expected that prophecy would flourish under these circumstances. The prophet was under royal control as the priest was. Jer. 29:25 ff. can only mean that in Jeremiah's day prophets were considered to be under the high priest's jurisdiction and so indirectly under the king's. It seems probable that this had been the case in Judah all along. Down to the time of Elijah prophets seem to play little part in its history. Asa's treatment of Hanani (II Chr. 16:10) suggests that he little expected any such interference from a prophet.

In the North the priests were a royal creation, and full well the people knew it. If we may lay any stress on Scripture's silence about the northern priesthood and on the Samaritans' later willingness to accept an Aaronic priesthood from Jerusalem (Josephus, *Ant.* XI, viii, 2), we may infer that Jeroboam's priests received little respect from either people or king. An outstanding weakness from the latter's standpoint was their lack of oracular power due to their non-possession of the Urim and Thummin.

Under these conditions the prophet became more important than the priest in Israel, but by virtue of this very fact he became more debased than in Judah.

Probably from the first there had been prophets attached to the local sanctuaries. After all, the worshipper was apt to come with problems that were not covered by the existent revelation known to the priest. With the inrush of Canaanite customs under the Judges we may take the sanctuary prophet for granted.

However genuine his prophetic call and gifts, any man who held such a position was exposed to the gravest temptation. The priest could rely on a

[1] Cf. Robertson: *The Old Testament Problem*, pp. 176 f.

fairly constant income; the prophet's payment would depend largely on his "delivering the goods" (cf. Amos 7:12). In addition the priest in charge of a sanctuary would normally look with no favourable eye on the un-popular prophet, who diminished his income by causing some of the worshippers to go elsewhere. The natural tendency would be for the prophet to phrase the genuine oracle so as to make it as attractive as possible, and even to follow the voice of reason, when the voice of God was silent.

Royal patronage proved disastrous. By the time of Ahab we find those crowds of prophets we are familiar with from Babylonian and Assyrian sources, and which were doubtless normal in Phoenicia, if we may judge by Jezebel's Baal prophets (I Ki. 18:19), whether they were a home product or imported from Tyre. If Elijah's attitude is any guide (I Ki. 19: 10, 14), the prophets saved by Obadiah (I Ki. 18:4) were distinguishable from those we later find round Ahab (I Ki. 22:6) only by their unwilling-ness to compromise with Baal worship. It may indeed be that after Elijah's victory on Carmel they simply slipped back into the positions they had formerly held in Northern sanctuaries.

For those who functioned under such conditions the prophetic office will often have been a question of birth or training ("the sons of the pro-phets"). The "divine oracle" was more and more sought by means sug-gestive of magic and divination, until Jehoshaphat, looking on Ahab's prophets with horror, asked, *Is there not here another prophet of Jehovah of whom we may inquire?* (I Ki. 22:7). Over two centuries later Jeremiah was to sum up the whole tragedy of these debased prophets in the words, *And the prophets prophesied by Baal* (Jer. 2:8).

Tragically enough, these sanctuary prophets obviously carried convic-tion with their hearers. Ahab can greet Elijah with the words "You troubler of Israel" and "Have you found me, O mine enemy?" Speaking of Micaiah ben Imlah (I Ki. 22:8, 18) he casts doubt on the genuineness of his prophetic claim by using the form *yitnabba'* (hithpael) instead of the more usual *yinnabe'* (niphal). For him it was self-evident that through his sanctuary prophets he heard the indubitable voice of Jehovah. As we shall see, not all these prophets were corrupt and deceivers, but they had tied the will of Jehovah to what they considered the best national interests of the country.

CHAPTER V

ELIJAH

THE SUDDEN APPEARANCE OF ELIJAH BEFORE AHAB (I Ki. 17: 1 marks the beginning of a new chapter in God's dealings with Israel.[1] Prophecy could never be quite the same again. One small incident underlines this. When Elijah stopped Ahaziah's messengers as they went to inquire of Baal-zebub in Ekron, and returned them with a message of doom, the king had no difficulty in identifying him from the description, "a man with a garment of hair" (II Ki. 1:8, RV mg., RSV, Moffatt, etc.) and a leather girdle. This, the dress of the average poor peasant, could not have served for identification unless it was strikingly different from that worn by the sanctuary prophets. Yet in the twilight of Old Testament prophecy after the Babylonian exile we find that the garment of hair had become an indispensable badge of the prophet (Zech. 13:4).

It is doubtless just because he was the initiator of something new and better that Elijah appears in Mal. 4:5 as the precursor of the day of Jehovah. Similarly, on the Mount of Transfiguration he is present as the representative of the canonical prophets with Moses, by whom the law came.

He came from Tishbeh in Gilead (I Ki. 17:1, LXX, Josephus, RSV), a small place not far from Jabesh-gilead among the hills of Trans-Jordan. We may infer from his dress that he was a poor tiller of the ground or more probably a shepherd, which would explain his knowledge of the secure retreat in the torrent valley of the Cherith, safe from the eyes of Ahab's spies. The fact that his father's name is not mentioned shows that he came from a family of no standing. Somehow during his humble toil the Spirit of God awakened in him a vision of the absolute demands of Jehovah, those demands that are mirrored in the Decalogue and the other apodeictic laws of the Pentateuch, laws which consist of bare demand or prohibition and know nothing of a perhaps or peradventure.

Ahab never consciously forsook the worship of Jehovah. This is best seen in the fact that all his children whose names we know, even the notorious Athaliah, bear the Divine name in one combination or another. His marriage had been purely a matter of international politics. Even his

---

[1] The essential truth of this statement is not influenced by the possibility that ch. 21 comes before ch. 17 chronologically.

father, the great Omri, had had the worst of his struggles with Damascus
(I Ki. 20:34) and needed allies. Then too Assyria under Shalmaneser III was
pressing south. It would not be long before Ahab would share in the desperate drawn battle at Qarqar (853 B.C.) against him, and in 841 B.C. Jehu
would pay him tribute. It seemed obvious to him that his Phoenician wife
Jezebel would continue her worship of the Tyrian Baal (cf. I Ki. 11:4-8);
if like Solomon, he would sometimes graciously be present himself, that
was surely a mere matter of courtesy, which only a fanatic could object to.

There is no evidence that Jehovah worshippers as such were persecuted
during his reign. The prophets of Jehovah whom Jezebel cut off were
doubtless in royal eyes fanatics who threatened the stability of the state by
criticizing the royal religious policy. There may have been even some
excuse for her. It is certainly noteworthy that her doom was pronounced
in connection with the murder of Naboth (I Ki. 21:23, II Ki. 9:36 f.) and
not because of her persecution of the prophets.

The real evil was that ever since the time of Jeroboam ben Nebat most
in the North had been thinking of Jehovah as a god not strikingly dis-
similar to Baal. So it seemed quite natural to them that Jehovah and Baal
should "gang up" against a common enemy, the gods of Assyria. Since
Jehovah had done this, for this was how most understood the alliance
between Israel and Phoenicia, He would obviously expect respect to be
shown to His ally.

Elijah was not interested in abstract questions about the existence of
Baal, or even in royal marriages; he was perhaps the least political of all the
prophets, and was concerned solely to demonstrate the absolute power of
Jehovah. As the excavations at Ugarit have shown us, Baal was above all
the god of the winter rains. But let Jezebel, her priests and prophets howl
to Baal as they would, there would be no rain in Israel, no, not even dew,
until *Jehovah* gave it, and He would announce its giving beforehand
through His servant Elijah, lest any should give the glory to others. There
is no suggestion that the famine was punishment, though punishment it
was at the same time; it was above all an undeniable proof of Jehovah's
power and Baal's impotence precisely in that realm which was considered
Baal's speciality.

He allowed the lesson to sink in thoroughly. Three winters passed without rain and three summers without harvest (I Ki. 18:1).[1] We can easily
imagine how the worshippers, prophets and priests of Baal were reduced
to despair. Only then did God tell him to come out of hiding and tell
Ahab that Jehovah would have mercy on a land that must have been near
its last gasp.

It was not enough, however, to give rain in the name of Jehovah. The
war had to be carried into the enemy's camp. This Elijah did by challeng-

---

[1] Elijah will have given his message just before the autumn rains were due, so the three year
and six months of Jas. 5:17 includes the previous summer.

ing Baal on his own ground. Not only was the seaward end of Carmel claimed by Phoenicia, but it was considered especially sacred to Baal. Here on Baal's own ground he was challenged to send his lightning flashes from heaven, for his worshippers looked on him as the controller of the thunderstorm. How successful Elijah was in his purpose may be seen by translating the cry of the people literally, "Jehovah, He is the Mighty One; Jehovah, He is the Mighty One!" (I Ki. 18:39).

In passing it may be mentioned that the traditional site of Elijah's sacrifice, however attractive it is to the visitor, lies too far inland, too clearly in Israelite territory, to suit the story. We must surely look for it much nearer the seaward end of Carmel, and this in turn will remove the problem of how Elijah could have wasted the water, for it could have been drawn from the sea. Then the altar will not have been broken down by apostate Israelites, but by Phoenician worshippers of Baal. The killing of Baal's prophets on the other hand suggests that most were apostate Israelites.

The story ends with Elijah racing through the plain of Esdraelon in front of Ahab's chariot supported by a power greater than his own. In part we are to see the victor in the context honouring his humbled king by assuming the slave's role of forerunner. To most who saw him, however, he will have been the herald of Jehovah's triumph, as the rainstorm swept along in his wake.

ELIJAH AND NABOTH

Modern man is apt to protest too much about Naboth. Today there would have been a compulsory purchase order and out Naboth would have been flung. Israel had not invented the perpetration of injustice by due processes of law.

Ahab was a man of whims. He pictured his winter palace at Jezreel neatly rounded off by a vegetable garden at the point where Naboth's vineyard jutted into it. That a vineyard would be little suited to his purpose hardly crossed his mind. Naboth was doubtless an old curmudgeon, who loved to stand on his rights. It is very hard to believe that in Israel at that time the laws of Lev. 25 were applied and that his objections were seriously religious. There can be no doubt that Ahab was honest in his offer, but Naboth, obviously quite a big man in Jezreel (cf. I Ki. 21:9), liked to show that he was as good a man as the king.

All would doubtless have been well, had not Jezebel been one of those – they are always with us – who maintain that at a time of crisis we cannot afford to weaken the executive power, and so the rights of the individual must always take second place. Obviously to a woman like Jezebel it mattered not at all whether her husband was kept busy and happy laying out a vegetable garden; it was the principle of the thing she was concerned with.

Equally it was the principle that Elijah was concerned with. The king, who had the responsibility of maintaining God's law, had wantonly allowed it to be flouted, and so the whole weight of the broken law would fall on him. He had involved Naboth's family in his fate (II Ki. 9:26) and so his own family would be involved in his fate. Repentance might post-. pone the vengeance of the broken law (I Ki. 21:29) but it could not deflect it.

By his two interventions Elijah established that the prophet stood above all earthly power. Neither the expediency of religious policy nor of social injustice could bind him. It did not matter what precedents the authorities might appeal to, or how much state religion through priest or prophet might support them; the man who could say "Thus saith the Lord" stood above them all.

ELIJAH AT SINAI

There are few scenes in the Bible that have received more conflicting interpretations than Elijah's sudden flight (I Ki. 19:3); suggestions of over-tiredness and loss of nerve are particularly common. The clue is surely given by Jezebel's boasting, defiant words, *So let the gods do to me, and more also, if I do not make your life as the life of one of them by to morrow about this time* (I Ki. 19:2). If in fact she really hoped to kill Elijah, she would hardly have put him on his guard, and it is difficult to think that Elijah, with his keen instinct for the heart of a matter, would not have realized this. We should rather see in her words a defiant challenge to Elijah, her claim that she had not been defeated after all. The sequel suggests that Elijah suddenly realized that she was correct, that his victory was a merely external matter that had not touched the heart of the people.

This has been excellently put by Stanley Frost:

> Then came Jezebel's message, and all Elijah's elation oozed away through the gaping hole she had made in his self-esteem. How right she was! How easily she could turn the mob against him! Naboth – the prophets of Baal – himself the next victim.[1]

So Elijah went off to Sinai, where God's covenant with Israel had been made at the first. On the way there the thought invaded his heart that the struggle was no longer worth while (I Ki. 19:4), but the provision of heaven-sent food showed him that his first impulse had been correct. At Horeb twice over he accused Israel of complete failure (note RV and modern renderings of Rom. 11:2), thereby suggesting that the original covenant had been not worth while.

God's rejection of storm, earthquake and fire as media of revelation in favour of "a sound of a light whisper" was an implied rebuke of much in Elijah's methods. But it was a rebuke of the exaggerated in them, and God

[1] *Patriarchs and Prophets*, p. 146.

immediately accepted the accusation against Israel as fundamentally co-
rect. He revealed to His prophet that he had been an instrument of judgment and that the judgment was to continue at the hands of Hazael, Jehu
and Elisha until a mere remnant of 7,000 would be left (I Ki. 19:18 – the
mistranslation in the AV seriously obscures the meaning). For the sense in
which Elisha fulfilled this prophecy see p. 45.

When we read this in the light of Isa. 6:9–13, we realize that Elijah
stood at the same point in Israel's history as Isaiah in Judah's. I Ki. 19:18 is
as much a foretelling of the end of the Northern kingdom as Isa. 6:9–13 is
of Judah. It is true that over 140 years were to elapse before the judgment
went into full effect, but an exactly similar time lies between the divine
doom spoken to Isaiah and the destruction of Solomon's temple.

If we grasp the inner significance of Elijah at Sinai we shall understand
the work of his followers better. They strove not so much to save the state
as to increase the size of the remnant, for there are probably few who will
regard the 7,000 as anything other than a symbolic number.

We must not anticipate our conclusions before we study Hosea's
message, but if he is to be understood in the light of the doom spoken at
Horeb, it may well be that the view that the remnant of Israel was taken up
into Judah and found its fulfilment there is not as foolish as many would
claim.

I have never been impressed by the view that the command to anoint
Hazael, Jehu and Elisha was the expression of God's disapproval of
Elijah's flight from Jezebel, and that thereby his prophetic work was as
good as terminated. He had a considerable period of activity still before
him, and there is absolutely nothing in the story of his departure to justify
such a conclusion. For Elijah to anoint those who were to carry on his
work, whether he did it personally or by proxy, is rather to stress with
what authority they would act, when they brought judgment and destruction on Israel.

ELIJAH AND AHAZIAH

The least attractive of the Elijah stories is that contained in II Ki. 1. To us
it seems altogether unreasonable that two captains and their companies of
fifty should be liquidated simply because they were trying to do their
duty. If, however, we cease to look at it from our standpoint and see it in
the light of Biblical statements, we shall realize that we are dealing with
one of the most important incidents in the history of Biblical prophets. Of
all his legacies to the future this was perhaps Elijah's most important.

T. H. Robinson wrote:[1]

To the ordinary government official their message was nothing short of high
treason. Indeed, it is quite clear that they must have been under some special
protection, or their lives would not have been worth a moment's purchase.

[1] *Prophecy and the Prophets in Ancient Israel*, p. 45.

The ecstasy made it obvious that the speaker was justified in claiming the authority of Yahweh Himself, and therefore he must not be injured. It is noteworthy that in the whole of the Old Testament there is only one instance of the execution of a prophet. That is the case of Uriah, put to death by Jehoiakim.

This is a more scholarly way of putting the opinion often met, that since prophets behaved like mad men they were given the protection and toleration that the Near East has always afforded the mad. But what are the facts?

We find that Samuel went to anoint David in fear of his life (I Sam. 16:2). Nathan's parable (II Sam. 12:1-6) suggests that his task was not without risk to himself. Jeroboam was prepared to do violence to the prophet from Judah (I Ki. 13:4). Asa put Hanani in prison (2 Chr. 16:10), as did Ahab Micaiah (I Ki. 22:27). In addition not only did Ahab allow Jezebel to kill many of the prophets of Jehovah, but his international search for Elijah (I Ki. 18:10) could have meant nothing less than his intention to kill him (cf. also I Ki. 19:2). All this hardly adds up to the picture suggested by Dr. Robinson.

Ahab, though he was a weak man, was not without his better traits. Once Elijah had been able to impress his authority on him, Ahab respected him, even though he hated him. But Ahaziah seems to have inherited all the weaknesses without any of the virtues of his father. Though the doom on his house was working itself out, he would show his disregard for Jehovah by consulting Baal and by executing Elijah. The fifty men were not intended to be a guard of honour! It was an open declaration of hostilities, and Elijah treated it as such.

He had plenty of time to disappear, but instead he took his place on a hilltop, where Ahaziah's men were bound to find him. It was like master like man. The first two captains were too lazy to climb the hill to arrest him, but their insolence fairly oozes out of the words they use. Elijah's answer, "If I be a man of God, let fire come down from heaven . . ." stresses that their words had shown that they had given him the title only in mockery, but they were now to experience its reality.

The fire from heaven burnt itself into the inner consciousness of Israel. From now until the long shadows of coming night fell across Jerusalem the person of Jehovah's prophet was to be inviolate.

ELIJAH'S ASCENSION

It lies outside the purpose and scope of this book to discuss the theological implications of Elijah's removal from the human scene. As with Moses, there was no grave and no corpse for men to reverence or to wreak their vengeance on. It is usual to state that Elijah was taken up into heaven in a chariot of fire, but in fact we are told that it was a whirlwind that carried him up. The chariots of fire (so RV, mg. correctly) and horses of fire were rather the outward sign and guarantee of God's care and protection over

His servant, whom He was now taking away. No more need be implied than that the whirlwind carried him off, no man knowing where, to be buried by the hand of God (cf. II Ki. 2:16).

The parallels between Moses and Elijah are too many to be accidental. From Elijah's dress we may infer that both had been shepherds. Both had spoken with God on the mount of the covenant. If Moses lived from God's gift of the manna, Elijah knew the miracle of the ravens and of the widow's meal-barrel that did not run out. If Moses stood before Pharoah and challenged the gods of Egypt, Elijah stood before Ahab and challenged the gods of the Canaanites. Both showed their control over nature in different ways; if Moses crossed the Red Sea dryshod, Elijah crossed the Jordan. Neither left a last resting place on earth for men to make pilgrimage to. We started our study of Elijah with the realization that he marked the beginning of a new chapter in prophecy. As we continued we found that in fact he marked the beginning of a new and vital chapter in Israel's history, the chapter of the remnant. When he returned to Horeb he implicitly wrote *finis* to the chapter that had been begun there by Moses.

It was the failure of the scribes and rabbis to understand the role of Elijah, a failure that involved an inadequate comprehension of the later prophetic message, that prevented their grasping the limited role of the Torah. By making the revelation at Sinai the be all and end all of God's revelation they made themselves incapable of recognizing the full and final revelation when He came.

CHAPTER VI

SONS OF THE PROPHETS AND OTHERS

ELIJAH GIVES US THE IMPRESSION OF BEING PERHAPS THE most individualistic and solitary of the prophets, though the mention of his attendant in I Ki. 18:43; 19:3 – the Hebrew *na'ar* is too indefinite to justify the rendering "servant," and it is not clear whether we are dealing with a young man who had attached himself to him or with a slave – should warn us against jumping to conclusions. For all that, we find Elijah towards the end of his life linked in some undefined way with the sons of the prophets (II Ki. 2:3–7). Their immediate and humble acceptance of Elisha as his successor (II Ki. 2:15) seems to prevent us taking their relationship to Elijah merely as one of respect.

The term "sons of the prophets" is known to us only from the Elijah and Elisha stories and from Amos' slighting remark (7:14, mg. of RV, RSV). Provided we do not assume an unbroken connection over the centuries, it is a reasonable suggestion that they correspond to the prophetic groups associated with Samuel (I Sam. 10:5, 10; 19:20–24), but this is incapable of proof. There is very little to be said for the suggestion that they were founded by Elijah himself. We are all too familiar with the rapid decline of godly institutions when the founder's influence is removed, but if the sons of the prophets had really been the embodiment of Elijah's and Elisha's teaching, it is hardly likely that Amos would have so disdainfully disclaimed any relationship with them. After all, it was little more than a generation from Elisha's death under Jehoash to Amos' appearance under Jeroboam II.

The probability is that the term is not explained because its meaning was obvious in the age in which the Scriptures were written. Archæology has made us familiar with "guilds" of prophets attached to the great sanctuaries of Mesopotamia. We gain the impression that physical perfection was demanded of them, and that they were specially trained for their task, especially in the production of an ecstatic state, and that they conformed to traditional models and rituals. We have already seen something analogous in Jezebel's Baal prophets and Ahab's four hundred "prophets of Jehovah" (I Ki. 22:6 f.). While there is no certain evidence for them in Judah, and it is illegitimate to assume their existence there merely by analogy, there can be no reasonable doubt that there were "guilds of prophets" attached to the main sanctuaries in Israel and that their members were trained for their task.

This is not to say that in the popular mind a son of the prophets and a prophet were synonymous terms. It is hard to believe that when Amos turned on the threatening figure of Amaziah, the high priest of Bethel (7:14–17), he was not speaking in prose, even if his indignation had made it rhythmic. In other words, for him "prophet" and "son of the prophets" were two different things, not alternative designations for the same office as might have been the case had he been speaking in poetry. This is borne out too by Hebrew idiom. The commonest metaphorical use of "son" (*ben*) is possessing in some degree the attributes of the "father". They were sons of the prophets because they were learning the externals of prophecy and were able to show something of the spirit of prophecy. As Pedersen says:

> In order to be one of the prophets one must normally become a member of their societies. . . . It is possible that some few individuals might receive the spirit and see visions without associating themselves with others. . . . But everything . . . would seem to indicate that the prophet belonged to or had issued from a society in which he was taught the prophetic experience as an art . . .[1]

To some extent the term was probably used because so many of the members of these "guilds" will have been literally prophets' sons. Once it is believed that the irresistible might of the Spirit can be led into the orthodox channels of man's making it becomes natural to regard the prophetic office as hereditary, even as the priestly office was. It may have been as a protest against this natural supposition that we do not find God using the sons of the great prophets to follow their fathers – the one case mentioned is Hanani (II Chr. 16:7) and Jehu (II Chr. 19:2).

It need hardly be argued that Elijah was not a "graduate" of one of these prophetic societies. To me it seems obvious that he would have considered it absurd, if it had been suggested that he could pass on the power that had made him a prophet of the Most High through ecstatic exercises and other traditional rites and rituals. It is no coincidence that his successor, Elisha of Abel-meholah, was a prosperous farmer and not one of the sons of the prophets.

To me then the most probable explanation of the relationship between Elijah and the prophetic "guilds" is that some of them, sincere even if misguided men, were so won over by his witness that they placed themselves under his control. Elijah did not belong to that type, so common in certain circles of Anglo-Saxon Protestantism, which thinks the very fact that some custom of institution has had a long history is the best reason for abolishing it. When we come to study the work of Elisha we shall have grounds for thinking that he used the sons of the prophets not for training up prophets but for moulding the remnant that God had spoken of at Horeb. If that is

[1] *Israel III–IV*, p. 108.

so, it is only reasonable to think that the policy started with Elijah. He will
have gladly accepted the chance of turning these zealous men from make-
believe prophets into true servants of Jehovah.

It must be insisted that only a minority will have acted in this way. This
is sufficient to explain Amos's depreciatory attitude. The majority will
have gone on in their old futile ways, while the minority will soon have
dropped a name that no longer had any real applicability to them.

AHAB AND THE SONS OF THE PROPHETS

Whatever the power that may be operative in it, if a false religion is to
endure, it must have some effectiveness. This power may come from a
shrewd use of human nature by its leaders, or from a tapping of occult or
even demonic influences, or in some cases even from God's pity towards
those who are in darkness. Similarly the prophetic "guilds" must have
shown some fruit to have continued. We have only a few detailed
examples of their work. In I Ki. 22:22 Micaiah ben Imlah claims that their
wrongness in that particular case was due to the deliberate act of God, not
to their inherent ignorance and impotence. The great canonical prophets
condemned them more for the general trend of their prophecies and less
for their failure to answer the questions put to them.

In I Ki. 20:35–43 we have a most interesting oracle given by one of the
sons of the prophets to Ahab. It must not be assumed that he belonged to
one of the groups that had accepted Elijah's authority, for no such suggestion is made.

The setting of this chapter is probably not long before the battle of
Qarqar in 853 B.C. between a West-Semitic league, in which Ben-hadad
and Ahab were leaders, and Assyria under Shalmaneser III. It may very
well be that the Syrian king tried to use the forces he was collecting to
make a vassal of Israel and so bring it into the anti-Assyrian league, even
as Damascus and Samaria tried to force Jerusalem in the time of Ahaz (II
Ki. 16:5). The grace of God was still operative, for the judgments
announced to Elijah at Horeb had still to run their course. God does not
outlaw a nation; if He pronounces doom, He also names the executioner,
and no one else can carry out His work for Him. So twice over (vv. 13,
28) Ahab was saved by prophetic intervention.

The magnitude of the second victory faced Ahab with a serious problem
(vv. 30–34). He could wreak his vengeance on his defeated and humiliated
enemy, and it is evident that this is what Ben-hadad expected, for he
would doubtless have done so had he had the chance. But Ben-hadad dead
would not mean Syria captured, and, even if it did, Syria was a welcome
barrier between Israel and the Assyrian steam-roller coming steadily
southwards. So once again expediency triumphed and Ben-hadad was
treated as an honoured royal brother. Was this perhaps the reason also for
Jehoash's half-heartedness in carrying out dying Elisha's command (II Ki.

13:14–19)?

As so often in Israel, there were zealots who were scandalized that the Lord's enemies should have escaped. One of the sons of the prophets subjected himself to a symbolic wounding (vv. 35–37), the meaning of which is passed over in silence by most commentators. The only meaning that suggests itself to me is that he wished to stress the inescapable force of God's commands, even when they seemed to be without reasonable motive. With a headband (v. 38, RV) or bandage over his forehead he waited by the roadside for the king. This served two purposes; it suggested that he had been wounded in the battle – there is no suggestion that the wound received from his friend was in the head – and it hid the mark which his "guild", at any rate, wore on their foreheads (cf. v. 41). Just as Nathan did with David, he used an imaginary incident to win the king's attention and then to turn it against him.

How far was he really God's spokesman? He claimed that God had put Ben-hadad in *cherem*, in the ban, had devoted him to destruction (v. 42), as He had the Canaanites and Agag, king of Amalek. Quite remarkably, however, there is not a word suggesting it in the earlier part of the story. Ahab would have had no grounds for thinking that this was God's will unless he had been expressly told so. God is not as arbitrary as the prophet was trying to suggest.

There is an interesting factor in the history here which seems to support this conclusion. It is universally agreed that chs. 20 and 22 are closely linked, and it is widely believed that ch. 21 is in fact chronologically out of place and that it should come after ch. 19. (This seems a more probable place than before ch. 17). If there has been a transposition, as I consider probable, this will have been deliberately done by the compiler of *Kings* for a special purpose.

Such by no means infrequent chronological transpositions have a spiritual significance. Here it ensures that the doom spoken by the unnamed son of the prophets should stand as near as possible to Jehovah's own outline of the future as given to Elijah at Horeb. In this setting how far the son of the prophets is from grasping the purposes of his God!

It is precisely here that we find the deepest weakness of the popular prophets. Many of them were honest men with a deep zeal for Jehovah; they were willing, if necessary to suffer martyrdom at the hands of Jezebel rather than give up their convictions. But they could not abandon the belief that God was bound to and by His people. What seemed best for Israel had to be God's will. This became so marked that finally Jeremiah (23:16–22) could show the difference between the popular prophet and the true one by saying that while the former prophesied peace, i.e. prosperity, the latter prophesied judgment.

There are those who will object to this on two grounds, first that we are given the story without adverse comment in Scripture, and second that the lion was surely proof enough of his bona fides. More often than we perhaps realize the Bible leaves it to the Spirit-led reader to infer the Divine judgment. As regards the second point, one of the most difficult of the lessons the great prophets had to bring home to the people was that the reality of a prophet's call had to be judged by his message and not by his miracles.

MICAIAH BEN IMLAH

The story of Ahab's death introduces us to perhaps the most unexpected of the minor prophetic figures of the North, viz. Micaiah ben Imlah of Samaria (I Ki. 22). He was well known to Ahab, who hated him because in his prophesying he had only messages which ran counter to the king's wishes. At the same time there is no suggestion that his attitude was bringing him into any particular difficulty.

Our first impulse is to ask how Elijah could have ignored his existence when he complained to God at Horeb, that he alone was left of the Lord's prophets (I Ki. 19:10, 14). The difficulty would not be entirely removed by assuming that Micaiah was a young man, who had only recently begun to prophesy, a supposition that has little to commend it on other grounds.

When Elijah returned from his hiding-place in Zarephath to speak to Ahab, Obadiah, the God-fearing controller of the royal household, took for granted that he would know how he had rescued a hundred of the prophets from Jezebel's vengeance (I Ki. 18:4). Seeing that he had a wholesome fear of Ahab's anger (v. 14), he was not likely to have flaunted his act in public, for he knew that Jezebel would not have forgiven him. In other words, he took for granted that Elijah had a close knowledge of what was going on in the world of the prophets. For all that there was no mention of this rescued hundred (surely there will have been others as well, when Elijah voiced his complaint at Horeb. It seems clear enough that while a dead sanctuary prophet might be for Elijah a martyr, he had little time for live ones.

We think lightly in terms of black and white, right and wrong, good and bad, but life is seldom as simple as that. We have already seen that those whom we, but not the Old Testament, call "false prophets" were not uniformly bad or deceivers. The Bible can give us only general spiritual principles to guide us in judging the validity of an individual's message and his claim to be a prophet (cf. especially Deut. 13:1-5; 18:17-22, Jer. 23:9-32, Ezek. 13:1-16). It did remain true, however, that the very professionalism of the sanctuary prophets' position acted as a constant downward drag, which reformers could check but not eradicate. Elijah must have been very conscious of representing an entirely different concept of prophecy, and he will have been indifferent to the small proportion of Ahab's sanctuary prophets who may really have given the Divine message without adapting it to a greater or less degree to their royal patron's wishes. He knew that they held out no lasting hope for the future spiritual welfare of his people.

So Obadiah's hundred meant little to him, and that included Micaiah ben Imlah as well. Whether or not he belonged to this hundred, there can be little doubt that he belonged to their class – he had a known domicile and he could be called on for an oracle whenever one was needed. I do not doubt that he was the greatest and most loyal of his class at the time, but he left neither disciples nor successors. The spiritual future of prophecy lay with those who were freed from all bonds of professionalism and human control.

Micaiah's isolated position between Ahab's prophets and Elijah seems early to have been felt as a problem. There can be little doubt that the end of I Ki. 22:28 "And he said, 'Hear, you peoples, all of you'," is a scribal addition from Micah 1:2 made with the intention of identifying Micaiah with the Judean prophet of the same name, who lived over a century later.[1] The half verse is lacking in the pre-hexeplaric MSS of the LXX, i.e. in those dating from before Origen's "correction" of the LXX on the basis of the Hebrew in the years A.D. 230–240. The use of the singular in AV hides the incongruity of the words in their context.

We are not told what motivated Jehoshaphat's question, *Is there not here another prophet of the* LORD *of whom we may inquire?*" (v. 7). He was not denying that the four hundred were prophets of Jehovah, but he was suspicious, perhaps because of their enthusiastically wholehearted unanimity. After all, Zedekiah ben Chenaanah's iron horns (v. 11), however crude and rough and ready, suggested a certain degree of premeditation.

It was doubtless Micaiah's tone of voice that told Ahab that his apparent agreement with his colleagues was not to be taken seriously (v. 16). The real oracle was greeted by Ahab with a mixture of scorn and superstitious fear. On the one hand he shrugged it off as "I told you so" to Jehoshaphat (v. 18), on the other he thought it wise to try and bamboozle God by disguising himself. He thought that God would not recognize him in his officer's armour – a private would not have served in a chariot – and so could not guide his fate to him.

Micaiah's vision has all too often been the derision of the liberal and the puzzle of the conservative. Yet it is merely one more expression of the fundamental riddle behind true monotheism – true monotheism, that is, and not merely thinly veiled dualism. We find it in the hardening of Pharaoh's heart (Ex. 4:21) and of Judah's too (Isa. 6:9 f.), in the evil spirit from God that troubled Saul (I Sam. 16:14), in Satan's moving of David to a census (I Chr. 21:1, cf. II Sam. 24:1), and in God's challenge to Satan over Job (Job 1:8; 2:3). We see it in God's giving up of idolaters to their lusts and passions (Rom. 1:24, 26, 28) and in His claim to be behind all

---

[1] Micah is only an abbreviated form of Micaiah, cf. Jer. 26:18, RV; RSV should not have obscured this fact.

(Isa. 45:6 f.). We hear its climax in the words on the cross, "Eloi, Eloi, lama sabachthani?" (Mk. 15:34). We are standing before that same mystery of God which lies behind predestination as well. We seem to think that we can in part hide our ignorance by boggling at the vigour of Micaiah's presentation of the mystery. With all our refinements we shall either take refuge in dualism or say the same as Micaiah, only in an obscured way. The simple fact remains that those who had repeatedly preferred the promptings of their own psychic powers – "The prophets prophesied by Baal" (Jer. 2:8) – to the leading of the Holy Spirit, and who had almost always placed the favour of the king before that of their God now reaped the harvest of their deceit by being deceived. As for Ahab, since he had willed to live by the flattering answer and had hated those that did not give it, he was to be led to his death by the flattering answer.

We are not told when Zedekiah fled from chamber to chamber (v. 25, RV, mg.) in a desperate bid to save his life, but it will probably have been during those grim years when Israel reeled beneath Syrian blows, as told us so graphically in the Elisha stories. Of Micaiah's fate we know nothing, but with Ahaziah on the throne and Jezebel, as queen mother, the power behind it, we may well imagine that he never left the prison alive.

We are told no more of the sanctuary prophets in the North. Indeed the fiasco of Ahab's death must have discredited them almost as badly as the fall of Jerusalem did those in the South. But they pass into silence gilded by the glory of their greatest representative, who reveals what they might have been had they been willing to be used completely by God.

true proportions. In just under forty years Israel, which had seemed to reach almost Solomonic glory under Jeroboam II (II Ki. 14:25, 28), collapsed into nothingness, like the wooden house whose vitals have been devoured by termites. We have some analogy in the quarter of a century that followed Josiah's death, and also in the last agonized years of Jerusalem before A.D. 70, but in both these cases the catastrophe was less unexpected, and its results were less complete. It is quite insufficient to appeal to the political and military genius of Tiglath-pileser III for an explanation of this collapse. The capture of Samaria in 723 B.C. marked not merely the end of a state but also the virtual end of a society. Whenever this has happened in human history, external pressure and violence have been merely the means of revealing desperate inner corruption.

A study of his activity makes it clear that Elisha turned from the people as a whole and devoted himself mainly to those who had whole-heartedly accepted Elijah's message – some evidence for this will be suggested later. Elijah's link with the sons of the prophets suggests that he himself began this activity, once God's judgment had been pronounced on the people at Horeb. It is a purely academic question why this task had to be passed on to Elisha and could not be carried out by Elijah himself. There is no need to give heed to those who love to run down great men and who see the cause in Elijah's flight to Horeb – age, temperament, upbringing all suggest themselves as possible and preferable reasons. The vital point is that whenever true religion is rejected by society as a whole, when it has to turn inward to little groups and to go underground, then the deadliest corruption begins at the roots of a nation's life. It was not the social depravity of the Neronian period but the deliberate rejection of Christianity by the Flavian and Antonine emperors that sealed the fate of imperial Rome. The conversion of Constantine came too late to undo the damage. Wherever national nerve has failed, where corruption has reigned both high and low, where the horrors of the Inquisition, of Nazism or Communism have ruled, we can easily establish that such a rejection of true religion has first taken place.

It was in this sense that Elisha was to slay those who had been spared by foreign enemy and dynastic upheaval. By being the human embodiment of God's turning from the people as a whole, he was the most effective instrument of judgment on them. We find a very close parallel in Isaiah's life. Once his message had been rejected by the court (Isa. 7:1–17) and the people (Isa. 8:1–8), he turned to his disciples (Isa. 8:16–18), thus preparing the way for the judgment that God had already pronounced (Isa. 6:11–13).

GRACE AND JUDGMENT

The average modern commentary on *Kings* or introduction to the Old Testament is apt to regard the Elisha stories as a collection of popular tales about prophets that crystallized around the name of Elisha, or even as sheer fiction. Quite apart from the failure of these theories to explain why the name of Elisha should have exercised such an attraction for stories, whether traditional or completely fictitious, they normally overlook that they have often an appositeness in Elisha's life that they could not have had elsewhere. This is strikingly seen in the first two stories told of him after Elijah's removal.

Recent excavations have shown that Jericho is the oldest permanent human settlement of which remains have so far been discovered.[1] This is due partly to its position near the fords of the lower Jordan, but even more to its excellent water supply in a water-starved area (the "ditch" in which the Jordan flows here makes it of little value in this respect). Though the old city *tell*, i.e. artificial mound created by city after city being built on the same site, had remained probably unoccupied and certainly unfortified from the time of Joshua till that of Ahab, until Hiel of Bethel defied the curse laid on the site to his own undoing (I Ki. 16:34), there is ample evidence that the oasis round the spring will have remained an important centre of population. It seems that just about this time the spring became contaminated. The language of the people certainly suggests that their plight was a recent one (II Ki. 2:19). The nature of the contamination is hidden from us, and its effects are far from clear. It was bitter, and apparently it caused miscarriages – "the land" (II Ki. 2:19) may very well refer to its inhabitants. In any case, the people could hardly fail to interpret it as meaning that Joshua's curse on the site had not been exhausted with the doom that fell on Hiel's family. In fact the contamination was probably Divinely brought about for that very purpose.

The healing of the spring was clearly miraculous. Had the salt been thrown in by anyone else it would certainly have been ineffective, while the newness or otherwise of the cruise or bowl could have had no influence on the result. This is a clear invitation to us to interpret the means used by Elisha symbolically. The newness of the cruse was to be contrasted with the age-old curse on Jericho, while the salt spoke of preservative power in the midst of putrefaction.

It was true that Elisha was the instrument by whom the curse of God was to be brought on the land, but for all that he was offering to all, even to a Jericho which had been under a curse for centuries, a new beginning. None were of necessity excluded from the remnant which God was beginning to form for Himself. Then there was the guarantee that in the growing putrefaction of the people God would be able to preserve His remnant uncontaminated. In the midst of a people for whom symbolism was a commonplace, it is hard to believe that the message was not understood by some.

The reverse side of Elisha's work is seen in the story of the lads of Bethel. Few incidents in the Old Testament have been more scoffed at and

[1] Cf. K. Kenyon: *Archaeology in the Holy Land*, pp. 39–42.

objected to, but this is due partly to mistranslation, partly to superficial reading.

The Hebrew offers no justification for translating *ne'arim qetannim* as "little children". *Na'ar* is one of those words which have, thanks to changing social circumstances, no exact equivalent in English. Apparently it was first used of retainers dependent on a lord; it was then extended to those who by age or status were dependants in the home. A study of the available evidence suggests that it was not used of the child, in contrast to the adolescent, except where previous reference or the context made its meaning absolutely clear. This is borne out by the few uses of *na'ar qatan*, or *qaton*.

Even if we made full allowance for oriental hyperbole, Solomon was not "a little child" (I Ki. 3:7), when he came to the throne, for he was already a father (cf. I Ki. 14:21). The story in I Ki. 11:17 does not really justify the traditional interpretation. In Isa 11:6 a lad old enough to drive animals to pasture seems to be intended, while in I Sam. 20:35 the translators realized that "a little child" was impossible. Even in II Ki. 5:14 we may well pause; the mighty Syrian warrior with a child's flesh would be a trifle incongruous! In fact "young lad" seems to be the most appropriate translation of *na'ar qatan* wherever it is found, and it is so translated in the RV margin to II Ki. 2:23. That the boys were young is clear enough from v. 24, where they are called "children" (*yeladim*). If we think of them as between ten and twelve, we shall probably not be far out.

The boys came from Bethel. This was the city that saw the beginnings of Jeroboam's corrupt worship and cherished the memory of the prophecy of coming doom upon it. It was the seat of a royal sanctuary and of a group of the sons of the prophets that once followed Elijah and now Elisha. From it had gone out the insolent challenge to God, when Hiel went down into the Jordan valley to rebuild Jericho. Bethel was one of those focal centres where the two conceptions of Israel's religion clashed most fiercely. The mockery of the boys was not the expression of the idleness and wantonness of youth, but of their parents' fierce rejection of all that Elijah had stood for.

Baldness is rare in the east, and so, many have thought that the prophets had some form of tonsure. Even if this were so, and it is unprovable, those who would so explain the story have yet to prove that Elisha was walking bare-headed. It is far more likely that "bald head" was a rude and lewd insult. But Elisha was to "go up" – Moffatt's "walk up" seems to be based on a failure to note all the details. They were telling him to follow his former master Elijah!

There is also a small point that is often overlooked. Elisha had to turn round to see them. He had not run up against a gang of youngsters looking for a bit of fun; they had probably been lurking behind a wall waiting for him and jumping out when he had passed. In v. 23 Hebrew grammar allows us to translate "there had come forth".

As the details of the story have been added one to another, we have obtained the picture of a large gang of young adolescents, who are expressing their parents' feelings of hatred and contempt, and who may well have been acting with their full knowledge and approbation. From v. 25 we gather that Elisha was making a formal round of the groups of the sons of the prophets who had accepted the leadership of Elijah. The story of the miracle at Jericho will not have taken long to reach Bethel, and the excitement of the sons of the prophets will have been enough to let the citizens know that their new head was expected. *Go up, thou bald head!* was Bethel's greeting for Elijah's successor, and his rejection brought inevitable judgment with it.

The modern man, even if he accepts the validity of this argument, remains unhappy. If God is to punish, the punishment should fall on those who were really guilty. We may well ask ourselves, however, whether it would have been all that mercy on God's part to spare the young mockers so that they might grow into the hardened sinners to whom we are introduced in *Amos* and *Hosea*. Quite apart from that, however, the Old Testament (and the New as well) repeatedly shows us the sins of the fathers being visited upon their children. In addition, God always deals with men as man is best able to understand His dealings. For the men of Elisha's day it was natural that since the people of Bethel had used their boys to challenge Jehovah and Jehovah's prophet, Jehovah should answer their challenge through the very boys who had expressed it.

So we see Elisha stepping into the limelight simultaneously the prophet of grace and hope and of judgment and doom.

ELISHA'S MIRACLES

Our exposition so far in this chapter has aimed at showing Elisha in a position where the work of the Exodus is being undone. Instead of God's people being redeemed from captivity they were being handed over to judgment and captivity, that a remnant for His name might be gathered out. It is entirely in accord with the Biblical revelation of God that this new period of Divine activity should be ushered in by a new outbreak of miracles, as was the case at the Exodus and the setting up of the Church. It will be seen that the stories told about Elisha are entirely consistent with this explanation. No attempt seems to have been made in *II Kings* to arrange them chronologically, and they are only partly grouped by subject matter. I have discussed their chronology in NBC, but here the Biblical order is followed, except where there is some definite gain in leaving it.

No direct indication is given in II Ki. 3 why Elisha was present with the army of Israel in its joint attack on Moab, but we are given a strong hint by which it can be inferred. Quite apart from the date (3:1, 6), it is clear that we are in the early years of Elisha's activity, for to the court he had as yet no independent status as a prophet (3:11). His complete indifference to the plight of Israel's army (3:14) shows that it was no concern for his country that had brought him along. Though he may at first have been ignorant of the reason why the Lord had sent him, it is clear that he was there to give instructions how Moab was to be treated. The barbarity of his orders (3:19) has always been a stumbling-block to his admirers. Strangely enough, the almost certain explanation is given to us in the only historical document to come down to us from Moab, viz. Mesha's inscription, commonly known as the Moabite stone. In it he tells with deep satisfaction how he had been able to cast off the yoke of Israelite rule, and how

> I fought against the town [Ataroth] and took it and slew all the people of the town as satiation (intoxication) for Chemosh and Moab. And I brought back from there Arel its chieftain, dragging him before Chemosh in Kerioth. . . . And Chemosh said to me, "Go, take Nebo from Israel!" So I . . . fought against it . . . slaying all, seven thousand men, boys, women, girls and maid-servants, for I had devoted them to destruction for (the god) Ashtari-Chemosh.[1]

The three kings were merely concerned with re-establishing Israelite rule over a rebellious vassal, but Jehovah had designated them as His executioners.

It is not easy to interpret 3:15 with certainty. The English versions (including RSV, but not Moffatt) tacitly assume a small scribal error in the Hebrew text. As they translate, this is a description of what happened on this occasion. There is no difficulty in seeing Elisha needing the calming influence of music after his stormy confrontation of Jehoram. As it stands the difficult Hebrew can only mean that Elisha habitually had recourse to a musician when he wished to prophesy. In the absence of any other evidence to this effect, the rendering of the English versions must be regarded as very probable.

The thought of the remnant is not far to seek in the story of the widow and the oil (4:1–7) and also in that of the borrowed axe-head (6:1–7). These are not just fairy-tales, miraculous stories of God's providing through His prophet. In both cases those whose need was met were among those who had joined the small groups around Elisha. These were not indiscriminate acts of charity, but were done for the sorely tried loyal remnant. The method by which the need was met is beyond our understanding, but in each case it was based on means already to hand. Repeatedly God's "little flock" of loyal ones has found God meeting their needs by means which were in the truest sense miraculous, but which so issued from the circumstances around them, that the heedless and hostile mob that saw them were hardly aware that anything out of the ordinary had happened. We should note too, that God's way of answering the need

[1] ANET p. 330b, also DOTT pp. 196 f.

C

was a wordless rebuke to those whose lack of faith had led to the borrow-ing of money or tools.

At first sight there would seem to be no more in the story of the Shunamite (4:8-37, 8:1-6) than quite understandable gratitude on the part of Elisha, but the moment we look at it more closely we find there are some obvious question marks in it. Why did Elisha advise the Shunamite to leave her home (8:1)? If any in eastern Esdraelon could have survived the famine, surely it was this rich woman. Then again, why was her property confiscated during her absence (8:3)?[1] The story of Naomi and Ruth shows how absence abroad did not break a claim to ownership of land.

A careful study of the story suggests very strongly that the earlier part is to be dated in the reign of Jehoram. Shunem lies on the slopes of Little Hermon at the east end of Esdraelon, only a few miles across the plain from Jezreel, where Jehoram had his winter palace. It is altogether reasonable to suppose that a leading citizen of Shunem would see to it that he was on good terms with the court of Ahab and his sons. Only so can we under-stand the completely subordinate role played in the whole story by her husband. He would not refuse the prophet hospitality, if his wife insisted, but he was not going to let the court think that he was in any way a supporter of Elisha. This also explains the strong expression in 4:8, "She laid hold on him to eat bread"; though we should probably regard this as merely metaphorical, it does imply pressure well above the normal. Elisha did not want to involve the home in difficulties with the court, and the mother's later reluctance to tell her husband of the child's death supports the suggestion that he had never really welcomed the prophet. 4:13 is no real contradiction of this, for a man like Elisha could easily have found those who would have acted for him.

Then the time drew near for the sending of Elisha's emissary to anoint Jehu ben Nimshi as king in Jehoram's stead. Foreseeing the ghastly blood-bath to follow, which would engulf not merely the royal family but all in its confidence (10:11), Elisha removed the friendly family from the threat while there was yet time. The famine came, but it was ultimately a pretext, for he could not reveal the thunderstorm that was to break so soon. Such an explanation amply explains the confiscation of the land, a decree promptly reversed by Jehu, once he was assured that the owner, now probably a widow, was in fact a friend of Elisha's. So once we grasp the undercurrents in the story we see that we once again have a picture of blessing on and protection of those who were prepared to link their lives with God's prophet.

---

[1] Miss K. H. Henrey (*Land Tenure in the Old Testament* – Palestine Exploration Fund Quarterly, Jan.–Apr. 1954, p. 12) suggests that the land was held as a military fief. Since the widow with only a young son could not fulfil the conditions, she forfeited the land. Note the special mention of the commander-in-chief in II Ki. 4:13.

The story of the poisonous "pottage" (4:38–41) comes doubtless from the period of the famine foretold to the Shunamite. The "gourds" have been identified with "the coloquintida, *Citrullus colocyntis*, with its little leaves and yellow apples, resembling melons, which Elisha's disciples, who were evidently not natives of the district, wanted to cook as food, but are only of value as an aperient".[1] Obviously Elisha did not take "death in the pot" too seriously – after all, it was more a matter of unpleasantness of taste and of certain after-effects than of poison – but the food was not to be wasted. Once again we see that for the remnant God can supply from the means that are to hand.

The remnant concept is underlined even more strongly in the equally brief story that follows (4:42–44). It is apparently unconnected with it. There is no suggestion that the people were in need; indeed we are not told, and we need not necessarily infer, that the hundred who were fed were sons of the prophets. They may have been only a group that had come to hear Elisha. The vital point of the story is that the unnamed man of Baal-shalishah had brought the *bikkurim* to Elisha. *Bikkurim* is the technical name for the first-fruits that had to be brought to the priest (Ex. 23:16, 19, etc.). The not really parallel passages Num. 13:20 and Nah. 3:12 hardly justify the contention of the ICC that the word is used here in a purely secular sense. The man was recognizing Elisha as the one true representative of God in the land; he did not wish to bring the first-fruits to the priests who had been contaminated by the Baalized worship of Jehovah, or even with Baal worship itself. By a gesture reminiscent of Mk. 3:31–35 Elisha, by sharing the *bikkurim* with his hearers, proclaimed that they too shared in his relationship to God.

The healing of Naaman needs no other explanation than that it was done for the glorification and hallowing of God's name. The slave-girl's words to her mistress (5:3) do not mean that Elisha had cured other lepers. They were merely an expression of her confidence in his powers. It is doubtful, however, whether our normal explanations really explain all angles of what happened. Above all, since Naaman was not likely to hear of the fate that had overtaken Gehazi, the punishment would hardly undo the mischief where we normally conceive it to have been worst. In addition they do not try to explain Elisha's question *Is it a time to receive money, and to receive garments, and olive yards and vineyards, and sheep and oxen, and manservants and maidservants?* (5:26).

If we put together the available data about Gehazi, viz. II Ki. 4:12, 25–31; 8:2, 4; 5:20–27 (it should be clear that chronologically 8:1–6 comes before ch. 5), it is clear that Gehazi had served Elisha for quite a time – we can hardly put it at less than fifteen years, and it may well have been longer. His relationship to his master is never clearly defined, though for

[1] Dalman, *Sacred Sites and Ways*, pp. 81 ff.

his contemporaries there was doubtless a clear understanding for it. He is always called Elisha's *na'ar*, a teasing word that defies exact definition, but never his *'ebed*, or slave. The simplest explanation seems to be that he voluntarily gave Elisha the service normally performed by a slave.

It may be that he hoped one day to be Elisha's successor, as Elisha was of Elijah. It may be that in his imagination he foreshortened the period of judgment, and hoped, as did the apostles, that in the new order he would occupy a position of distinction. But all this is mere speculation. The fact remains that "the heart is deceitful above all things and incurable" (Jer. 17:9). The moment of temptation found a man embittered by the passing years that had brought him no material reward. It is true that Moffatt and the ICC follow the LXX and Vulgate in rendering Elisha's question, "You have taken money and you mean to get garments . . . ?" – the change in Hebrew is one of vowel points. But it is precisely in a context like this, where the deeper meaning can so easily be overlooked or forgotten, that the Massoretic tradition, followed here by the English versions, is more likely to be correct.

When we think of the tragic figure of Gehazi, we would do well to place beside it the equally tragic figures of Judas, of Ananias and Sapphira, and to remember Paul's warning in I Cor. 7:29–31, a passage the Church in its days of prosperity is always apt to forget.

There are four stories which show Elisha as the controller of Israel's national destiny. The doom of the North had been foretold at Horeb (I Ki. 19:15–18), but it had to come as it had been foretold, not through the chances of history, but by the working out of God's purposes. That is why we see Elisha not merely as the one who announces the moment of destiny to Jehu and Hazael, but also as the restrainer of forces that would anticipate or exceed God's purposes.

The armies of Ben-hadad (6:24) might foreshadow the bitter sufferings that Hazael (8:7–15; 10:32, 33; 13:7) would bring upon Israel, but they might not go beyond that. So Elisha sat at home in Samaria (6:32), the living token both of its temporary inviolability and of God's judgment. That this interpretation is not far-fetched is shown by the way Jehoram – the name is not mentioned, but none other will fit – finally lost his head (6:31–33). It was not by chance that it was four lepers who discovered that the invading army had melted away (7:3–10); the spiritually minded at least were to grasp that Jehovah, who had given them a moment's respite, had not changed His opinion of them.

We are apt to think of a prophet as a grim man rejoicing in the message of doom he was commissioned to deliver, even as there are modern preachers quite capable of preaching hell with smiles on their faces. The simple face is that the prophet was commissioned to proclaim not his feelings, but God's message, and it is only rarely that the prophet's feelings

– Jeremiah's heart-outpourings to God are the best example – are part of God's revelation. From time to time, however, the veil is lifted, as it is in 8:7–15 with Elisha. We are not told what impulse or command from the Lord sent him to Damascus; there is not even any indication that, as Hazael waited on him, Elisha knew that here was the man whose destiny had been fixed years earlier at Horeb. To the straight question "Shall I recover of this sickness?" he returned a straight answer, "Go, say unto him, Thou shalt surely recover." It is a pity that the translators of the AV thought they had to save the prophet's reputation by the impossible rendering, "Go, say unto him, Thou mayest certainly recover." (An even more striking example, going back to pious improvements in the Greek text, will be found by comparing the AV with RV mg. and RSV, NEB of John 7:8).

Suddenly God deepened the prophet's vision; he knew to whom he was speaking, and with breaking heart he saw that the beginning of Israel's doom had come. It was not the first time, as it was not the last, that the ruthless will of man was cutting across what should have been, but then, as always, man's sin and rebellion were blindly working out God's purpose.

There can be no doubt that 6:8–23 is later in time than the two stories we have just been considering, though there is no obvious reason for the inversion. There are two periods only in which we can reasonably date it. It might come from the earlier years of Jehu's reign before the full effects of the awful blood-bath of Jezreel (Hos. 1:4, II Ki. 10:1–31) had made themselves felt, and the full power of Hazael had not yet fallen on the land. On the other hand, the obvious impotence of Israel, with the Israelite forces more concerned with avoiding the Syrians than with fighting them, and the Syrian ability to march to Dothan in the heart of the country point almost irresistibly to a date late in the reign of Jehoahaz or early in that of Jehoash. This enables us to give full weight to 6:23b as well.

We are not told anything of Elisha's work during the grim years when Hazael was the scourge of God. It has left as little record on the pages of history as has the remnant to which he ministered. Now there was to be a lightening of the load, and the man who had unleashed Hazael on Israel in God's name had now the duty of ending the ordeal.

There is a paradoxical element in the story, for it is distinctly humorous to see the king of Syria sending his troops raiding through the valleys of Israel to catch a prophet who had known his every plan and so could have played blind-man's-buff with them. How human it all was! We are always apt to recognize God's power in one area and yet to deny it in another. And so Elisha sat tight in Dothan, the bait in God's trap, knowing full well that "the angel of the Lord encamps around those that fear Him, and delivers them" (Psa. 34:7). His servant might need to see them, but Elisha knew they must be there.

We are finally introduced to Elisha on his death-bed, an old man between eighty-five and ninety years old. It was not sufficient that the Syrian bands no longer roamed the land. Israel had to have one more lease of prosperity, that it might be seen whether it had learnt its lesson and repented, and if not, that its conduct might amply vindicate God's final judgment. The story of Jehoash and the symbolic arrows is easily understood, when we grasp that the easing of Syrian pressure and the subsequent Israelite victories that led to the prosperity of Jeroboam's reign were due primarily to the increasing pressure of Assyria on Damascus. Jehoash knew that Elisha was offering him the annihilation of Syria, but that would mean that there would no longer be a buffer state between him and the menace of Assyria! He might take leave of Elisha (13:14) with the same words as Elisha had used in taking leave of Elijah (2:12), but there was no living faith in the God of Elijah and Elisha.

The fact that we have no tradition of a miracle-working tomb of Elisha in a land in which traditions can be surprisingly tenacious makes me think that the man who was dropped into his tomb (13:20, 21) was not actually dead. The burial of the apparently dead has become almost impossible in this country, but it can happen much more easily in the Near East, where burial is carried out wherever possible on the day of death. In either case the miracle is of minor importance. It was a final message that death had not finished the work that Elijah and Elisha had done, for the God who had spoken and worked through them was still all-powerful to accomplish His purposes, even if there were but few that proclaimed the word of God in the next forty years or so.

Before we leave the work of Elisha we should ask ourselves whether it had any lasting effects. From Elisha to Amos is only about half a century, yet neither in his words, nor in Hosea's, do we find any real trace of the promised remnant, but that may be just because it was a remnant. We have no way of estimating the population of Israel in the time of Ahab, but a million will be a conservative figure (cf. II Sam. 24:9). On that basis 7,000 is less than one in a hundred, and it was probably less than one in two hundred. When we further remember that there will have been few that were rich or mighty among them, it is easy to see why they played no part in the message of the later prophets.

That they did exist may be seen from II Chr. 30:11, 18, the more so as their acceptance of Hezekiah's invitation cannot have been without personal risk from their Assyrian overlords. Few, if any, will have been of sufficient social importance to be deported by Sargon and his successors, but in Samaria at least they will have kept the flame of true religion alight.

CHAPTER VIII

JONAH

FROM THE DEATH OF ELISHA TO THE PROPHESYING OF AMOS nearly forty years must have elapsed, during which the only recorded prophetic voice is Jonah's. Doubtless to prevent the people from taking the glory to themselves he had announced beforehand the coming victories of Jeroboam II (II Ki. 14:25).

He was the son of Amittai, from Gath-hepher, the modern Khirbet ez-Zurrac, a few miles north-east of Nazareth (cf. Jos. 19:13). Jeroboam II became sole king in 782 B.C. We do not know at what time in his long reign the great expansion of Israel's frontiers began, so we cannot date Jonah with any certainty. Indeed, he may well have prophesied under Jehoash, his predecessor. In any case it was fairly certainly during the period of Assyrian weakness in the half-century before Tiglath-pileser III seized the throne in 745 B.C.

This is not the place to discuss the date of the composition of the book that bears Jonah's name. There is no claim in it that it was written by Jonah himself. On the one hand, our complete ignorance of Galilean dialect under the Northern monarchy renders the linguistic argument for a post-exilic date of virtually no value, while the other arguments are strangely inconclusive. What really matters is the historicity of the book. It is abundantly clear that its literal truth was never questioned in Jewish tradition. Indeed, Philo of Alexandria, that great master of allegory, who would doubtless have eagerly seized on a symbolic or allegoric explanation had it been known to him, "took great pains to explain the marvel of the fish".[1]

Equally the canonicity of the book seems never to have been questioned. Whether the modern scholar explains the book as prophetic legend, symbolic narrative or didactic fiction, he is faced by the impossibility of explaining how the Jewish people, and in particular our Lord, came to regard it as historically true. The difficulty is the greater when we realize that our spiritual explanation of it as a historically true account will be, to a greater or less degree, significantly different from that we should give it, if we regarded it as fiction. We are asked to believe that the Jews not merely forgot that it was fiction, but even forgot its true meaning. It is not unfair to remember also that moderns are singularly in conflict as to its original purpose and meaning.

[1] König, HDB, Vol. II, p. 749a.

During the Middle Ages, when the Jews came in great measure to share the credulity and superstition of the medieval Church, the average Jew came to look on the Haggadic legends from the early rabbinic literature as literally true. This was helped by the widespread belief that the Talmud and the Midrashim were as inspired as the Old Testament itself. It should be clear, however, that the average far-fetched story in the older rabbinic writings was normally told with tongue in cheek and twinkle in eye. The old rabbis were far from being credulous men prepared to believe anything because it was edifying. Indeed, many would hold that one of their weaknesses was an unduly rationalistic strain. In addition their treatment of the Song of Songs shows that they were not averse to symbolic and allegoric interpretations. Those then who deny the book's factual truth must bear the onus of explaining how a book so very different from the other prophetic books ever came to be included in the prophetic canon, how it was forgotten that it was symbolic or didactic fiction, and above all how our Lord was incapable of realizing its true nature. It is one thing on the basis of the *kenosis* theory to suggest that our Lord may have been ignorant of this or that fact (the truth is that the New Testament ignores all such theorizings as completely irrelevant, and to argue about them is merely an attempt to support one's own *a priori* views); it is quite another to suggest that His authority as spiritual teacher is in any way defective.

Let us face a simple fact. From Eichhorn[1] onwards the denial of the book's historicity was in the first place the result of the then dominant rationalistic view of the world, in which there was no room for miracle or for Divine interference in things physical.

The conservative must bear part of the blame, however. For him, all too often, the first half of the book is all that has mattered. He has tended to overlook that God's miraculous dealings with Jonah were but a preparation for the revelation of the Divine character. If we want the literal truth of the book to be taken seriously we must both give it an adequate spiritual interpretation and justify the exceptional miraculous element in it.

Just about the time that the dynasty of Jeroboam ben Nebat was swept away by Baasha, Assyria under Adad-nirari II began to wake up from a sleep that had lasted over a century and a half. He and his successors gradually extended the Assyrian empire amid some of the worst cruelty recorded in human history.[2] Already in 876, while Omri was still on the throne, the Phoenician cities and Hamath had to submit to Ashur-nasir-pal II. By 853 Shalmaneser III was proving such a threat to Syria that Ahab joined in an alliance in which Hamath and Damascus were the other two leading figures. The Assyrians were checked at Qarqar and the alliance

---

[1] His *Introduction to the Old Testament* dates from 1780-83.
[2] H. W. F. Saggs, *Everyday Life in Babylonia and Assyria*, p. 118, tries, not too convincingly, to justify it.

was dissolved. But in 841 Shalmaneser was back, Syria was ravaged and Jehu became tributary. Again in 803 Jehoahaz paid tribute to Adad-nirari III, and it was from this time that Damascus began to lose its power over Israel as it reeled under Assyrian blows. The unnamed saviour of II Ki. 13:5 is probably the Assyrian king. It is most likely that the victories of Jehoash (II Ki. 13:25) and Jeroboam II (II Ki. 14:25, 28) were won in alliance or at least understanding with Assyria.

The proud kings of Assyria were willing to co-operate with former tributaries, because from the closing days of Shalmaneser III they were increasingly involved in a struggle with Urartu to the north, in which the frontier was pushed south until it was less than 100 miles from Nineveh. Assyria was in a position in which anything could happen. Occasional campaigns against the West were a warning that she was still a power to be reckoned with, but Assyria itself knew that if the fierce mountaineers of Urartu, Mannai and Madai were to venture down into the plain of the Tigris the ensuing battle might well mean its end.

It is in this period, probably after the death of Adad-nirari III in 782, that we are to place Jonah's visit to Nineveh. It would explain the readiness of its citizens to listen to his message. In addition his *yet forty days and Nineveh shall be destroyed*[1] ceases to be a vague menace. For speaker and hearers alike it meant a sudden, swift and decisive attack by the Northerners.

Nothing could have suited Israel better. Though Jeroboam can hardly have captured Damascus as early as this, Syria had already ceased to be a danger. All the other states, bigger and smaller, of the Fertile Crescent had been too badly mauled by Assyria to be able to take over its empire, while there were no indications that Urartu had dreams of empire-building in the plains. Many must have been the hearts that longed for Assyria's downfall, especially as Israel would have been the one to gain the most.

Morally too Jonah's message was justified. Assyria had earned itself lasting infamy by its inhuman conduct. Ashur-nasir-pal II decided to use terror as a means of enforcing submission and loyalty. To quote Hall:

His usual procedure after the capture of a hostile city was to burn it, and then to mutilate all the grown male prisoners by cutting off their hands and ears and putting out their eyes; after which they were piled up in a great heap to perish in torture from sun, flies, their wounds and suffocation; the children, both boys and girls, were all burnt alive at the stake; and the chief was carried off to Assyria to be flayed alive for the king's delectation.[2]

Though his successors did not go to the same lengths, cruelty remained the outstanding feature of Assyrian warfare and conquest. The people of Nineveh did not need to be told for what they might expect sudden

[1] It may be that LXX "three days" is correct. It fits the picture better.
[2] *The Ancient History of the Near East*, p. 445.

judgment.

We must resist the temptation of minimizing Jonah's mission to Nineveh, even though its major effect will have worn off quickly enough. After all, it was an act of God's grace, but it suffered from the same weakness which every call to repentance under a threat must share, even though we are unwilling to recognize the fact. The warning that God will do so and so, if we do not mend our ways, should it be effective, always produces the after-thought, "Would it really have happened, if I had gone on as I was going?" But such a thought is normally the first step to a return, partial it may be, to the past which we thought we had abandoned.

Jonah's mission has left no mark on extant Assyrian records. That is sign enough that its effects were not very deep. But it would be rash to infer that there were none, or that they did not last. Though the abominations of Assyrian cruelty continued, we have the impression that their worst excesses were over. Quite clearly too, when Tiglath-pileser III once again set the Assyrian arms moving west he no longer relied on sheer intimidation for the maintenance of order and loyalty.

Thus in the truest sense Jonah may well have achieved the main purpose of his mission. This was unique in the Biblical record, and it had as its deeper purpose the preparing of the rod of God's anger against Israel and Judah; it was to be a rod that would chastise and not exterminate.

While this explains Jonah's mission, it does not sufficiently explain the existence of the book in its present form; indeed, it does not even explain the personal story in it. He would be a bold man who would affirm that God had no one else to send, once Jonah ran away. He would be a rash Christian who, basing himself on the story of Jonah, would reckon on a second chance when he had deliberately run away from his duty and God's call. It is true that many have suggested that the story of Jonah's deliverance had reached Nineveh before him, and that it was this and the physical signs of his sufferings that so mightily affected his hearers. It would be rash to deny this possibility merely by arguing from the silence of Scripture, but it is surely much rasher to make the central point of the story depend on something the Bible does not mention.

No; the repentance of Nineveh does not sufficiently explain Jonah's experience. It is only when we grasp that Jonah's mission was not merely for Israel's ultimate good, but that the recording of it was for Israel's learning, that we begin to understand the deeper message of the book.

The symbolic school of interpretation has seen clearly enough that Jonah represents Israel. We may reject their interpretation as a whole and yet accept this without question. Jonah is a historical character, but he does typify his people. The disobedient prophet is dispensable; as an individual he may be laid aside or broken. But however much the individual Israelite may rebel and fail, God reaches His purposes in and through Israel, even though it involves judgment, exile and its reduction to a mere remnant. Therefore Jonah, just because in God's wisdom he has become a type, must carry through his mission, whatever may be the cost to him. He even serves as a type of Him, the true Israel (Isa. 49:3, RV, RSV), who for three days and three nights lay in the grave because of the unfaithfulness of those He represents. Furthermore, because in Abraham all nations were to be blessed, Jonah, as the representative of Israel, had to go even to the nation that would gladly swallow Israel alive.

Though it is rather foreign to our purpose, we may do well to note how Jonah's experience with the fish has so often found a parallel in Jewish history. It is a commonplace in modern Old Testament study that the psalm in ch. 2 is quite unsuited to its setting, for it is a thanksgiving before deliverance, and it commemorates rescue from the sea and not from the fish's belly. All this is very true, though it would be interesting to learn why the man who "inserted this psalm" did not choose or compose something more suitable. The simple fact is that this psalm is a thanksgiving for rescue from drowning or destruction. I know neither what sort of a fish it was nor how the miracle worked, but the fish, however uncomfortable it may have been for Jonah, was the means of his preservation. Jonah, once he had been preserved from drowning, knew that his life would be preserved. Scripture is not so foolish or naïve, as some would have it be. So repeatedly it has been in the long history of the Jews. There have been so many peoples that would gladly have swallowed up Israel for ever, yet in God's providence they have been the means by which Jewry has been preserved and moulded for God's purposes.

But let us return to Jonah. Why did he flee from God? It is true enough that he feared he would be successful, and he did not want to be (4:2), but we should be foolish to take a runaway prophet's self-motivation as the complete truth. In addition it does not explain why he ran away. I can hardly believe that he had such a high opinion of himself, that he thought that if he disappeared God would have to give up His purpose. In any case, all he had to do was to dig in his heels and say "No!"

There have been those who have suggested that he thought Jehovah's power did not extend to distant Tarshish. If this were true, it would certainly tell against a post-exilic date for the book, when all such ideas had vanished among those who had returned from exile, but there is no indication that he really did so think. It is hardly fair to quote his words to the sailors (1:10), for while they are true they express only part of the truth. Jonah did not want to go to Nineveh just because he recognized God's control over Nineveh, His power to destroy and His power to bring to repentance. It is absurd to think that he believed that Jehovah did not have the same power over Tarshish, because it was somewhat farther off.

One would have to be a Frenchman, who three times, or a Russian, who twice in a lifetime has felt the might of Germany tearing at his country's vitals, fully to grasp how a man like Jonah must have regarded Assyria. Three times at least the threat had drawn near, three times the hot breath of destruction had been felt, three times the threat had spent itself on others. Men were hoping and praying that the scourge might be vanquished, but here was God holding out His hand of mercy to the threatened city. Jonah must have known that this could mean only one thing, that God was preparing Assyria to finish the work of judgment foretold to Elijah at Horeb some seventy years earlier. Sick at heart and with the usual foreshortening of the future we repeatedly meet among the prophets, when they foretell the coming judgments of God, he wished to escape, not beyond the power of Jehovah, but beyond the stage on which He was working out His purposes and judgments.

In the old mythologies of the Fertile Crescent, basically the same in spite of all their variation in detail, creation was looked on as the fruit of the victory of the gods of order over the powers of chaos. Though chaos had been conquered, it had not been annihilated, and it ever threatened to overthrow order once again. It was symbolized by the sea, with all its disorder, and by the great monster, Leviathan, which was supposed to live in it. Though the old mythology had become merely metaphor in Israel, at least for the true servants of Jehovah, it was metaphor the meaning of which was still alive.

God's power over the sea and over the great fish, which must have recalled Leviathan to the prophet's mind, was the guarantee to Jonah, and through him to Israel as a whole, that His power was absolute. It was not merely that there was no land or realm where His writ did not run, but that He controlled them, even though He was neither recognized nor worshipped there. If He was turning once again to Assyria, that He might turn it as a mighty stream of judgment over His land, it was not that it should come merely as a torrent in spate. Even as He had sat as King at the flood (Psa. 29:10), so He would control all the waves and billows of the king of Assyria. Indeed Assyria might swallow up Israel as "Leviathan" had swallowed Jonah, but it would be as God's blind servant accomplishing a purpose beyond its ken.

It was not only power but also love that God revealed to Jonah. It matters little how we interpret the six score thousand persons who could not discern between their right hand and their left (4:11), whether they are the population as a whole or only the children. The Lord's "tender mercies are over all His works" (Psa. 145:9); even the cattle are partakers of His mercy.[1]

---

[1] Modern Arabic usage suggests that in 4:9 we should translate ". . . to be grieved for the gourd? . . . to be grieved even unto death," cf. v. 10. This does not apply to 4:1, 4, when there is a minor difference in idiom. I owe this point to Dr. R. L. Lindsay of Jerusalem.

Brought up on an age-old theology that prosperity was the reward of godliness, first Israel and then Judah were to pass through the crucible of affliction and exile until only a very small remnant was left. But that remnant, without the cross to explain and transform suffering, was to learn that all it had passed through was not evidence of God's impotence but of His sovereignty, not merely of His wrath but of His far greater love. Swallowed up by the power of Babylon the great, it could look forward to the days when the gates of brass would yield and the bars of iron would be cut asunder.

I do not doubt that behind the visions of Amos and Hosea, Isaiah and Micah, Jeremiah and Ezekiel, behind the faith and steadfastness of the remnant, whether in place of power as Daniel or in utter obscurity as most, the lessons that Jonah learnt were the basis of the faith with which they received God's word and awaited the fulfilment of the promises in faith.

CHAPTER IX

AMOS

THE GLORIES OF JEROBOAM II (793–753 B.C.) WERE AT their height when for discerning men a warning cloud appeared in the sky. There came on Israel in fairly quick succession a series of natural visitations, which were traditionally associated with the wrath and judgment of God. As they are detailed for us in Amos 4:6–10 they were famine (v. 6), caused by drought (vv. 7 f.), excessive *khamsin* wind from the desert, mildew and locusts (v. 9). We shall see later that there is no need to take this as an exact chronological list. Then there was a visitation of the plague (v. 10), which was doubtless that mentioned in Assyrian inscriptions as ravaging the Near East in 765 B.C. It is not clear whether Amos implies that this was accompanied by military disaster. It could well be God's sword which is meant here, the more so as there is otherwise in the book no suggestion of a military disaster of this magnitude.[1] In addition, in 763 B.C. there was an eclipse of the sun (8:9), which for popular belief was a sign of trouble to come. The only effect in Israel seems to have been a multiplication of sacrifices (4:4 f.), but for at least one in Judah they were a warning that could not be ignored.

Amos seems to have been a simple shepherd (*noqed* – 1:1) of Tekoa. Some have thought that he was the owner of his flock, because the same word is used in II Ki. 3:4 of Mesha, king of Moab. This may well be, but no Tekoa sheep-master is likely to have been rich, and the fact that we are not told the name of his father shows that he did not spring from a family of importance. The English translation "herdman" in 1:1 (AV, RV) is a deliberate mistranslation to agree with 7:14. In the latter, however, as is shown by the LXX, we have merely a scribal error by which the very rare *noqed* has been replaced by the very common *boqer* (the ease of the change will be obvious to all who are familiar with the Hebrew alphabet).[2] The correctness of this assumption is shown already by 7:15 and by the fact that herds could never have been kept in the environs of Tekoa. We realize something of how poor Amos was by the fact that when he led his flock into the lower western hills in search of grass he added to his income

---

[1] The earthquake in 4:11 must either have been still future and be referred to by a prophetic perfect, i.e. a perfect expressing a certain and unavoidable fact in the future or a later insertion by the prophet after the fulfilment of 8:8, 9:5, cf. 1:1.

[2] The suggestion that *noqed* and *boqer* are technical expressions referring to certain groups of cultic prophets may be ignored.

by tending the fruit of sycomores (*Ficus sycomorus*). This has no connection with the sycamore, as it is incorrectly rendered in AV. It belongs to the fig genus and was valuable both for its wood and fruit. It was common in the plains and lower hills.

Tekoa lies some ten miles south of Jerusalem and to the east of the main mountain backbone of the country with its north-south road.[1] It is situated on a detached hill about 2,700 feet high. While to the west the view is bounded by the somewhat higher hills of the central ridge, to the east the ground falls rapidly 4,000 feet to the Dead Sea. Owing to the very steep drop from the central range a "rain shadow" is formed, and the steep slopes are so waterless that the Wilderness of Judah or Jeshimon (= devastation) is one of the most inhospitable regions of the world. The only sure sources of water are the rare springs, and the shepherd must know the rugged slopes like the palm of his hand if he is to find sufficient grass for his flock.

This then is one side of Amos's background. He was a man of the desert with all its contrasts of light and darkness, of life and sudden death, in which luxuries played a very small part indeed and the dividing line between the essential and the inessential could be easily drawn.

For all that Amos was no nomad. He had his home in the little fortified hill-top town with its self-government and its inequalities. In addition Tekoa lay near enough to the main road to the west for the news of the day to reach it easily. We have seen too that when the grass gave out once the summer heat began in earnest, Amos had to move to the gentler western slopes, where nature turns a milder face to man. There is little doubt in addition that G. A. Smith was correct when he suggested that Amos would have gone from time to time to the fairs in the northern cities to sell his wool.[2] So while Amos thought largely in the blacks and whites of the desert dweller he knew something of the complexities of urban life and civilization.

THE CONDITION OF THE PEOPLE

How are we to judge the welfare and prosperity of a people? Are we to gaze in open-mouthed astonishment at the mansions of the rich and to look with jealous eyes at the wares displayed in the luxury shops, or are we to turn to the houses of the poor and to try to understand how they live? While we may not ignore the rich and mighty, surely it is the level of the poor that will best reveal to us where a country stands.

The superficial, and sometimes the more than superficial, reader allows Amos to take him on an escorted tour of the luxury of Israel and fails to realize that these things are being denounced against a background of

---

[1] There is some evidence for a Tekoa in Galilee (V.T., Vol. III, pp. 305 f.), but it is insufficient to shake the traditional identification.

[2] *The Book of the Twelve Prophets*, Vol. I, p. 79.

grimmest poverty that embraced the bulk of the population. Writers of text-books are fond of describing the prosperity under Jeroboam II, but for the most part they seemingly fail to realize that it was a very small proportion of the population that profited from it. Not so many years later Menahem could find only some 60,000 from whom he could raise his special levy of fifty shekels a man (II Ki. 15:19, 20), or about the value of two normal slaves.[1]

The inescapable and regrettable fact is that the institution of the monarchy meant the collapse of Israel's ancient system of land tenure. There were many ways in which the royal domain could be enlarged. It could be by purchase; I Ki. 21:15 f. suggests another. It is, however, certain that whatever came into the king's hands was no longer subject to the law of Lev. 25:8-34, and the same will be true of the estates he gave to his courtiers. If for any reason they fell vacant, it would be to the king that they would return. The law of Ezek. 46:18 is sufficient to indicate how much suffering was caused in this way.

We may be sure that where the monarchy had driven a coach and four through the provisions of Lev. 25 the mighty will have found ways and means of circumventing them too. That is why I suggested earlier, when dealing with Naboth, that it is far from certain that the law of Lev. 25 was still in operation in the days of Ahab (see p. 31).

Over a period of at least a generation Syria, under Hazael and Benhadad, had devastated Israel (II Ki. 13:3-7). It needs an effort on the part of the modern city-dweller to grasp what this must have meant for the small farmer with no reserves to fall back on, once the raiders had swept away his harvest and livestock. Some, in sheer despair, will have sold themselves as slaves. Jer. 34:8-11, though two centuries later, is doubtless a true picture of how it will have been in Israel; the "Hebrew slaves" (cf. Ex. 21:2-6 Deut. 15:12-18) will have had no hope of freedom in the seventh year, unless indeed some national disaster should touch their masters' conscience. Others will have sold their land, remaining as tenants paying a heavy rental and under the continual threat of being thrown out if unable to pay. Isa. 5:8 gives us a picture of the parallel development in Judah some twenty-five years later than Amos. Mic. 3:1-3 gives us a dramatic idea of the cruelty with which the rich used their power over their tenants. In other words the prosperity of Israel was merely a thin veneer over a mass of poverty and misery.

There have always been those who have condemned the possession of superfluities as being in itself evil. One such was Jehonadab ben Rechab, who condemned his descendants to a life as nomads, refusing them even

---

[1] H. J. Cook in his article *Pekah* in V.T., Vol. XIV (1964), pp. 121 *seq.* argues quite convincingly that the Northern Kingdom was divided at the time between Pekah and Menahem, so this to some extent diminishes the force of the argument.

the fruit of the vine as a solace (Jer. 35:6, 7). But there is no evidence that Amos shared such an outlook. Rather, like all the prophets in the long line that ended with John the Baptist, he looked on the one hand on the need of those who have not, while we have more than we need, but on the other hand considered that wealth might well have been entrusted to some by God to be used for Him.

◢ Manifestly the reason why Amos condemned some things was that in an agricultural society they could be obtained only by the oppression of the majority by a minority. When he called the rich women of Samaria "fat cows of Bashan" and rebuked their pleasure in wine (4:1) he was not speaking as a temperance advocate. The luxurious living of these rich women was made possible only by oppression, and it was only this that concerned him.

When, however, he gave a picture of the idle rich in 6:4-6, though the thought of oppression may have been in the back of his mind, his real stress was on how little their luxury was earned. The Israelite was glad to see a king who ably bore the full weight of government rewarded with the good things of life. The same applied to the man who risked his life in the field at the head of the king's forces. But luxury and ostentation on the part of those who had not even earned a crust of dry bread was an abomination. Such an outlook is deep-rooted in all true religion. Paul expressed it pregnantly when he said "If any will not work, neither let him eat" (II Thess. 3:10). It is most important that we should be clear on this matter, for we shall miss the real point of Amos' message if we look on him merely as a wild man of the desert condemning civilization just because it is civilization.

THE CALL OF AMOS

The sheer logic of prophetic service as enunciated by Amos in 3:7 f. makes it unlikely that his call was an all-shattering and life-transforming event like those of Isaiah and Ezekiel. This is borne out when we come to study the five visions of chs. 7-9, which almost certainly formed his call, though this is not expressly stated.

It will be an exaggeratedly developed critical outlook that will refuse to link the first two visions, locusts (7:1-3) and drought (7:4-6), with the beginning of the roll of judgments in 4:6-9, even if here the order has been reversed.

The news of a major locust invasion travels rapidly in the Near East, for there is no saying in what direction it may turn, and all, even many miles away, feel themselves threatened. To Amos, however, came the vision that these, like Joel's, were no ordinary locusts, for they were being made by God Himself; in other words there was no limit to the destruction they might do. To the shepherd, for whom every blade of grass was precious, came the shocked realization that they were being turned loose on their devastating course just after the royal first-fruits of the grass had been mowed. The period of herbage in Palestine is so short that once the locusts had done their work there would be no more hope of grass for that year. In his deep understanding of the desperate plight of the northern peasants his voice rose in intercession: *O Lord Jehovah, forgive, I beseech Thee: how shall Jacob stand? for he is small.*

This is no mere artificial interpretation, invented for the occasion. As was made clear when we were looking at the story of Jonah, Israel at the time was probably outwardly the strongest and richest kingdom west of Assyria. To have called Israel as a kingdom small would have had little meaning. The very use of Jacob may point in the same direction. The name Israel had been pre-empted by the northern tribes and had become a political term. Its true meaning and use had for the most part to lie dormant until after the destruction of Samaria. Though we cannot be certain why Amos uses Jacob, it seems as though he was doing so that we might look away from the magnificent political exterior of Israel to the reality of the small struggling farmers who were its real strength, little though the rich nobles realized it. It is not likely that he is thinking of the original antithesis between Jacob and Israel.

God listened to Amos' prayer, but probably a year later, after a winter almost without rain, with the growing summer heat began a second visitation, that of drought. Once again Amos was given to see that this was no mere passing lack of rain. Possibly, as he sheltered with his flock behind a rock to escape the desert wind coming like a breath of fire, he saw a vision of fire drying up the great deep on which in popular imagination the land floated, and which supplied the springs with their water. When its work was done it prepared to attack "the portion" (RV, mg.), the piece of land owned by the small farmer. It is needless to underline that the drought is here pictured as fire. Once again Amos prayed, and once again the visitation was stayed.

The third vision was not of punishment, but of inescapable doom (7:7-9). For a westerner it is enigmatic. The Lord stands with a plumbline by a wall and says that He will set a plumbline in the midst of Israel. That was all, but it was more than sufficient for Amos.

Most commentaries seem to find unnecessary difficulties here, even resorting to textual emendation. The wall is, as G. A. Smith rightly tranlates, a city wall, not that of a house.[1] Such walls could be, roughly speaking, of two types. During the middle and late Bronze Ages many had been either of beaten earth, showing a very steep slope outwards to hinder attackers, or of somewhat sloping stone-work making the wall wider at the bottom than the top. Such walls were absolutely solid, but required much labour to build. Under the Israelite monarchy, they were of vertical masonry of the type we normally associate with city walls. Obviously, if

[1] Op. cit., p. 114.

such a wall is to be of any height, it must be built with great care, especially
if it is of the casemate type or if its core is filled with rubble, both methods
being common in Israel. All this need for care is expressed by the wall seen
by Amos being called "a plumbline wall".[1]

In the vision Jehovah was not building the wall, but was testing it with a
plumbline. It is left for us to infer that it was seriously out of the perpen-
dicular. When that happened there was no hope of saving it. Isaiah
describes graphically what was to be expected:

> *Therefore this iniquity shall be to you*
> *like a break in a high wall,*
> *bulging out, and about to collapse,*
> *whose crash comes suddenly, in an instant;*
> *and its breaking is like that of a potter's vessel*
> *which is smashed so ruthlessly*
> *that among its fragments not a sherd is found*
> *with which to take fire from the hearth,*
> *or to dip up water out of the cistern* (Isa. 30:13 f. RSV).

Amos' silence at this point is characteristic of an attitude we find
repeatedly in the Old Testament. It was not caused by disgust at Israel's sin
or by secret satisfaction that the hour of Judah's rival had at last come, as
some have suggested. Repeatedly we find it stressed that a point can be
reached where the wrath of God must be given free course. Abraham
rightly ceased to intercede for Sodom when he had reduced the number of
potential righteous to ten. Samuel's mourning for Saul (I Sam. 16:1)
doubtless included intercession, but God commanded him to go and anoint
Saul's successor – an action which effectively inhibited any future hope for
the king. Jeremiah was three times forbidden to pray for contemporary
Jerusalem (Jer. 7:16, 11:14, 14:11). It should not be thought that this is
peculiarly an Old Testament attitude. It lies behind our Lord's words as
He wept over Jerusalem (Lk. 19:41–44). We find it expressed in words in
I Jn. 5:16 and in action in the story of Ananias and Sapphira.

So, just as did Isaiah a generation later (Isa. 6:9–13), Amos went out to
his task as a prophet knowing beforehand that his message could not be
accepted by the people as a whole. Things had gone too far for that. Hence
his message is more a commentary on judgment to come than a call to
repentance.

Two more visions were given to mark the nearness and completeness of
the coming judgment. The sight of a basket of autumn fruit (*qayits*),
probably figs, brought the divine word that the end (*qets*) had come for
Israel (8:1, 2). The link between the fruit and the coming end is often

---

[1] It must be confessed that there is this great difficulty in this interpretation, that it was not
recognized by the old versions, cf. Brunet, V.T. Vol. XVI (1966), pp. 387–95. His interpretation does not carry conviction.

explained by their ripeness. This is improbable, because no comment is made on their condition. The real link is suggested by my rendering autumn rather than summer fruit for *qayits*. The Gezer calendar[1] makes it certain that the time for *qayits* fell approximately in August, but that does not mean that we should reckon it as summer in our sense, for any merely mechanical attempt to superimpose our seasons on the Palestinian year is apt to land us in serious misunderstandings. There August is essentially the end of the agricultural year; what is not ripe then will not ripen. We have this note of finality in *qayits* again in Jer. 8:20, where our versions translate it as summer though autumn is demanded by the sense. For good or bad Israel had borne her fruit, and now there remained only God's judgment on it; there was no reason why it should be postponed.

The final vision, which in spite of a slightly different introduction G. A. Smith is surely incorrect in seeing as being somewhat later in time,[2] was of God standing by the altar and commanding doubtless His attendant angels, *Smite the capitals* [of the columns supporting the roof] *till the thresholds shake and shatter them* [i.e. the fragments] *on the heads of all the people; and what are left of them I will slay with the sword; not one of them shall flee away, not one of them shall escape* (9:1).

In spite of virtual unanimity on the part of commentaries there is no real reason to suppose that the sanctuary at Bethel is particularly intended here. Any and every Israelite shrine was involved. There is no compelling evidence in Anos or elsewhere to make us think that the sanctuary in Bethel held the same unique position in Israel that the temple on Mount Zion held in Judah.

We may take it for granted that Israel shared in Judah's fatal delusion about organized religion. Just as in the days of Jeremiah men were sure of their safety as long as they were near the temple (Jer. 7:4), so in A.D. 70 many fanatical defenders of Jerusalem and the Temple against Titus believed to the last that God *must* intervene on their behalf even at the last hour. So too it must have been in the Northern kingdom.

It may very well be that the Bethel temple was destroyed by the earthquake Amos foretold, but if so it was no more than a symbol of the uselessness of their religion to protect them from the wrath of God. The altar was the symbol of the bringing together of God and man, of the creating of an at-one-ment, but now in the vision it had become the place of judgment. Marx and Engels might maintain that "religion is the opium of the people", but in fact they had only picked up and misapplied the dictum of one of the old Levellers in the time of the Commonwealth. He had meant that religion, in contrast to living, active faith, lulled the soul of men to sleep as nothing else could. All the discussion on the theological doctrine of righteousness will not necessarily lead a man to live righteously, and the

[1] DOTT pp. 201 ff.
[2] Op. cit. p. 187.

reiterated proclamation of righteousness by faith in Christ is no guarantee that the hearers, in spite of their intellectual assent, enter into the gift of God offered them.

Amos learnt from his last vision that nothing had sealed the fate of Israel more surely than its religion; not because it was a "false" or "perverted" religion, in our sense, but because it had in fact taken the place of humble and active faith and obedience to God. By its very existence it had encouraged the worshippers to refuse the prophetic message. That is why in the words of Amos there are no condemnations of the Northern shrines or priesthood and no summons to accept the Davidic monarchy and the true temple in Jerusalem. All the religious reformations in the world would have resulted merely in deeper inability to apprehend the will of God.

As he was later to express it to his critics (3:8), *The Lord God has spoken, who can but prophesy?* So he entrusted his sheep to some fellow townsman and went north to face the meretricious glitter of Israel's shallow civilization with the message of God's judgment at the doors. He had been admitted to the secrets of God (3:7), so he needed not to fear what man might seek to do to him.

CHAPTER X

AMOS AT BETHEL

WITH MANY OF THE PROPHETS WE CAN ONLY SPECULATE on the original order and setting of their oracles. With Amos, however, there are no grounds for reasonable doubt that we have his prophecy in the order in which it was spoken,[1] and that we have what amount to three separate "sermons", viz. 1:3–2:16, 3:1–6:14, 7:1–9:10 (this last including the report of an interruption, 7:10–17). This is a slight over-simplification, for it ignores the question, of no great interest to the ordinary reader, whether Amos caused minor additions to be made in the written version of his message. We shall see later that the closing promise (9:11–15) must be regarded as an appendix added by him after he had returned to Judah. Views of extensive interpolation, popular earlier this century, are today treated with far greater reserve. Those familiar with Moffatt's translation will know that he is in the old tradition and has bracketed many verses as later additions.

If, however, this interpretation of Amos is correct, we should ask ourselves how it was that the style and manner of his prophesying was so different from that of the other eighth-century prophets with their much shorter prophetic "units". We repeatedly gain the impression that they were not able to hold the attention of those to whom they prophesied for any great length of time. The position does not change until we reach Ezekiel and the post-exilic prophets.

In the first place it is easy to exaggerate the difference between Amos and his later contemporaries. The three main sections of his prophecy break up into short oracles in every way comparable with those of the others. Though I have used the word "sermon", I do not doubt that each shorter section was repeated a number of times until Amos could hope that some of his hearers at least knew them off by heart. We need not even assume that the longer second section need have been confined in its delivery to a single day though it probably was. What is vital, however, is the impression forced on us that Amos, unlike his later contemporaries, was able to hold the attention of his hearers for a considerable period of time, although we can trace signs of mounting hostility, of which the outburst of Amaziah, the priest of Bethel (7:10–13), was merely symptomatic.

---

[1] J. Morgenstern in his *Amos Studies* argues for an inconsiderable rearrangement that would transform the bulk of the book into one address, but he gives no convincing explanation for the present order, which cannot be accidental.

This can be most easily explained by assuming that Amos's oracles were delivered at Bethel at the great autumn festival in the eighth month (I Ki. 12:32), which was the New Year festival of the Northern Kingdom. There seems no adequate reason for not dating the prophecy shortly after the eclipse of 763 B.C. (cf. p. 62). The predominant tendency today is to date it about 750 B.C., but this does not seem to allow enough time for the breakdown of society pictured by Hosea. Morgenstern's dating in 751 B.C. involved hazardous suppositions.

It is only by assuming the background of the New Year festival that we can explain why the prophecy was delivered in Bethel rather than Samaria. We shall see that this supposition helps to explain the form and initial success of the message. The seven-day festival offered ample time for the delivery of the message.

Though we are not in a position even to guess at the details of the New Year festival, from the fact that Canaanite influence was so strong in Israel we may be certain that it stressed Jehovah's sovereignty and the renewal of nature under His control. Whether it was an actual "enthronement feast" as Mowinckel and others postulate for Judah, with far less probability (except possibly in the reigns of Ahaz and Manasseh), is in itself immaterial. There will have been a thrill of hope each New Year's Day, as the reaffirmation of Jehovah's rule was celebrated, that He would at long last rise in wrath against His enemies, who were Israel's enemies too, and destroying them bring in the long-desired day of Jehovah.

When Amos' voice rang out in the ears of the pilgrim worshippers, solemnly in the name of Jehovah consigning the neighbours of Israel one by one to destruction, the immediate response must have been one of incredulous and almost delirious joy. If Amos was a prophet indeed, his words could only mean that the longed-for day was at hand. It has for a long time been a commonplace of criticism that certain parts of 1:3–2:3 are later additions, and Moffatt in his translation has even gone so far as to bracket those sections he did not consider original. The grounds adduced in support of this view have always been suspect, because of their extreme subjectivity, and the very purpose of the oracles demands the mention of *all* of Israel's neighbours. They are not prophecies to be carried to the nations named and threatened, but recitations of unavoidable judgment to make it clear that the day of Jehovah was at hand.

The fact that neither Egypt nor Assyria is mentioned, to say nothing of Babylon and the tribes of the Iranian and Anatolian plateaus and the Ionians across the waters of the Mediterranean, does not militate against this interpretation. These played little part in popular thought in the Indian summer of Israel's glory under Jeroboam II; in the thinking of the time the complete enumeration of Israel's neighbours implied a completeness of judgment that would embrace those further peoples that found no mention by name.

The first troubling of the ecstasy, the first loosening of the spell, came with the mention of Judah (2:4 f). While the North doubtless considered itself the true Israel, it is clear that it never placed the South outside the covenant loyalty of Jehovah, and now the word of judgment had been spoken against Judah, vaguely it is true, but clearly for all that. Before the people could focus on this new concept, the storm broke, and incredulously they realized that the strange prophet was proclaiming that Israel would be the chief sufferer in the judgment to come. It seems, however, that something of the old enchantment lingered on, so that Amos was able to deliver a sustained message of judgment such as no other of the eighth-century prophets was apparently able to pass over to his hearers. The one major exception to this seems to be the incident recorded in Jer. 36:9–16.

We must now look at the leading thought of this the first part of Amos's message. We should first note that there is no question of nationalism in the condemnation. It is true that Syria (1:3–5) and Ammon (1:13–15) had sinned especially against Israel, and Edom (1:11 f.) against Judah, but Moab's evil act had been against Edom (2:1–3), and there is no ground for thinking that the slave trading of the Philistines (1:6–8) and of the Phoenicians (1:9 f.) had necessarily involved Israel. Though this is generally taken for granted, the failure to mention Israel or Judah points the other way; the marginal note to 1:9 in RV mg. may with advantage be ignored.

The clue to the six condemnations of the neighbours of Israel is given by the last. Moab's sin is to the average modern man so venial and so common – let us think of how many Jewish cemeteries were desecrated by the anti-semite – that it seems absurdly out of place in the list. For antiquity, however, the desecration of tombs was universally regarded with abhorrence. Here the matter had been made worse because the motive was not greed, which motivated the ordinary tomb robber, but sheer spite, the wish to revenge oneself on one who had passed beyond the conflicts of this life.

Conscience is not the voice of God in the sense that it provides a revelation of God's will to man. Its demands vary with the centuries and with the society of which the individual forms a part. But whatever the demands of conscience they come as a categorical imperative until a man deliberately blunts and sears his conscience. All the things condemned by Amos were recognized as evil in themselves, not merely in Israel, but by all the nations of the western Fertile Crescent.

Syria stands accused of cruelty for sheer delight in cruelty. Raiding, war and slavery were all taken for granted in the ancient world. A blood feud might cause a man to strike one who could no longer defend himself, but in warfare the victor's hand was normally stayed by surrender. He who yielded was spared, even if he was enslaved. But here the prisoners were doomed to a ghastly death by being bound, laid on a threshing floor and crushed and cut to pieces by having heavy threshing sledges, their undersides studded with sharp pieces of basalt rock, driven over them (cf. also II Ki. 8:12). In perhaps cruder form they were guilty of the same evil as was Assyria, an evil that made God's judgment inevitable, even if delayed.

As we have already said, slavery was taken for granted in the ancient world. In all the uncertainties of life, constantly threatened by warfare, nomad raiding, famine and plague, slavery was for those broken the only hope of life and often the way of mercy. It came the more easily for them, since the kings looked, at least in theory, on all their subjects as their slaves. Slave trade was quite another matter, especially when, driven by greed for gain, it was not content with a glut of prisoners of war or the fortuitously kidnapped adolescent. It was the Phoenician, more and more enslaved by the conscienceless commerce that had become his life, who had made it a reality in the western Fertile Crescent, until in the craze for gain solemn treaties (*the brotherly covenant*) were swept away. Evidently the poison had spread to the Philistines astride the great land trade-route as well, and on them fell the same condemnation.

For the Bne Ammon the condemnation comes, as in the case of Syria, for wanton cruelty and barbarity with the superficially strange remark *that they might enlarge their border*. A reference to II Ki. 15:16 suggests that the ripping open of the pregnant woman was not simply an act of sadistic cruelty, but the final act in the barbarous extermination of an entire population. The two other passages where this practice is mentioned, viz. II Ki. 8:12, Hos. 13:16, are certainly consistent with this interpretation.

In some ways the most remarkable of the condemnations is that of Edom, and it has been thought by many to represent too advanced a stage of thinking to be attributed to Amos. It is said that we have passed from the realm of actions to that of motives. Such an objection comes from interpreting the oracle in the setting of today and not in that of the ancient Near-East. The concepts of honour and of the need to avenge insult and injury formed an integral part of the life pictured in the Old Testament. The Law of Moses moderated it with an insistence on "eye for eye, tooth for tooth, hand for hand, foot for foot, burning for burning, wound for wound, stripe for stripe" (Ex. 21:24 f.), i.e. the revenge must not exceed the injury; a further modification was the institution of the cities of refuge for the accidental homicide. But revenge as such is never forbidden. But while the neighbours of Israel might show less moderation in revenge they clearly deprecated excess. Excess was the sin of Lamech, "I have slain a man for wounding me, and a young man for bruising me: if Cain shall be avenged sevenfold, truly Lamech seventy and sevenfold" (Gen. 4:23 f.). Such excess brought a curse with it. Edom had no grounds to love Judah and had long scores to pay; but the desire for vengeance had become a consuming fire that took no account of measure or moderation and would destroy him who sought vengeance.

GOD'S JUSTICE

By implication at least, God affirmed through Amos that man's conscience comes from Him. Man's feelings of a compelling must, however varied his standards of right and wrong, are not merely the effects of economic and other material causes, are not merely an effort by the "haves" to keep the "have-nots" in their place. However dimly and falsely men may draw the boundary, there are such things as absolute right and wrong based on the nature of the Creator and Ruler of all.

Among the complications of life and the sophistries of society, man, his conscience damaged by past sin and heredity, is always tempted to think relativistically, to tone down black and white to shades of neutral grey. We have too often stood bemused by the complexities of our own situation to want to sit in judgment on those who want to ease the harshness of decision. But where a man once knows what is right and what is wrong, woe is him if he deliberately chooses the wrong. As Charles Kingsley so truly said of Hereward the Wake, when he had his marriage with his faithful Torfrida dissolved that he might marry another:

He had done a bad, base, accursed deed. And he knew it . . . he knew that the deed was evil, and chose it nevertheless. Eight hundred years after a far greater genius and greater general had the same choice . . . and he chose as Hereward chose. But as with Napoleon and Josephine, so it was with Hereward and Torfrida. Neither throve after.

What is true of the individual is true also of nations. When a society acquiesces in and welcomes an evil, knowing it is evil, that society is doomed. What Amos proclaimed of the small neighbours of Israel, later prophets affirmed of Egypt, Assyria and Babylon, and in apocalyptic language of the Seleucid kings. John in the Apocalypse foretold the same of imperial Rome (even though Babylon the great is more than the Rome he knew).

Amos' message was welcomed by the worshippers at Bethel not merely for its own sake, for its apparent foretelling that the day of Jehovah was at hand. They welcomed it because, until it was turned against themselves, their conscience told them that if Jehovah was a personal and moral Being and not merely a blind force, if He was in any way Judge and Ruler over whatever other gods there might or might not be, He must act in this way. Modern man's indifference to the preaching of hell is a sorry tribute not merely to the false way it has so often in the past been preached by the church but also to the fatty degeneration of the modern conscience.

THE SIN OF JUDAH

Many have thought that we may not see Amos in this short oracle (2:4 f.), because its terms are too vague and general in contrast with the specific accusations against Israel's neighbours and Israel itself. This is an objection that has the fusty smell of the study hanging about it. The oracle is not one for Judah's consumption, but it is a preparation for the message to Israel, which is the goal and purpose of all that goes before. To have omitted Judah altogether would have been to lay Amos open to the charge of partiality; on the other hand, to have started an enumeration of specific sins would have so entranced many of his hearers that they would have had little attention left for the oracle against Israel. It is brief, but very much to the point.

When faced with the superior might and riches of the Northern Kingdom, Judah will always have answered, "But *we* have the true worship of Jehovah, the sanctuary He has chosen for His abode!" It was not a question of how great Judah's sins were compared with Israel's, though Isa. 5:8–23 shows they were bad enough. Because Judah gloried in having what Israel did not have, Judah would be judged by its lack of loyalty to that which it gloried in. As our Lord said to the Pharisees who asked Him whether He was calling them blind (with the clear implication that they did not consider themselves to be), "If you were blind, you would have no sin, but now that you say, 'We see' your sin remains" (Jn. 9:41).

THE SIN OF ISRAEL

The men of Israel, as always in the prophets the rich rulers of the people, are accused of two things: a denial of the moral nature of Jehovah and ingratitude for His goodness.

One of the most remarkable passages in the Pentateuch is Ex. 22:22 ff., "You shall not afflict any widow or fatherless child. If you afflict them in any wise and they cry at all unto Me, I will surely hear their cry; and My wrath shall wax hot, and I will kill you with the sword; and your wives shall be widows, and your children fatherless." The Law of the Covenant was not merely an ideal; it was the basis of the existence of Israel. However much God might work through judges and kings, making them His representatives, He never abandoned His claim to be Judge and King of Israel. In theory the judges and rulers of the people never forgot this and gloried in their Divinely given position. If then God's representative, who knows and glories in the fact of being God's representative, deliberately perverts the law given by God, he is in fact claiming that this law is only a mere façade, and that the God behind it is arbitrary and without interest in justice. He is the God of the big battalions, of the "haves"; poverty and want are a sign of Divine displeasure, therefore kick and trample on the man who is down.

It is to be noted that we are not dealing with men who had fallen into great temptation. It is not here a question of every man having his price or of some social climber trying desperately "to keep up with the Joneses". The bribe (2:6) had been the price of a pair of shoes, or as we would say today "the price of a packet of fags". The same attitude is revealed by the fact that their immorality – whether with a temple prostitute or a common harlot matters not – from which any normal sensualist would shrink (2:7), actually took place on sacred ground, implying that of course Jehovah was quite indifferent.

Their ingratitude was shown by their attitude towards Nazirite and prophet. In a society where service for Jehovah was virtually confined to a hereditary caste, Naziriteship offered the simple man an opportunity for showing his love for God by his long hair that marked him out, by his renunciation of wine, the one luxury of the poor man, and by the care in his walk to avoid touching any form of corpse. For the rich, cynical rulers of Israel any form of religious "enthusiasm" was an abomination.

It is hardly necessary to say that it has been most rare for men to say to the prophet *Prophesy not* (2:12). Above all, in a land like Israel, where there will have been a superabundance of prophetic groups, of prophets and of sons of the prophets, this will not have happened. More subtle are the means by which the proclaimer of the word of the Lord is silenced. Where position and rank and even daily bread depend on the message given, there will have been all too many who will have known how to blunt the sharp edge of the message given them by God. Even today we are sadly familiar with the preacher who preaches the whole Bible most faithfully but yet so that none of his hearers are ever shaken out of their sins. I myself have been told by a sincere Christian man, who was motivated, as he thought, purely by concern for my well-being, "You mustn't say that kind of thing here, or you will not be invited again." How many a man of God has been passed over when a minister has been wanted: "He is not the man for *us*." There are many ways of saying to the prophet *Prophesy not*, and one and all they are an abomination to God and bring judgment on God's people.

The Second "Sermon"

The first shock of Amos' message will have created a dual reaction. On the one hand many grumbled that it was entirely unfair to compare Israel with its pagan neighbours. Even though it undeniably had its faults, they could not reasonably be placed in the balance with the fact of Israel's knowledge of Jehovah and of its consequent keeping of the law and its sacrificial system. Then on the other hand some, while granting that Amos was a prophet, suggested that this particular message will hardly have come from Jehovah, but was a mere expression of Judean bitterness at having to play second fiddle to Israel. As a result Amos began his second message with a devastating answer to both attitudes, *You only have I known of all the families of the earth; therefore I will visit upon you all your iniquities* (3:2).

These words demolished for ever any justification for the idea that there
: leavage between the grace and the righteousness of God; that God by

a legal fiction can bestow on a man a standing that is not reflected in his life; that He can ignore sin because He loves the sinner.

This is not the place to write an essay on the Atonement, but a few remarks seem called for. One of the greatest tragedies of the Reformation controversy was that in the mind of the common man (not, be it insisted, in that of the theologian) there grew up the idea that when the Protestant rightly insisted on interpreting "being justified freely by His grace" (Rom. 3:24, etc.) as "being accounted righteous" and not "being made righteous", the latter idea was being turned out of doors. The teaching of the Roman Church was that, when a man was made righteous by a combination of God's grace and his own effort, then God would also finally account him righteous. The reformer said "No; through trust in the death and resurrection of Jesus Christ, man by God's grace alone is accounted righteous in order that by the work of the Holy Spirit he may finally be made righteous." There is nowhere in the New Testament a suggestion that status without fulfilment is sufficient, though the fulfilment is as much the work of God as the conferring of the status. "I am sure that He who began a good work in you will bring it to completion at the day of Jesus Christ" (Phil. 1:6).

As might be expected, this is the teaching of the Old Testament as well, though the terms used may be somewhat different. Particularly in *Deuteronomy* (7:7, 9:6, etc.) it is repeatedly stressed that Israel's standing as God's people is purely an act of God's grace and election love and in spite of the people's character. Having elected him, God had given him the most perfect of laws (Deut. 4:8), and He expected him to keep it (Deut. 10:12, etc.).

You only have I known. When used of persons *yada'* does not mean a mere collection of information about them. It involves an imparting of one's own person to the one known, for true knowledge of another person can come only by the sharing of personalities. This knowledge is best expressed and pictured by marriage, where *yada'* is regularly used of the sexual act, cf. Gen. 4:1, 17, 25, etc. That is why Israel is so often shown as the wife of Jehovah. Amos does not attribute ignorance of other nations to God or even indifference to them. It is simply that He has given Himself in a special way to Israel, and this in turn has caused Israel to know Him as the nations do not and cannot.

Modern study of the Old Testament, in spite of its shortcomings, has provided a valuable antidote to the flaccid "Christians before Christ" attitude of much older exegesis. But however much it has shown the close parallels between the popular religion of Israel and that of its neighbours, it has also, often apparently against its own wish, borne testimony to the fact that, however much Israel was attracted to the religions around it, it always maintained its distinctiveness. Even during the depths of Manasseh's apostasy one gets the impression of an artificiality and exaggeration about it, which differentiate it from the "natural" paganism around it. We see the religion of Israel more clearly than ever, in spite of so much human frailty, as something that cannot be explained by evolutionary theories. This is due to the fact that God's knowing of Israel involved Israel's knowledge of God. The Exodus and Sinai had changed Israel; he could never again be the same, nor could he be "like all the nations", however much he might wish to be.

Much anti-Jewish prejudice fastens on the Jews' alleged claim to be "the chosen people". But, as Maritain has said,

> Thus from the first Israel appears to us a mystery of the world and the mystery of the Church. Like them it is a mystery lying at the very core of redemption. . . . Israel, which is not of the world, is to be found at the very heart of the world's structure, stimulating it, exasperating it, moving it. . . . If the world hates the Jews, it is because the world clearly senses that they will always be "outsiders" in a supernatural sense, it is because the world detests their passion for the absolute and the unbearable stimulus which it inflicts. It is the vocation of Israel that the world execrates.[1]

The simple fact is that God has placed His mark on Israel, and he cannot help being different.

Therefore I will visit upon you all your iniquities. This is in itself no threat of extra or severer punishment. It is the statement that when God passes Israel's history in review every iniquity will be marked up against it. The difference between sin and iniquity (*'avon*) is not hard to grasp. Sin is the failure to meet God's requirements; it may be conscious or unconscious, deliberate, accidental, or even unwanted. Iniquity implies that there is a degree of deliberation or of distortion of mind and will. The dim and enfeebled conscience of the nations may not have recognized many of their sins for what they really were, but Israel has so known God that it cannot fail to recognize its deliberate sins, its iniquities, though it may often shut its eyes to them. For the world, for Israel and above all for the Church the principle has always held good: "And that servant, who knew his Lord's will, and made not ready, nor did according to His will, shall be beaten with many stripes; but he that knew not, and did things worthy of stripes, shall be beaten with few stripes. And to whomsoever much is given, of him shall much be required: and to whom they commit much, of him will they ask the more" (Luke 12:47 f.).

THE DIVINE LOGIC OF PROPHECY

We are as prone as the men of Israel in Amos' day to discredit the word of prophecy when we hear it. However highly we may value the speaker as a general rule, we are always ready to suggest, when it suits us, that in this case he has exaggerated or misunderstood.

Amos reduced the logic of prophecy to its simplest terms. For him there

[1] *Anti-Semitism*, pp. 17, 20.

was fundamentally no mystery about it. If two men travel together it must be by prior agreement (3:3) – something more obvious in the relatively sparse population and unsettled conditions of Amos' day than it would be in the crowds and security of England today. The hunting lion does not roar or growl in satisfaction until its prey is caught, otherwise the prey would only be startled and the lion left supperless (3:4). The bird caught in the net presupposes a bait set for it; nor do the flaps of the net jump up unless something has been caught in it (3:5). Up to this point Amos has been enumerating everyday sights and sounds from which obvious deductions would be drawn by all. What follows is not so obvious to us.

When the sentinel's alarm horn has sounded, fear grips the town's inhabitants. Just as surely the coming of outstanding catastrophe and misfortune points to God at work. At this point commentaries underline that the ancient world "often took no account of what we term 'secondary causes'" and that "Amos is here omitting the intermediate chain of causation". Modern man is so conscious of the laws of nature, of the means used by God in blessing or judgment, that he seldom, if ever, sees God's hand in the disasters that smite him. When the preacher laments the lack of a prophet to interpret God's signs in history and nature, it is generally because men do not want to have them interpreted. It is seldom that the prophets claim a special revelation in this field. For them, since God is the God of law and order, it is obvious that the catastrophic and chaotic must be the expression of His will in judgment on sin, which is lawlessness.

But even in Old Testament times there are no grounds for thinking that most catastrophes of nature were taken by the ordinary man as a call to repentance. Certainly Amos 4:6-10 does not create the impression that the disasters that had spoken so vividly to the prophet had had much effect on the men of Israel. Right through the canonical prophets from Jeremiah (2:30) to Haggai we find the same insensitivity to God's judgments through nature. Amos' principle was given lip-service but seldom taken to heart.

As obvious as these normal facts from life is that God will not do anything – in the context calamity and punishment are uppermost – without revealing His secret purpose to His servants the prophets. It need hardly be mentioned that the "nothing" of 3:7 has its elements of exaggeration, cf. II Ki. 4:27, but the vital principle is that all God's acts among men reveal and are intended to reveal His character and will. It should stand to reason therefore that God will not leave Himself without men able to interpret these actions.

Now Amos comes to the climax of his series (3:8). Even in these days of modern firearms there are few who can hear the lion's roar, when they are in the open, without a contraction of the heart. God has spoken – the lion's roar of 1:2 – and the prophetic oracle is the prophet's trembling response. There has for long been a tendency to draw a distinction between

Jeremiah and the other canonical prophets, to find in him a sensitivity and a sense of compulsion (cf. Jer. 4:19–21, 15:15–18, 20:7–9, etc.) that are lacking in the others. They may well have been more marked in Jeremiah, but here Amos is claiming that prophecy is the outcome of an awesome compulsion. The nature of the prophet's message should be the best guarantee of its genuineness.

Where the people of God's choice are concerned, judgment on them is involved in an inescapable problem. In a world where the sovereignty of God is denied either in the interests of polytheism or because the forces and laws of nature are virtually deified, for man's sake it becomes necessary for God to safeguard His honour, when He punishes His people. Otherwise their sufferings will be attributed to His weakness and inability to control the forces around Him.

Hence Amos invites the Egyptians and Philistines (Ashdod – but the LXX Ashur, i.e. Assyria, so RSV may very well be correct) to come and see what is taking place in Samaria, so that when the hour of doom arrives they may agree that justice, and only justice, has been done (3:9–11). If the invitation is to Assyria and Egypt, it is to the only two powers of the time through which judgment could well come. If it is to the Philistines and Egyptians, it means that the small and the great alike are invited.

When the judgment fell there would be a small remnant left (3:12). This would not be as an act of grace – this statement is no necessary denial of 9:8, 9, for in prophecy there is never any hesitation to make extreme remarks, which can be modified later – but to demonstrate that the judgment had happened with God's full knowledge and permission. Under Palestinian conditions it was considered unavoidable that a shepherd would lose an occasional sheep snatched by a lurking beast of prey. To demonstrate his watchfulness, however, he was expected to bring home some part of the victim – *two legs or a piece of an ear* – snatched from the devourer. If he failed to do this, he was under suspicion of having eaten the sheep himself and was expected to pay its price to its owner. Lest any might think that some irresistible power had overwhelmed Israel, Jehovah would present His trophy to show that all had happened under His control.

Lest there be any doubt as to those on whom judgment should fall, Amos adds, *So shall the children of Israel be rescued that sit in Samaria on the corner of a couch and in Damascus on a divan.* This rendering, rejected by the RV and RSV mainly because II Ki. 14:28 was not taken seriously, shows that not the poor peasantry, but the rich, lording it both in Samaria and in vassal Damascus, would bear the brunt of judgment. There is, however, much to be said for I. Rabinowitz's rendering,[1] involving a different division of the Heb. consonants: "So shall the Israelites who dwell in Samaria be 'rescued' – in the form of a corner of a couch and of a piece

[1] V.T., Vol. XI (1961), pp. 228–31.

out of the leg of a bed!" So it would be that summer house and winter
house with all their panelling of ivory would perish (3:15). So in fact it
was, for the 27,290 whom Sargon removed into exile (II Ki. 17:6)[1] were
for the most part the remnant of those richer men to whom Amos had
pronounced God's judgment.

It may have been the scornful toss of the head or laugh of a group of
rich women passing by or listening at a discreet distance that turned Amos
for a minute from his main theme to throw perhaps his bitterest oracle of
all at them,

Hear this word, you Bashan cows,
who live on the hill of Samaria,
who oppress the poor, who crush the needy,
who say to their husbands, Bring that we may drink.
The Lord Jehovah has sworn by His holiness,
that behold the days are coming upon you,
when you shall be taken away with hooks
and the last of you with fishhooks.
And you shall go out through the breaches,
everyone straight before her,
and you shall be thrown into the dung-pit[2]
– oracle of Jehovah (4:1–3).

Bashan was famous for its cattle (cf. Psa. 22:12), and so Amos is calling
the rich women of the capital "fat cows". If the placing of Amos'
prophecy at the New Year festival is correct, there is nothing surprising at
their being in Bethel at this time.

The word rendered "oppress" is used particularly of defrauding, e.g.
Lev. 19:13, Deut. 24:14, I Sam. 12:3f. Amos is not suggesting that the
women were directly involved in oppression, but that their continual
demands on their husbands for luxuries and wine in plenty drove them to
the wrongs and injustices of which they were guilty. While this in no way
excuses the men, it does remind us that the real cause of many a wrong
rests with unnoticed people behind the scenes. Though they are far from
being the only ones involved, that mad contest, today popularly called
"keeping up with the Joneses", which is as old as civilization, has normally
derived its main drive from the women, and they in turn are ultimately
the main sufferers from it.

The fate Amos foresees for the women is terrible, but common enough
in the long history of Assyrian conquest and cruelty. He sees them led out
like a long line of cows through the breaches in the walls of captured

---

[1] cf. ANET, pp. 284 f., DOTT, pp. 58 ff.
[2] Heb. has the meaningless "to the *harmon*"; I follow T. H. Robinson's emendation, based
on Duhm, which may have some support in LXX.

Samaria, hooks in their noses according to a frequent Assyrian custom (cf. Isa. 37:29), going straight ahead, unable to choose the smoothest path. There is a darker shadow too, if T. H. Robinson's emendation and explanation of the unintelligible *harmon*, adopted above, is correct.[1] He sees others as corpses dragged out to the mass burial pit, where the dead are thrown as so much rubbish without even the minimum of burial rites. How certain their fate was is shown by God's oath by His holiness, that aspect of His nature so separated from man that man cannot possibly move or influence it in any way.

THE FOLLY OF ISRAEL'S RELIGION

Already before he had broken off his message to turn on the rich women, Amos had made it clear that in the hour of calamity Israel's religion would fail them, for such is the most likely reason for his saying (3:14) that the horns of the altar of Bethel would be cut off. Whatever their original symbolism – and they were not peculiar to the worship of Israel – they were evidently seen as providing asylum (I Ki. 1:50; 2:28). But even earlier he had rejected the whole popular religion. In his shocked picture of their defiance of Jehovah he had said (2:8): *In the house of their god they drink the wine of such as have been fined.* We must stress "their". This is no half-expressed accusation of idolatry, but an indication that where men challenge God in their worship of Him, He refuses to acknowledge that He is the object of their worship.

Now Amos turned and mocked the whole glittering ceremonial of Bethel (4:4,5). Let them heap ritual upon ritual and sacrifice upon sacrifice until every day became a New Year's Day, and so their tithes, due every third year (Deut. 14:28), would be brought every third day. Let them even try innovations in the cultus and make leavened bread part of their thankofferings. It would all mean no more than an increase of transgression, for they had ignored God's earlier rejection of their sacrifices as revealed by their misfortunes (4:6–11). To persist in and to multiply that which God has refused to accept is one of the deepest possible insults to God. It implies that He is a being of whims, that He may be bribed, or may yield to sheer importunity. Though v. 12 seems to be final, like all prophetic threats it is the offer of forgiveness, if there is a turning to God.

It should be specially noted that Amos did not find fault with Bethel's golden bull (I Ki. 12:28 f.), nor with the lack of an Aaronic priesthood (I Ki. 12:31), nor with many other things that doubtless did not agree with the ritual laid down in the law of Moses. These things were all symptoms, not causes. Had he preached against them, it would have been easy for a powerful king like Jeroboam II, who had nothing to fear from Judah, unlike the former king of the same name, to make a clean sweep of all these things and to return to a pure ritual and cultus, as did Hezekiah in

[1] Robinson–Horst, *Die Zwölf Kleinen Propheten* (H.A.T.), pp. 84 f.

Judah about half a century later. But had he done so the effect would have been as superficial as it was in Judah under both Hezekiah and Josiah, for it would not have touched his subjects' inner attitude to God. Regeneration and not reformation should always be the Church's task.

All the distresses that had come on Israel were merely God's forerunners, the dust that heralded His coming. Israel's obduracy would merely cause the judgments to continue until, metaphorically at least, it met its God face to face (4:12). What sort of God would it find Him?

He that forms the mountains, and creates the wind,
and declares unto man what is his thought.

Modern man is so fascinated by his own skills that he increasingly forgets or belittles God the Creator. He forgets that he is merely the child in the nursery playing with the building blocks that God has provided for him. All the energy he turns out in his power houses in a year, if transported to the sun and released in a moment of time, would scarce provide enough additional energy to be recorded by the measuring instruments of man on earth. All the marvels of scientific instruments sent up in space satellites are but small compared with those of the insect born today and dead tomorrow, its appointed task completed. An example of man's megalomania was the widespread belief a few years ago that his nuclear tests were materially altering the weather.

Amos depicts God as the former of the mountains. Whether we reckon the existence of *homo sapiens*, of true man, on the earth in thousands or in tens of thousands of years, the mountains are the one essentially unchanged feature in the landscape of the world as he has known it. Geology has taught us that mountains too change and vanish, but that happens on a time scale too vast for us, even could we prolong our lives to the years of a Methuselah. But He is also the creator of the wind, often the shortest lived, the least predictable and the least tamable of God's creatures. Whether it be the cooling zephyr, or the seasonable winds on whose regularity man relies, or the gale and hurricane, all are called forth by God at His will.

Even when man has to bow to the forces of nature he can neither tame nor control, he prides himself at least on the creativeness of his spirit, on his thoughts, autonomous and hidden until he chooses to reveal them. But God declares and reveals man's thought to man, for not even there can man rule free from the sovereignty of God.

He that makes the morning darkness
and treads upon the high places of the earth;
Jehovah, the God of hosts, is His name.

Both eclipse and earthquake (cf. Mic. 1:3 f.) are in God's control. The

predictability of the one (to us at least, though not to Amos) and the un-
predictability of the other are both expressions of His rule and sovereignty.
In brief, His title is Jehovah, the God of hosts. He is the self-consistent,
fundamentally unchanging, infinitely beyond man's grasp, though He
makes Himself known to him. Added to this every power and lordship in
the universe is at his beck and call. He is the Controller of all created
hosts within His creation.

For Israel to have to meet such a God, when He comes in judgment, can
have only one outcome. So Amos lifts up the funeral lament over Israel
(5:1, 2) and declares that the most that can hope to escape are God's
tithe (5:3).

How foolish in the light of all this is the cult of sanctuaries and holy
places (5:5)! We do not doubt that God in His grace appeared to Jacob in
Bethel, but He was equally with him in far-off Haran in Padan-aram. The
stone circle in Gilgal commemorated God's power over Jordan in the days
of Joshua, but He showed it equally, or even more strikingly, in Egypt by
the ten plagues and the dividing of the Red Sea. The Patriarchs experienced
the protection and guidance of God in Beer-sheba, but so they did in
Egypt and Mesopotamia as well. The gracious revelation of God in space
and time does not bind Him to any given spot or season. These can at the
best serve to stir up our memories, but never as fetters by which men can
bind the Lord. They may be set apart for His worship by grateful men, but
they can be no more holy than any other place, for "the whole earth is full
of His glory". The hardened sinner was no safer in Bethel, or Gilgal, or
even Jerusalem, than he would be in Samaria, where there had never been
a theophany, a manifestation of the glory and presence of God.

Lest there might be some lingering hope that God might yet allow
himself to be persuaded, bribed or cajoled, Amos reminded them once
again (5:7) that the real charge against them was that they had turned
judgment to wormwood and had thrown away God's standards (righteousness) in disdain. Already in the story of Abraham we find Jehovah recognized as the righteous Judge of all the earth (Gen. 18:25). But these men,
who represented Him among His own people, were not merely unjust;
they had made the very thought of justice bitter and an abomination to
those who were wronged. LXX, however, suggests that the Heb. text is
corrupt. Watts may be correct in rendering:[1]

It is Jehovah who pours out justice from above
and who grants righteousness to the earth.

Amos looked to the great uniformities of nature (5:8 f.), the star con-
figurations that have remained unchanged ever since there was life on our
globe, and the change of day and night that never fails.

[1] V.T., Vol. IV (1954), pp. 215 f.

(Seek Him) that has made the Pleiades and Orion
and turns deep darkness into day
and darkens day into night;
that gathers the waters of the sea
and pours them upon the earth;
that makes Taurus to shine forth after Capella
and Taurus to set hard on the rising of Vindemiatrix,
His name is Jehovah.[1]

There are no more fitting pictures of the unchangeable nature of Jehovah. He had revealed Himself to Israel as the one sitting enthroned upon the cherubim, with the tables of stone engraved with the ten commandments safely guarded under His feet in the ark of the covenant, so there could be no question of the fate of those who had trampled underfoot the standards He Himself had revealed.

THE CALL TO TRUE RELIGION

Amos summed up the situation by showing justice turned upside-down (5:12). It was the great transgressors who accused the just, i.e. those with right on their side, "in the gate", i.e. in the sessions of public justice, and because they bribed the judges they could be sure of the verdict. The poor man was pushed to one side, his plaint not even heard. So evil was the time (5:13) that only a fool or a prophet – not that there was much difference in public estimation – would lift his voice in protest.

Modern bribery is subtler in its nature, but it can therefore be even more effective. Oppression is often made respectable by its being done in the name of the community or some association. Refuge is even taken behind the letter of the law, while the whole spirit of the law is outraged. Doubtless oppression was never as blatant in Israel as the words of the prophets suggest. But lawlessness that wears the mantle of respectability is even worse than the open force of a society that knows no law.

So evil was the time that judgment could not be averted. At the best repentance would bring grace solely to *the remnant of Joseph* (v. 15) that would be left when the judgment of God had passed over the people. Repentance is pictured as the choice and love of the good, the rejection and hatred of the evil. In agreement with very much in prophetic religion, however, the good is equated with a right attitude to man rather than to God (cf. Jas. 1:27). Even as Isaiah in his great appeal (1:17) interpreted learning to do well by relieving the oppressed, judging the fatherless and pleading for the widow, so the good for Amos was establishing judgment in the gate.

[1] So Hoffmann (Z.At.W. III, pp. 110 f.), reproduced by G. R. Driver in JTS, 1953, pp. 208 f. Taurus, Capella and Vindemiatrix are constellations. The emendations to the Heb. are minimal.

The actual terms chosen are conditioned by the fact, as was pointed out earlier, that the prophets addressed their message first and foremost to the rich and mighty, but the underlying principle surely holds good for every class of society at every time. It is a sad misunderstanding of "true religion" when good works are looked on as a mere outward adornment of saving faith. The brutal fact is that "faith apart from works is dead" (Jas. 2:26). Where there is no living faith, man can at the best produce a sterile, legalistic imitation of the will of God. Where there is true faith he will seek and love the good, and this will inevitably reveal itself in his attitude to his fellow men. Since, however, Amos could see that there was no response to his call, he closed it with a picture of mourning and lamentation (5:16, 17), covering town and country alike. We should translate "They will call the farm-labourers to mourning . . . and among all vineyard-workers there will be wailing."

If we ignore the prophecy of Joel because of uncertainties as to its date, Amos 5:18 ff. is the first in which the Day of the LORD is clearly mentioned. But it is obvious that the prophet is speaking of a concept well known to his hearers. It is likely enough that the idea was as old as Israel's religion; it may be referred to in Deut. 33:2 f., if we understand the past tenses to be referring prophetically to the future, as is not infrequently the case. This much is certain, however, that as soon as Israel's experience of God's grace fell short of what had been expected, there was a turning to the future to redress the balance of the present. Since Jehovah was all-sovereign, the time was bound to come when He would intervene to deal with His enemies.

Amos clearly accepted this concept, but since he knew that the necessity of God's final intervention was due to the sins of His people and not to the strength of their enemies, he underlined that the judgment was one that would overtake *them* in the first place. They thought that the worse conditions became the nearer came their salvation through God's intervention. Graphically Amos depicted a man racing away from a lion only to be pulled up in his tracks by an approaching bear. In his desperation he saw a hut near the road, dashed into it and slammed the door. As he leant against the rough stone wall panting and grateful for this last-moment, humble refuge, a snake put its head out from a crack in the wall and bit him. The final refuge of the godless Israelite would prove more fatal than the disasters from which it seemed to offer shelter. True, God would intervene, but He would intervene first of all as judge of His people, as Amos had already implied in 3:1 f. It must not be forgotten that, at least for the prophets, any major intervention of God in judgment could be looked on as a day of the Lord[1], and the fall of Samaria (II Ki. 17:9–11) was doubtless so regarded.

[1] Cf. my *Men Spake from God*, p. 21.

Some Christians are as complacent about the second coming of Christ as were the Israelites about the Day of the Lord. They forget warnings like those of Luke 12:45-48, I Pet. 4:17 f. I Cor. 3:12-15, and II Cor. 5:10. When they sing their rapturous second advent hymns, they forget that when He comes they will be the first to be judged – before the world that rejects Him – and it will be a true and faithful judgment.

Amos had already mocked at the splendid and increasing ritual of Bethel (4:4 f.) and had pointed out that its sequel showed clearly that God had taken no pleasure in it (4:6-11). Now he made it clear that it was worse than useless (5:21-24).

The vital verse is *Let judgment roll down as waters, and righteousness as a never-failing stream* (5:24). Amos made it clear that God was not concerned with the details of worship and sacrifice. These might well be of some importance when men were doing God's will in their dealings with their fellow men, but until that hour came God was not concerned with such trifles. The whole system, whether ritually correct or incorrect, was an insult to God, an expression of the hypocrisy of the worshipper, a statement of the underlying belief that God could be either bribed, wheedled, or magically compelled by ritual exercises. The whole lot, sacrifices and psalms (*your songs*) alike, were an abomination.

Amos reminded them that sacrifices and offerings played a secondary role in the wilderness. For at least a century now it has been a commonplace among scholars that Amos denied that there were sacrifices in the wilderness at all. Indeed this is the only way in which the renderings of the AV, RV, and RSV can reasonably be understood. The question obviously demands the answer, "No." It was therefore inferred that he was denying that the ritual had any Divine validity at all.

More recently, however, this interpretation has been seriously questioned. Some, e.g. Snaith,[1] have pointed out that at that early stage in Israel's history all meat-eating involved sacrifice and that Amos could not have been ignorant of this. Others, e.g. Pfeiffer,[2] have underlined that had Amos been attacking sacrifice as such he would have been advocating an entirely different type of religion to that known until then. To quote Pfeiffer:

Amos, however, did not, as has been maintained, advocate the abolition of sacrifices: he did not oppose the institution but its misuse, and did not introduce a new order of service. He moralized religion, but did not substitute morality for religion.

More important is the slowly growing realization that all our traditional

[1] *Mercy and Sacrifice*, p. 94.
[2] *Introduction to the Old Testament*[2], p. 582.

renderings do in fact do violence to the Hebrew original. They, of necessity, lay their stress on *did you bring?*, but the inverted order of the Hebrew demands that *sacrifices and offerings* should be the principal words in the sentence. The only really satisfactory rendering suggested is that by Macdonald, viz. "Was it (only) sacrifices and offerings that you brought me in the wilderness during forty years?"[1]

When he is so rendered, Amos occupies exactly the same position as Jeremiah in 7:22 f. A careful study of *Exodus* reveals to us the fact, undreamt of by many, that the Law is divided into groups of descending importance. First of all there is the solemn and unconditional affirmation in advance of obedience to all God's commands (Exod. 19:3-8, cf. Jer. 7:23). There follow as a separate entity the Ten Commandments as the essence of God's will (Exod. 20:1-17). This was the only part of God's law-giving heard by all the people (Exod. 20:18 f.). Then we have "the Book of the Covenant" (Exod. 20:22-23:33; cf. 24:4, 7) as a sort of commentary on the Ten Commandments. It is to be noticed that ritual matters have virtually no mention in the Book of the Covenant. There follows the sealing of the covenant (Exod. 24:3-8). This was crowned by a sacred meal, the prototype of the peace offering, in which representative figures from Israel took part (Exod. 24:9-11).

Then and only then we get the ritual commands of God in most of the rest of *Exodus* and in the first sixteen chapters of *Leviticus*, as well as in numerous chapters of *Numbers*. They are, as it were, by-laws as binding as the covenant legislation because given by the same legislator but none the less secondary. The covenant was not created by the ritual; the ritual existed to maintain the covenant. The ritual did not and could not bring a man within the covenant, but was intended to maintain him within it. Thus even the rabbis in the days of the second temple demanded of the proselyte baptism, circumcision and sacrifice in this order. He could not bring sacrifice until he was within the covenant.[2]

So Amos is saying that before there was any question of sacrifice in the wilderness there had to be the unconditional acceptance of God's will. But how was it with Amos' contemporaries in Israel? For once he turned from their sins against their fellow men and looked more closely at their worship. Even in ancient times 5:26 presented major difficulties to those for whom the names of the defunct Assyrian deities were at the best but the vaguest of memories. So in Acts 7:43 we find Stephen quoting the best the LXX could make of the passage. Quite apart, however, from the rendering of the Hebrew, there is nothing anywhere else in the Bible to link such a false worship with the wilderness. Today there is fairly general

---

[1] See Rowley, *From Moses to Qumran*, footnote, pp. 73 f.
[2] Should any plead that the argument is invalid, because the Pentateuch is composed of varying sources of differing date, it is sufficient to remark that "the unknown editor", by the order he adopted, obviously held the above view.

agreement that we should translate, *You shall take up Sakkuth your king, and Kaiwan your star-god, your images which you made for yourselves* (RSV). Both Sakkuth and Kaiwan are found in Assyrian inscriptions as names of the planet-god Saturn.[1]

It may be that the worship of Saturn was brought into Israel, as a token of loyalty, when Jehu paid tribute to Shalmaneser III, or it may have been voluntarily adopted by the ruling classes in admiration for the power of Assyria. But there it was, an open avowal of disloyalty to Jehovah in the midst of Israel. Amos tells them they will carry their heathen symbols as useless lumber (cf. Isa. 46:1, 2) into exile beyond Damascus, i.e. to Assyria or whatever power might in the interval replace it. It was not revealed to Amos to what part of the Assyrian empire the exiles would be taken, and his hearers did not need to know.

LUXURY BLINDS

Amos ended his second "sermon" – we can be sure his hearers were growing very restive – by trying to show how utterly foolish Israel's, and indeed Judah's (*them that are at ease in Zion*), complacency was (6:1) All around their borders lay the ruins of city states (6:2) which had once appeared as possible formidable rivals to Israel: *are you better than these kingdoms? or is your border greater than their border?* As they had fallen so would Israel fall.

But so little could the rulers of Israel see the warning signs that *you summon the evil day, and cause the rule of violence to come near* (6:3). Luxury that leads merely to self-indulgence and concentration on the trivial – students of European history will find a parallel in the court of Louis XV of France – is bound to end in dire disaster. Little though they wanted the evil day, their whole lives were an invitation to it.

There can be little doubt that v. 7 was fulfilled to the letter. It was the survivors of the luxurious, idle rich who were in the vanguard of the 27,290 captives that Sargon II deported (cf. p. 159).

In the ancient Near-East, epidemics were a standing threat to man's welfare, and they were virtually unavoidable in a long-drawn-out siege like that of Samaria, which withstood Shalmaneser V for three years (II Ki. 18:10). So the final agonies of Israel are depicted in terms of starvation and plague. In a graphic picture a near relation (v. 10 – "uncle" is too specific) comes to carry out the last rites and finds the dead man mere skin and

[1] The Hebrew of vv. 25, 26 is difficult, and the explanation given is far from receiving universal acceptance. There are still those, e.g. H. Kruse (V.T., Vol. IV (1954), pp. 395 f.), who maintain that v. 26 refers to the wilderness wanderings. But there was no reason why Amos' contemporaries should be punished for their ancestors' idolatry. In any case Exod. 32:5 shows that the golden bull was a misguided attempt to worship Jehovah. The only other form of idolatry hinted at is the worship of desert demons (Lev. 17:7). Others, e.g. H. H. Hirschberg (V.T., Vol. XI, pp. 375 f.) seek to interpret the cult terms in v. 26 of the sexual Canaanite worship that was so rife in Israel. This may very well be correct, but it has not won sufficient acceptance to be introduced in the text.

bones. He cannot be buried, but must be burned, for the enemy are round about the city. As he calls out in the great, rich house, asking if there is yet someone alive, a weak, and it may well be dying, voice answers from a back room, "Yes! but don't mention the name of Jehovah!" To do so might be to attract His attention, and so bring even greater judgment. At last, but too late, the hand of God stretched out in judgment has been recognized.

Such a fate was inevitable, for the behaviour of Israel had been as sense-less as setting horses running over rocky ground or ploughing the sea with oxen (v. 12 – so RSV correctly).[1] So Amos closes this section with the invader swarming over the whole of Israel from north to south.

"YOU MUST NOT PROPHESY" – THE THIRD "SERMON"

If the reaction to the first "sermon" was "This cannot be God's mes-sage," the reaction to the second will have been "You cannot be a prophet at all." So Amos told them the visions that had constituted his call, which we considered earlier (cf. pp. 65–68).

We can be sure that Amaziah, the chief priest of Bethel, had little love for turbulent prophets. It is fairly certain that he had authority to deal with them (cf. Jer. 20: 1 f.; 29:24–27 and pp. 27 f.), but he had hesitated to inter-vene with one who had so strikingly caught the public ear. At last he decided that enough was enough, but thought it well, if possible, to push the responsibility over to the king. *I will rise against the house of Jeroboam with the sword* (7:9) sounded remarkably like high treason, especially if *the house of Jeroboam* were suitably modified to "Jeroboam" (7:11). So he sent a warning to the king.

The story demands that the king must have been in his palace in Bethel; Samaria would have been too far away. This is in itself a further strength-ening of the suggestion that the background is the New Year feast. We may imagine the king at table, when the messenger arrived, giving his loyal subjects an object lesson in how to guzzle and booze (6:4, 6). "Tell Amaziah to do his own dirty work. I'm too busy to deal with mad prophets" will have been the gist of his answer. Jeroboam II was too sure of his position to be afraid of any possible prophetic plots; and as for God's warnings, he was no more concerned than the rest of the people.

So even as Amos finished repeating his vision of the plumb-line and its application, Amaziah broke in: *Seer* – at one time the normal title for a prophet (I Sam. 9:9), it had, for reasons we can only partially discern, largely dropped out of use. Though it was justified by the recital of his visions, in Amaziah's mouth it was doubtless used with a mocking note. *Visionary! go, flee to Judah! you can earn your living there.* Amaziah was suggesting that Amos was sufficiently unbalanced to think that such an

---

[1] This rendering is obtained by a different division of the Heb. consonants.

unusual message would loosen the purse-strings in Bethel.

I am no prophet, nor am I one of the sons of the prophets, but I am a shepherd[1] *and a dresser of sycomore trees, but the Lord took me from following the flock; and the Lord said to me, 'Go, prophesy against My people Israel.'* The Hebrew is equally capable of being translated "I was no prophet, nor was I one of the sons of the prophets," but in spite of H. H. Rowley's defence of this rendering the present tense seems preferable. Amos denies not merely that he is a professional prophet by upbringing and training, but also that he has become one. He is expecting to return to the work he had left. He is indifferent whether any financial reward comes to him as a result of his words. God's messenger must always move in the tension between I Cor. 9:4–14 and I Cor. 9:15–18. In the moment when even inwardly he begins to think of his financial prospects he has become virtually useless to God. On the other hand, however, he has no right to dictate to God how he is to live. If God moves his hearer to open his purse to him he has no right to refuse.

Then in burning words came God's judgments on Amaziah. His wife would be a harlot with the enemy,[2] driven to such a life by dire need, for her husband would be impotent to help her. He would be childless, his children killed by the sword of the invader, and he would die a captive, knowing that his fields had been parcelled out by the conqueror, and that his people shared his lot.

Such a shattering answer will have swung the crowd, always glad to see a man in high place rebuked and shamed, to Amos' side. While Amaziah smoothed his ruffled dignity and collected the temple police, Amos had time to round off his message.

He turned on those who had enjoyed Amaziah's discomfiture most, the traders and middlemen. They were as bad as the powerful rich, and the poor had as much to suffer from them (8:4). They were not the great lords riding roughshod over justice, but the small men using every form of petty deceit and taking every advantage of the desperate need and debts of the poor, selling them into slavery for a trivial debt. They were weaker than the great, but they were also more rotten. The former took their religion seriously, even though it was fundamentally misconceived; for the latter it was a burden and a hypocritical cloak. The love of gain had so twisted them that every moment spent without the possibility of further gain was abhorrent to them. Nothing less than an earthquake could adequately symbolize Jehovah's hatred of such a perversion of human nature.

There are not many references to commerce in the Old and New Testaments, but they are virtually all condemnatory. The reason is not far

[1] For this rendering see p. 62.
[2] For this rendering see S. Speier, V.T., Vol. III (1953), pp. 308 ff.

to seek. There is nothing evil in trade and commerce as such. The whole of human history and civilization suggests that God never intended men to live purely self-sufficient lives. But all too often the motive that has driven a man from his native hearth and home has been the wish to "better himself" and not his fellow men. In the terrific competition of the home market, or facing the dangers and risks of other lands, all motives other than those of gain are apt to be submerged. Modern capitalism may perforce be more ethical than in past centuries, but its tendency is to have even less soul. In the passing glimpse given us by Amos we see that in Israel too, although it must have been predominantly an agricultural country, the cancer of the lust for gain had gained a firm footing.

There had been a day long before when it seemed that the sun of Israel was sinking before it had properly risen. In the days of the boy Samuel, when the Israelite amphictyony entered ever deeper into the shadow of growing Philistine power, and the amphictyonic sanctuary at Shiloh was a centre of immorality and the despising of God's will, we are told that "the word of the Lord was rare in those days; there was no frequent vision" (I Sam. 3:1). As it was then, so it should be when the sun of Israel was setting for ever. Its worst affliction would be a famine of the word of the Lord (8:11 f.).

One last word had to be said before Amaziah's police escorted Amos from the temple courts. The prophet was being driven out and with him went the glory of Israel. The one thing that marked out Israel from the nations was that it was the people of God. Once it turned its back on God's word and will it was no different in God's sight from the Negroes living in the far Sudan, and the Exodus shrank to an historic event of no greater importance or significance than the national movements of the Arameans or Philistines; these had been willed and led by God, as are all major events in human history, but they played no part in the history of salvation.[1] There is no colour prejudice or racial pride in Amos' mention of the Ethiopians; it was simply that they were the remotest people of whom Israel knew anything precise. The promise to Israel before Sinai had been, "If you will obey My voice indeed and keep My Covenant, then you shall be a peculiar people unto Me from among all peoples: for all the earth is Mine" (Exod. 19:5). Israel had rejected God in rejecting His prophet and so had dropped to the same level as all the nations.

God's judgment on the nations is always a just judgment (cf. Rom. 2:4–11), so His judgment on Israel would be just. It would be *all the sinners of My people* that should die by the sword (9:10). Nor would it be purely the negative judgment of the withdrawal of His protection and blessing. In the sifting of Israel *No pebble shall fall upon the earth* (9:9, RSV). The most useless and hardened sinner would remain under the control of the

---

[1] Kir is still unidentified; Caphtor is either Crete or Cappadocia – for the latter cf. G. A. Wainwright, *Caphtor Cappadocia* (V.T., Vol. VI (1956), pp. 199–210).

God he had slighted and disobeyed, until his God-willed fate overtook him.

AT HOME IN TEKOA

Ever since the rise of modern critical scholarship it has been a commonplace that the last five verses of Amos could not be by the shepherd prophet, though there have always been those who were prepared to defend the possibility of his authorship with more or less reserve. In fact the only really valid argument against them is that it is incredible that the prophet of unreserved judgment should suddenly weaken his whole message by speaking of restoration and blessing. I accept the force of the argument, but do not consider that it proves what it is thought to.

We have no grounds for thinking that Amos continued in Israel or was even allowed to remain. News travels fast in the East, and it will not have been long before his native Tekoa and indeed Jerusalem knew of the shepherd prophet who had bearded the king of Israel and his grandees at the royal sanctuary at their most solemn feast. Then some two years later came the prophesied earthquake, so disastrous that it was still remembered in the days of Zechariah after the Babylonian exile (14:5) – it is probably also referred to in Isa. 9:10. We can easily understand that Amos should have been urged to leave a permanent record of his message.

As he wrote or dictated it the question must have presented itself relentlessly: "Is this all? Have God's purposes been finally frustrated by the sin of Israel?" So it is that he ended his message on a note of hope, less for Israel for whom there was now no hope and more for those to whom his unchanging message of an unchanging God should come.

There is no need to see the hand of an exilic or post-exilic writer in *In that day I will raise up the booth of David that is fallen and repair its breaches, and raise up its ruins, and rebuild it as in the days of old* (9:11, RSV). It is out of line with the language of later prophecies and gives every indication of being earlier than the much more drastic prophecy in Isa. 11:1. Once the complete split between North and South had taken place, the Davidic kings had lost their proud claim to be king of Israel, king of God's people, and the proud empire, the fulfilment of the promises to the Patriarchs of old, had become merely a nostalgic memory. The present promise goes no farther than to imply the reunion of the divided kingdoms and the restoration of the boundaries of the Davidic empire, as it includes merely *all the nations over whom My name has been called*. We have not reached the level of Messianic expectation we find in Isaiah.

Though the figure of the Messiah remains embryonic, we are introduced to the Messianic age (9:13–15). Here again many object to the apparently purely materialistic picture that contrasts so oddly with Amos's spiritual message. They overlook that the thought of Psa. 107:33–38 seems to be basic in the Old Testament. Man and the land on which he lives are inextricably united. The condition of the land is evidence of the spiritual condition of those who live in it. Therefore such a picture of material blessing must imply the prior transformation of the people. It is this transformation that makes it morally possible for God to say, *I will plant them upon their land, and they shall no more be plucked up out of their land which I have given them.*

CHAPTER XI

HOSEA'S MARRIAGE

TEN YEARS OR LESS AFTER AMOS HAD STARTLED AND shaken Israel by his message a young man, Hosea ben Bichri, married Gomer bat Diblaim, certain that in his choice he had been obeying God's will.

We cannot tell whether as a lad he had hung on Amos' words, or whether they had been repeated in his home town by some startled but sceptical pilgrim. Then had come the earthquake two years later, and it will have shaken Hosea to the core. While most around him muttered "coincidence," he turned to seek the Lord even more sincerely. Gradually his eyes were opened to see how truly Amos had depicted the society in which he lived. Then the Lord spoke to him, commanding him to marry (1:2).

Before we look more closely at the command and its consequences, there are a number of technical points to be considered. I have taken it for granted that Amos prophesied before Hosea. On the modern conservative side E. J. Young does not even discuss it; it is assumed.[1] On the liberal side the only voice known to me raised in favour of the priority of Hosea is Snaith's and the impression created is that of a *tour de force* not taken too seriously even by the author.[2] Kaufmann's view of two Hoseas, the first in Ahab's reign, hardly calls for mention.[3]

The early scribes who put Hosea first in the Book of the Twelve may have been influenced by its relatively greater length or by the attractiveness of its proclamation of the love and loyalty of God in contrast to the stark denunciations of Amos. In any case the Talmudic discussion on the subject gives the impression that the original reason had been long forgotten.[4]

The reason for this virtually universally accepted order is not a comparison of Hos. 1:1 with Amos 1:1. Though the relative order is clearly indicated here, this is not an argument that would weigh very heavily with the liberal, who so readily writes off such statements as the work of later and often mistaken editors. The reason lies in the clear recognition that the picture of Israelite society given by Hosea shows a much greater degree of corruption than that depicted by Amos. It is surprising that

[1] *An Introduction to the Old Testament* (The Tyndale Press, 1964), see Table p. 199.
[2] *Mercy and Sacrifice*, pp. 9–15.
[3] *The Religion of Israel*, pp. 368 ff.
[4] Young, ibid., p. 250, Snaith, ibid., pp. 10 f.

some modern writers seem to minimize or ignore this element. If we accept that Jeroboam II died about 753 B.C., we shall probably not be far wrong in dating the call of Amos, Hosea and Isaiah about 760, 755 and 740 B.C. respectively. This early date for the death of Jeroboam II compared with the *c.* 745 B.C. that used to be given suggests that the story in chs. 1–3 to some extent antedates Hosea's main prophetic activity, as is indeed psychologically quite probable.

There has been unnecessarily much discussion about the dating of Hosea's activity in 1:1. That the two halves of the verse are disparate should be obvious to anyone who has ever taken the slightest interest in the chronology of Israel's monarchy (cf. II Ki. 15:8), but it seems easy enough to explain the fact without calling in post-exilic editors. In spite of the difficulties it contains, Hos. 1–3 must with reasonable certainty go back in some respects to the prophet himself. The reference to Jeroboam II is probably the prophet's own and refers only to these chapters – note that 1:4 clearly antedates the sweeping of the dynasty of Jehu into oblivion (II Ki. 15:8–12). It is even more certain that the book as a whole owes its existence to one or more of the prophet's disciples working in Judah after the fall of Samaria (723 B.C.), and to them we will owe the mention of the Judean kings.

It is impossible to establish how long after the death of Jeroboam II Hosea continued to prophesy, or how he met his end. There are no real grounds for thinking that he lived to see the beginning of the siege of Samaria, but there are even fewer for doubting that he experienced the internal dissolution of Israel's society that preceded it.

Few prophets have succeeded in maintaining their essential anonymity better. He came of a family of some standing, for his father's name is mentioned; he presumably lived in the heart-land of Israel in Ephraim or western Manasseh, in a provincial town rather than in the capital; his word-pictures tend to be more of the home than of the open country, as with Amos. Beyond this all is speculation – speculation so baseless that there is no point in mentioning the forms it has taken. The suggestion that he was a Levite, or in some way connected with a sanctuary, is purely subjective, based on what was felt to be fitting. There is perhaps one thing that may be said with reasonable assurance. It is difficult, if not impossible, to believe that the work of Elijah and Elisha did not leave living memories behind it. If so it is reasonable to suppose that Hosea will have come from circles where the memory of those men of God was treasured and their teaching obeyed.

GOMER

Hosea tells us that God's first speaking with him was in a command to marry (1:2). It is useless to speculate whether this command was linked with any manifestation of God to which we could legitimately give the

name "call". It is not stated, and it is not wise to infer it in the interests of
some theory of uniformity in God's dealings with the prophets. If there
was one, it will probably have been of much the same type as that of
Jeremiah, the prophet with whom Hosea has the closest affinities.[1]

The story of the marriage is told us in chs. 1–3. Unfortunately for us
moderns, Scripture is more concerned with the message that arose from
the marriage than with the human interest in it. As a result there is hardly
a feature in it that can be interpreted with certainty. What is more, *every*
interpretation offered is in the last analysis subjective, so there is no point in
counting heads and seeing which has the most and the most impressive
supporters. It is not even a question of conservative and liberal. The only
reasonable method for me to follow is to point out the main interpretations
and the difficulties that beset them, and to give the reasons that have moved
me to go one way and not the other.

The marriage story itself is told in 1:2–4, 6, 8, 9; 3:1–3 – the oracles
connected with it will be considered separately. There is no formal link
between the two chapters; in addition ch. 1 is told in the third person,
ch. 3 in the first. This has never found a really satisfactory explanation
either in the setting of a general theory about first and third person pro-
phetical biographical narratives or in one applicable to Hosea only. It is
probably connected in some way with the oracles contained in chs. 1, 2
and 3, for it seems clear that the stories are told, at least in the first place,
not for their own sake but as an introduction to and an explanation of the
oracles linked with them.

There are those who maintain that both stories are merely two versions
of the same incident. This is not impossible in spite of their deep dissimi-
larity, but the supporters of this view fail to give any real parallel elsewhere
in the Bible or adequate motivation for the phenomenon here. After all,
the editor or compiler of the book could hardly have been ignorant of the
facts, and no reason for deliberate mystification can be suggested. It is
significant that to maintain this view T. H. Robinson has to omit '*od*
("again", RSV, "yet", RV) as a gloss in 3:1.[2]

But if, as the majority hold, the stories are of two separate incidents in
Hosea's life, do they tell of one woman, who appears in both, or of two
different women? Though they would doubtless agree that the symbolism
is thereby somewhat weakened, the numerous supporters of the second
view would doubtless plead with justification that this would be an inadequate ground for rejecting their interpretation. A particularly vigorous
defence of it is offered by R. H. Pfeiffer,[3] who defends the character of
Gomer almost with the zeal of a knight errant. The actual evidence he

---

[1] Rudolph, *Hosea* (K.A.T.), p. 39, is of course correct in stressing that Hosea knew himself
a prophet before marrying.
[2] Robinson–Horst: *Die Zwölf Kleinen Propheten* [2] (H.A.T.) p. 14.
[3] *Introduction to the Old Testament*[2], pp. 567–9.

adduces seems, however, rather thin when it is examined more closely.

His translation of 3:1, "And Jehovah said to me a second time ['od], 'Go, love a woman beloved by a paramour and adulterous,'" is possible, but not so obviously correct as he maintains. The Massoretes did not so understand it, and both the position of 'od and possible metrical considerations suggest that the traditional rendering in some form is correct. Not much can be based on the indefiniteness of "a woman", the more so as Gesenius-Kautsch[1] may well be right in seeing in it the idiom of "indeterminateness for the sake of amplification", and in translating "such a woman", adding the comment "without a doubt to be referred to the Gomer mentioned in ch. 1".

Pfeiffer's positive treatment of ch. 3 seems to be even weaker. He claims that the woman purchased by Hosea was "a common street walker". Since, however, Hebrew has its standard and unmistakable term for such a woman, the terms actually used are, at the least, surprising. We may also reasonably ask how Hosea was to know that her degradation had included adultery. If it is pleaded that she was in some way known to Hosea, this cancels out the argument based on the indeterminacy of her description. Above all, however, he makes no effort to give an adequate meaning to 3:3, Surely Hosea's words mean literally and symbolically that he held out hope to the woman that she could become his wife. But Pfeiffer with considerable justification, maintains that Hosea could not have married a known prostitute. For him "the point of ch. 3, brought out by a symbolical action that has nothing to do with Hosea's family life, is that Jehovah still loves his adulterous nation and will take measures to bring it to its senses. . . . By an act of kindness to a wretched prostitute, Hosea symbolizes God, in His abiding love, endeavouring to redeem His wicked people." But quite apart from the fact that this hardly does justice to Hosea's words, the bringing in of the prostitute as a sort of family retainer can hardly be considered as an adequate symbol of the renewal of Jehovah's broken marriage with Israel.

This view has recently been defended by W. Rudolph,[2] who considers that v. 2b was expanded by the actual author of the book (not Hosea!), who read back into Gomer the character of the people she represented.

We are left then with the view that in chs. 1 and 3 we have two stages in the history of Hosea's life with Gomer, his wife. Immediately the question is asked whether we are dealing with facts or with an allegory or a symbolic dream experience. For our purpose the two latter need not be distinguished. Such a view has been held by Maimonides, Rashi, Kimchi and Ibn Ezra among Jewish exegetists, and by many commentators, both conservative and liberal, in the seventeenth to nineteenth centuries, though at no time was it the undisputed interpretation. In our days it has been

---

[1] *Hebrew Grammar*, § 125 c.
[2] Op. cit. pp. 39–49, 86–90.

defended by E. J. Young. Basically these interpretations are all derived
from revulsion against the idea that God should have commanded Hosea
to marry a harlot. This natural and laudable attitude will be little changed
if we accept the suggestion of some moderns that Gomer was a temple
prostitute (*qedeshah*), something that could so easily have been stated but is
not even implied. Young's additional arguments have only a limited
validity, and have little bearing on the suggestions made later.[1]

The validity of the chief objection will be considered later; but even if
it could not be met the supporters of an allegorical interpretation scarcely
seem to realize the difficulty of the view they support. Hosea, like Jeremiah
about a century and a half later, was prophesying at five minutes to midnight. His chance of saving Israel was almost non-existent; indeed it is
doubtful whether he himself had any hopes of it. His chance of impressing
the message of God's lasting loyal love on the survivors of the disaster,
whether in exile or left in the land, was problematic in the extreme. It is
hard then to conceive of his fundamental message being expressed in an
allegory. Particularly significant in this respect is the complete failure of
these commentators to find any convincing allegorical meaning in the
name of Hosea's wife or father-in-law though Rudolph may well be
correct on suggesting that the actual pointing of the names may have an
allegorizing tendency.[2] It is useless appealing to Ezekiel. It is not merely
that his allegories are cast in another mould – they do not involve the
prophet personally – and clearly reveal their nature. Ezekiel was not
prophesying to doomed Jerusalem like Jeremiah, but teaching the rescued
deportees in Babylonia what was the significance of and reason for the
coming destruction.

The supporters of a symbolic dream are little better placed. We have
come to realize that not the dreaming or relating of symbolism gave it its
effect, but the actual acting of it. The older view that the symbolism of
Jeremiah's girdle (13:1-7) or of Ezekiel's actions or immobility (4:1-5:4)
was lived out only in dreams has today been largely abandoned. They may
well have been carried out only in part – Jeremiah may not have gone all
the way to the Euphrates[3] and Ezekiel may not have lain rigidly all the
time[4] – but it was that carrying out, even if only in part, that for the
prophets' contemporaries gave the message linked with the symbolism its
more than human power.

But can we really believe that God would command Hosea to marry a
prostitute? Had she been a penitent one, perhaps, but under the circumstances I can only agree with those who find it impossible. God may
sacrifice the honour of His children and servants, but not in this way. But
does the Bible say that He did so command? His command was *Go, take a*

[1] Op. cit., pp. 252 f.   [2] Op. cit., pp. 50 f.
[3] Cf. E.Q., Vol. XL (1968), No. 1, pp. 36-39.
[4] Cf. my *Ezekiel: The Man and his Message*, p. 33.

wife of harlotry and children of harlotry: for the land has assuredly committed harlotry, departing from Jehovah. In what sense was Hosea to take "children of harlotry"? A few commentators, including Abarbanel, thought that Gomer had already given birth to illegitimate children. Though the language could mean this, seeing these alleged children are never mentioned later we can ignore this interpretation as too unlikely to merit serious consideration. In other words the children were still future.

Since it is both immoral and foolish to suggest that Hosea was to encourage Gomer in bearing illegitimate children, or even deliberately to bring up her children in a corrupt religion (the metaphorical sense of harlotry in Hosea), the "harlotry" of the children was future and only potential. This being so, we cannot exclude the possibility of Gomer's "harlotry" being future and potential as well. This possibility becomes a virtual certainty when we remember that Gomer is serving as a type of Israel in the time of its loyalty as well as its apostasy. In addition Hosea's subsequent behaviour is hardly comprehensible, if Gomer was merely behaving as might have been expected.

The Israel Gomer represented on her wedding day was that of 2:15. No matter that, as Ezekiel was later to make clear (20:5–10, 23:3), the seeds of future evil were already there at the Exodus and Sinai, Jeremiah was able to say of that period:

> *I remember the devotion of your youth, your love as a bride,*
> *how you followed Me in the wilderness,*
> *in a land not sown* (2:2, RSV).

So too it was with Gomer. God could see the bitter seeds that would yield a yet more bitter harvest, but for the wedding guests she was altogether fair. In other words, whatever the exact form of God's command to Hosea – we now have Hosea's reinterpretation of it in the light of experience – its implications lay in the womb of the future.

Some will remain unsatisfied. They cannot see any difference between a command to marry a depraved woman and to marry one who God in His omniscience knew would become depraved. We stand here on the brink of the unknowable and undebatable. There have been many tragic marriages over which God's blessing has been sincerely asked, but for all that God was being asked to bless man's own choosing. There have been others, however, where the vows and promises were made in full confidence that God had joined them together, and yet . . . It may well be that of God-willed marriages only a minority are struck by tragedy, but they exist. There will be few where Hosea's experience is in some measure re-enacted, but there are some. We cannot explain it, but we should not try to deny it. One thing we can say, however. Where under such circumstances humble faith persists, the sufferer is brought ever closer to God and finds in his loss gain, and salve for his broken heart in the love of God, the source of all comfort. So it was with Hosea, and as a result there seems to be no one in the Old Testament who drew nearer to an understanding of God's love.

There is an ultra-modern tendency to question whether Hosea's experiences had any effect on him. It is said that his marriage was an act of obedience for symbolic purposes, and that was all. It is strange that those who will not tolerate the suggestion that the prophets were mere channels through whom the Divine word came can yet suggest that they could be left unchanged by the message they had to speak and the circumstances that surrounded it. Even if God's messenger marries for symbolic reasons, he has married, and his marriage cannot leave him unchanged.

I am not suggesting that I have anywhere near covered all the suggestions that have been thrown out. There are many, like the bizarre suggestion by Y. Kaufmann (cf. p. 95) that the perfectly normal Hosea family had to act these things, which are not likely to be taken seriously except by their inventors and perhaps their pupils. But the main lines of exposition have been covered. As I said earlier, while some may be intrinsically unlikely, the final decision is likely to be subjective, based on what seems most consistent with the character of God and the unique spirit of Hosea's prophecy.[1]

HOSEA'S TRAGEDY

There are no reasons for suspecting the paternity of Hosea's first son. That he gave him a symbolic name, Jezreel ("God sows" – 2:22), which is essentially a name of hope, though first linked with judgment (1:4), means no more than Isaiah's action (7:3; 8:3). Whether the name of his daughter ("Not pitied" – 1:6), and of his second son ("Not my people" – 1:8), indicated on Hosea's side doubt and suspicion we do not and cannot know.

Then Gomer left him. Again we do not know why. Many a minister's wife has been his worst enemy, though not so openly and dramatically, and it will have been harder to be a prophet's wife than a minister's. Hard it is for any woman to accept that she must take second place in her husband's life, unless indeed she has accepted this in the sight of God before she says yes to his avowal of love. Was it incompatibility of temperament? Positive goodness and purity can become sheer agony to one who possesses these qualities at the best negatively, as a mere refraining from badness and impurity. Was it the cunning, wooing words of a neighbour with a roving eye? We do not know, but she left her husband.

Hosea was left broken-hearted with three little children. Doubtless his neighbours expected him to do the obvious, to divorce her and to find someone who would fill her place and care for his motherless children.

---

[1] A much fuller scholarly study of the question, which comes to much the same conclusion as I do, is H. H. Rowley, *The Marriage of Hosea*, ch. 3. of his *Men of God*.

They waited in vain until one day, as darkness fell, a veiled woman followed Hosea home. Though she would have been little out of doors and would have been given very little freedom, the news was soon round the little town, "Hosea has taken Gomer back! He has *bought* her back!"

The degradation and suffering that lie behind the necessity of Hosea's buying her back, his wife though she was, is a spur to our imagination, but we cannot pass from theories to facts. Some might question my statement that Hosea had not divorced her, but the vehemence of Jer. 3:1 (follow RV mg., RSV) shows that the law of Deut. 24:1-4 not only existed but was generally observed.[1] Christians who are all too ready to advocate divorce proceedings when fellow Christians find themselves in similar tragic circumstances would do well to pay more attention to our Lord's teaching, and to remember that divorce is the denial of love and reconciliation. It could be that payment was made to avoid dragging Gomer's name yet further in the dust by bringing a court case against the man who claimed authority over her. We might be able to pencil in some detail with reasonable assurance if two points of translation were clearer.

The description of Gomer in 3:1, if we base ourselves, as we are entitled to, solely on the Hebrew consonants can be translated in three ways: (1) beloved by a paramour, (2) loving a paramour, (3) loving evil (so LXX). Perhaps the second is the more likely; neither in the story nor in its application to Israel is there any suggestion of anything that could be called love on the part of the seducer.

Then we are not sure how much Hosea paid for her. It is usually assumed that the value of one and a half homers (about twelve bushels) of barley was fifteen silver shekels, so that he paid in all thirty shekels, the legal value under certain circumstances of a slave (Exod. 21:32). This has been questioned from two angles. On one hand it has been queried whether grain was so expensive at the time. In view of the speculations of the corn merchants (Amos 8:4-6) it probably was, so there is not likely to be much point in this argument. On the other hand we may well question whether he paid thirty shekels. This was the sum paid to the owner for a slave killed. Since no distinction is made between the sexes and no account is taken of age, it was probably a penal sum, considerably above the normal market price of a slave, and fixed to avoid interminable arguments about the actual value of the killed slave. In the time of Jeroboam II social chaos and debt would have multiplied the number of slaves and pushed down their price, so it would have been the exceptional slave who would have fetched as much as thirty shekels. Gomer had borne three children and had further diminished her good looks and strength by a dissipated life. It seems most improbable then that she would have fetched anything like thirty shekels in the open market. We must decide between supposing that

---

[1] The later Talmudic law forbidding the taking back of an adulterous wife (*Soṭah* 28a) is irrelevant here.

Hosea paid an inflated price for her out of love and the suggestion that we should render the Hebrew, *So I bought her for fifteen shekels of silver, even a homer and a half of barley*, i.e. she went fairly cheaply at fifteen shekels, which were paid in grain. On the whole I think the latter far more likely.

However, Gomer did not come home as Hosea's wife, but as his slave. Wife she was in law, but she had forfeited her rights. The position of wife was being offered her in loving grace, but on condition that her behaviour justified it. A long period of probation lay before her. *You shall sit still for me many days; you shall not play the harlot or belong to another man, and I will withhold myself from you.*

The rendering of the last clause assumes with the majority of moderns that by one of the easiest of scribal errors two words have dropped from the Hebrew text. If we leave the text as it is, it is probably Hosea's promise to remain loyal to her, but this was in any case implicit in his actions.

So the curtain falls on Hosea's personal life. Did Gomer finally yield to his unyielding love, or did she only hate him the more for it? As a lover of happy endings I should like to think the former, but as a realist in touch with life I fear the latter. Just as we do not know whether Hosea's love triumphed with Gomer, so we are left without an answer as to whether Jehovah's love will triumph with faithless Israel.

GOD'S LOVE AND MAN'S LOVE

Those who maintain the allegoric or symbolic-dream interpretation of Hosea's marriage in many cases justify their position by seeing in the oracles of chs. 1–3 one message based on Hosea's family experiences as a whole. I believe, however, that a closer study of them will show that they contain a definite progression. They grow clearer and deeper as Hosea's own experiences made the position of Israel in the sight of God clearer to him. In fact we have no justification for demanding that the whole of these chapters should be regarded as chronologically earlier than ch. 4, etc. The development of Hosea's family tragedy will have kept pace with his earlier message to Israel.

Our first oracle is in 1:4, linked with the naming of his eldest child, Jezreel, which means "El sows", but is also the name of a pre-Israelite town in Issachar (Josh. 19:18). Like Isaiah's somewhat later naming of presumably his eldest son Shearjashub (Isa. 7:3), the name is a combination of threat and promise. If God is to sow, it will be because there has first been a harvest of wrath and judgment. This is linked verbally with the town where Jehu began the blood-bath that led him to the throne (II Ki. 9).

The oracle, *Yet a little while, I will visit the violently shed blood of Jezreel on the house of Jehu, and I will cause the rule of the house of Israel to cease. It shall come to pass in that day that I will break the bow of Israel in the valley of Jezreel*, has been a major problem for many. The reason can be simply stated. If Jehu was anointed by the command of Elisha in the name of

Jehovah to destroy the house of Ahab (II Ki. 9:6–10), how could a later prophet condemn the work for which he had been raised up by God?

For the modern scholar the question is normally simply solved by an appeal to development. It is suggested that the prophetic understanding of the nature of God had so developed between Elisha and Hosea that what seemed obviously right to the former was seen in its enormity by the latter.

Quite apart from the question of prophetic inspiration, for which such a theory makes no adequate allowance, there are certain major difficulties raised by it. No student of the Bible should question that God's revelation through the prophets was "by divers portions and in divers manners" (Heb. 1:1); few will deny that in them is a growing depth of understanding for God's purposes and will. But this is not to say, or even to imply, that the later contradicts the earlier or suspends it. In a rare case like Isa. 16:13 f. there is the modification of a preceding prophecy, but this does not involve the contradiction of its spiritual principle. It falls rather into the category of contingency, which Jeremiah declares is inherent in every promise of blessing or threat of doom (Jer. 18:7–10).

However contrary to modern views it may be, I state flatly that within the prophetic tradition we never meet a repudiation of the prophetic past whether by word or by action, which we can never ultimately separate in the divine revelation. A truth which does not lead to action is sterile and harmful. Obviously, as the knowledge of God widens and deepens, the actions that result from it will change and deepen spiritually. But that does not mean that the earlier actions were in any sense wrong, any more than we condemn a child's acts because they do not conform to the standard we expect of a grown man. The incident recorded in Luke 9:51–55 is a rebuke of James and John and not a condemnation of Elijah.

We may rule out then any repudiation of Elisha's act, the more so as it would surely have been more explicit had it been so intended. But how then are we to understand Hosea's words? In Isa. 10:5–19 we have the condemnation of Assyria, the rod of God's anger against Judah, and in Hab. 2:2–19 of the Chaldeans, whom God had raised up against Jerusalem. In neither case is the condemnation for the harm done to Judah; in both cases it is for the spirit in which it was done. So it was with Jehu. Any change of dynasty in the ancient world was normally bound to be a bloody and beastly business, but any right-minded man must shudder at the hypocrisy of II Ki. 10:1–9 and the blood-lust of II Ki. 10:18–25, when Jehu's deceitful approach was bound to claim the maximum of victims. So we may reasonably infer that the judgment on Jehu's dynasty was for the manner in which he carried out God's command, and on Israel because there was no other to do it as it should have been done. For obedience Jehu had God's gift of four generations on the throne (II Ki. 10:30), but when they were over the harvest he had sown would be reaped.

The oracle linked with the naming of Hosea's second child goes very much farther, *Call her name Not-pitied, for I will no more pity the house of Israel in bearing their sins* (1:6). Whether his is Hosea's tacit denial of his paternity of the child we cannot possibly say, but it is God's tacit repudiation of the claim He put into the mouth of Moses, "Israel is My son, My firstborn" (Exod. 4:22). God now refused that pitying love which a father shows by bearing his child's misdeeds and so forgiving them. Judgment had come many a time on Israel before, but now behind it a father's pitying love would be no more discernible.

The average modern looks with suspicion on 1:7, and not without reason. An oracle addressed to Judah seems entirely out of place at this point. But it may well be considered doubtful whether any of the strikingly varied references to Judah in this prophecy were ever meant in the first place for the hearing of the southern kingdom. Just as Amos began his prophecy by passing judgment on Israel's neighbours in order to prepare Israel for her own condemnation, so Hosea uses Judah to place Israel in true perspective. The northern kingdom had arrogated the name of Israel to itself. It clung obstinately to the belief that its greater riches, area and strength showed that it was the true representative of God's people. The mention of Judah underlines the vital truth that the rejection of the North in no way involved God's complete repudiation of Israel's sonship.

The shadows are even darker when we come to Hosea's youngest child. Now it is not merely a refusal by God to behave as Father; it is a denial of paternity and of all relationship. *Call his name Not-My-people, for you are not My people and I am not* 'ehyeh *for you* (1:9) – *'ehyeh* is the title Jehovah gives Himself in Exod. 3:14; the form of Yahweh (Jehovah) apposite, when He speaks of Himself in the first person. In other words the covenant relationship is declared at an end.

It is hard to believe that this steady descent into the depths is not the result of a longer period of experience. The growing awareness of Gomer's disloyalty kept pace with a growing burden of Israel's sin and doom.

Light in the Darkness

Suddenly through this midnight darkness there flashes the bright light of hope. Perhaps nowhere else in Scripture is there such a drastic and dramatic juxtaposition of doom and salvation. There is neither motivation nor explanation; the "yet" of the RV, RSV is neither in the Hebrew nor implied by it. *And it shall come to pass that the number of the children of Israel shall be as the sand of the sea . . .* (1:10). This oracle of hope (1:10–2:1) marks the other pole from the oracles of doom, and in the antinomy between them the rest of 2:2 – 3:5, and indeed of the whole book, is played out.

Here the exile of both Israel and Judah is clearly foreseen, for *and shall go up from the land* can only mean the land of exile. While Israel is promised restoration from exile, the primacy in that restoration is given to Judah; Israel's restoration will depend on its recognition of its sister kingdom.

There seems little point in inquiring too closely who is to say *My-people* and *Pitied* (2:1). All parabolic, symbolic and allegorical language breaks down somewhere. Ultimately in the antitype we cannot draw the distinction we can make between Gomer and her children. There is no possibility of identifying the children with different sections of the people. There were, however, others besides Hosea who lamented the downward path of Israel. It is they, the faithful remnant, though the term is not used, who are to hail the coming day of redemption and who under the picture of the children are to "plead" with Gomer-Israel (2:2).

The ambiguity of *Plead with your mother, plead* (cf. Jer. 2:9 RV), retained even in RSV, is bound to lead to the popular interpretation that Gomer's abandoned babies are to plead with her to return. But like most other sentimental interpretations of Scripture it is impossible. We must render, *Bring your charge against your mother, bring your charge! For she is not my wife, and I am not her husband.*[1] Israel's one hope is that her own sons should stand up in accusation against her, as Ezekiel was later to do with Judah (cf. chs. 16, 20, 23), rebuking her not for her faults but for her fundamental unfaithfulness. At this point no more is to be read into the denial of the marriage relationship than that every effective link between God and Israel had now disappeared. That it was not irreparably dissolved is shown both by the threat (2:3), which only the husband could make, and the sequel. Whatever the harlotries and adulteries (v. 2) may have meant in Gomer's case – possibly ornaments given her by her lovers – they are clearly here the outward signs and symbols of Israel's apostasy.

THE SIN OF ISRAEL

When we compare Amos and Hosea we find that their picture of social conditions largely coincides, but at first sight there seems to be no way of reconciling their sketch of religious shortcomings. Amos mentions, almost as an aside, Israel's worship of the Assyrian planetary gods (5:26, cf. p. 89), but this finds no echo in Hosea. Probably, as in Judah under Manasseh, this foreign idolatry was confined to court circles, so this may be an adequate explanation of Hosea's silence, though there may be a tacit assumption of the practice in passages like 5:13; 7:11; 8:9; 12:1. On the other hand, Hosea not only mentions the golden bulls of Bethel and Samaria (8:5 f.; 10:5), which find no place in Amos, but apparently depicts the whole set-up of Baal worship, even though it had been so ruthlessly stamped out by Jehu. However much Amos was primarily concerned with social righteousness in Israel, it is hard to believe that he could have passed by such blatant religious disloyalty in silence had it

[1] *rib* is essentially a legal term, though this is not adequately recognized in RV, RSV.

existed. It is easy to see why Yehezkel Kaufmann in desperation should cut
the Gordian knot by attributing Hos. 1–3 to an earlier prophet who lived
in the days of Ahab.[1]

The explanation seems to be that God's judgments are not man's, and
it is only where special vision has been granted that we can see with God's
eyes. The Son of God Himself might call the Pharisees play-actors (hypo-
crites), but not so the apostles. It is the two most sensitive among the
prophets, Hosea and Jeremiah, who dismiss the religion of Israel and Judah
as Baal worship.

Though Jehovah condescends to use terms of human relationship to
express His covenant link with Israel, He is in fact far exalted above
human relationships and descriptions. Symbolically Moses may see only
His back (Exod. 33:23), the glory that remains, when He has passed by.
The forbidding of the making of any image to represent Him is not
merely because of the hopelessness of the task, but also because He lies outside the realm of human representation. He is not merely the ruler of the
universe, but also outside it, controlling it but uncontrolled by it. Of such
a God we may well say with Job,

> *Behold, I go forward, but He is not there;*
> *and backward, but I cannot perceive Him:*
> *on the left hand, when He works, but I cannot behold Him:*
> *He hides Himself on the right hand, that I cannot see Him.* (Job 23:8, 9).

He is knowable ultimately only through revelation.

But Israel did what men have ever since been doing, when they have
heard of Israel's God. They tried to bring Him into His creation, to make
Him graspable in terms of contemporary thought, to make Him conform
to the ideas of the age, to bring Him under control by human actions,
above all by sacrifice and prayer. If man is not lifted above the spirit of the
age by the Holy Spirit, he will, even without realizing it, be fashioned
according to it. So too it was with Israel.

The writers of the Old Testament turn with abhorrence from Israel's
perversion of the Mosaic revelation and do not describe it, except indirectly by their denunciations. Beyond assuring us that Israel respected
Jehovah's command that no image of Him be made (though they were
prepared to provide Him with a golden bull as a throne), archaeology has
little to tell us of it. Some things are, however, clear. As with some today,
psychic powers were regarded as a sign of inspiration (Jer. 2:8). Sexuality
was introduced into the concept of God, and if we may judge by the
number of female figurines found by the archaeologist, His "wife" was
worshipped as well. Jehovah became the great fertility God, more concerned with the fruits of the soil than with history, with sacrifice than
with morals. One of the more potent means of winning Him over was

[1] Op. cit., pp. 368–70.

ritual prostitution – probably dismissed by Amos as immorality of the worst type (2:7) – which represented sex offered to God (Hos. 4:13 f.). What other deities or powers attendant on Jehovah may also have been honoured we know not. The whole sorry affair is written off by Hosea as not different from the Baal worship proscribed by Jehu. The names were different, and so may have been the ritual, but fundamentally the same set of concepts was held up as sacred.

It lies outside our subject, but a little reflection will show how much both in the thought of liberal intellectual Christianity and in the popular practice of so many, not only in the unreformed churches and their imitators but also in so-called Bible-based churches comes under this condemnation.

Some will object to the interpretation given basing themselves on 2:7, *I will go and return to my first husband*, but this represents merely a slight exaggeration on the prophet's part. There seems to have been throughout the period of the monarchy a tension between the thought of Jehovah the God of history and Jehovah the God of nature. The stress on the Passover by Hezekiah (II Chr. 30) and Josiah (II Chr. 35:1–19) represents such a deliberate swing back to the God of history, instead of Tabernacles, when it was above all the God of nature that was worshipped. It was not Israel who saw two gods involved, but the prophet, for he knew that the nature God was not really the God of revelation in history, but a creation of man's fantasies and desires.

THE DOOR OF HOPE

The first step in Israel's rehabilitation was to rob her of the gifts of nature (2:6–13). Whether this was to be through drought and locust or through Assyrian pillaging is not stated. Probably both are involved, the latter being more prominent towards the end of the passage, for when we reach the second stage (2:14–17) Israel is in the wilderness of the exile (cf. Ezek. 20:35).

Here we are introduced to perhaps the most remarkable courtship in history. God says, *Behold, I shall seduce her*; the word used is that found in Jer. 20:7 and Exod. 22:16.[1] The "seduction" lies in the fact that *I shall bring her into the wilderness* is regarded by Israel as her abandonment by God, while in fact it is intended by God as an act leading to her restoration. *And I shall speak there to her heart*, as did once Boaz to Ruth (2:13, cf. Isa. 40:2). To see this in practice we must look from Israel to Judah. However much the Gentile may look with scorn on the Synagogue, and the Hebrew Christian remember the aridity he found in it that first detached his heart from the traditions of the past, it remains true that during the long centuries of dispersion, of deprivation of civil rights, of persecution and

---

[1] The translation "I will allure her" can be justified only if we remember the fundamentally bad meaning in "allure" as used in Heb.

the ghetto, it was God who lightened the life of His people and put joy into their hearts. Though the Synagogue may have been a sanctuary only in small measure (Ezek. 11:16) it was a very real one. Even Zionism, though avowedly secular, has never been able to free itself from the thought of God.

And I shall give her her vineyards from thence. Wine is for the Bible the one luxury the poorest man may hope to have to lighten his load and brighten his days. Because of God's presence, the Jew in the midst of ghetto conditions never became a helot or a robot. Some were broken, it is true, and became *Luftmenschen*, living as it were on air, but there has never been a time in the dispersion when Jewry did not produce that which was beautiful and noble, and which enriched its neighbours, if they were willing to be enriched.

And the valley of Achor for a door of hope. We do not know which of the *wadis* cutting into the eastern slopes of Benjamin or southern Ephraim may have been the valley of Achor, but the present passage suggests that it provided a way up to the central ridge – was it perhaps the route followed on the first attack on Ai (Jos. 7:2–5)? – and many who used it will have shuddered at the thought of the fate Achan had to suffer for the conquest to be possible. To Hosea is given the half-seen revelation that restoration would be possible only by one who would bear the curse, but, unlike Achan, not for his own sin.

Presumably at the time it was a matter of taste whether a wife called her husband *ba'ali* ("my owner") or *'ishi* ("my man"). The force of the promise is not primarily one of greater intimacy, but the utter forgetting of Baal and all his ways. On the other hand, as a name so normally the reality. As we conceive of God, so is His relationship to us likely to be.

The Christian sings,

> *Love so amazing, so divine,*
> *Demands my soul, my life, my all.*

The Old Covenant could never produce a really analogous act of God's love, for while it proclaimed God's grace, it was not so easy to show that it had cost God anything. That is why Hosea's message stands nearer to that of the New Covenant than any other part of the Old, because through the broken heart of a man, it gives an insight into "the broken heart of God". But this is left to be inferred rather than proclaimed. Hence we have here the proof of God's love as seen in His mighty acts to Israel.

God is seen as God of nature, *I will make for you a covenant on that day with the beasts of the field, the birds of the air, and the creeping things of the ground* (v. 18a). He imposes His will on His physical creation that it may dwell in peace with His people. But He is also seen as the God of history, *I will break the bow, the sword, and war from the land; and I will make you lie down in safety* (v. 18b). Exactly the same combination can be found in Isa. 40–48, only that the historical side is made more definite by the mention of King Cyrus, while the nature side is expressed in the transformation above all of the wilderness.

There follows a new betrothal, not a marriage, presumably because the old one had never been finally dissolved, one in which Israel is for the first time fully to know what it means to have God as husband. *In righteousness*: for the first time the relationship will really conform to God's pattern for it (cf. Jer. 31:32). *In judgment*: no longer would the past be merely covered over, ignored, not called to reckoning or even carried by God, but "I will forgive their iniquity, and their sin will I remember no more" (Jer. 31:34). *In covenant love* ("steadfast love", RSV): love will now have reached its goal and will be able to reveal itself unbrokenly. *In mercies*: the full, pitying love of the Father can now be shown unmixed with severity to the sinner. *In faithfulness*: Israel will experience how unwavering the love and loyalty of God are. The goal? *That you may know the Lord*. Election love and covenant loyalty, the outpoured blessings of a Father's hand, are never an end in themselves. They always have as their goal that the beloved may know the Lover. So when Not-My-people becomes My-people his adoring answer is "My God."

THE TIME OF PROBATION

Exile does not mean rejection, but the wife may fall till she becomes her husband's slave (3:2). The full meaning of marriage – and if God uses this picture for Israel, He cannot be satisfied with less than this – is not reached until physical oneness has led to the union of the whole being. However much God may care for Israel in exile, there must be proof of a change of heart before there can be restoration. The slave condition of exile is real. A slave has no privileges, and so all that Israel based its trust on must go (3:4), whether God-ordained or not. So too it has been down the long history of Jewry's dispersion; its political organization and both God-given and man-devised forms of worship under the monarchy have gone.

How long must Israel and God wait? Only he who claims to possess the foreknowledge of God will venture to interpret the *many days* (v. 3) beyond realizing that they run to "the latter days". But will these days have an end? Did Gomer yield to Hosea's love? Our answer must wait until the end of this book, if indeed we feel inclined to answer it then. For the North at least Hosea is clear that more than a return to God is involved; there would also have to be an acceptance of His judgment on the past. David is more than the messianic king; he stands also for the recognition that in the moment Israel rejected Rehoboam, David's grandson, they had also put themselves outside the main stream of God's historic purposes.

CHAPTER XII

ISRAEL'S INNER CORRUPTION

T HE ORACLES IN HOS. 4–14 GIVE THE IMPRESSION OF HAV-
ing been given against the background sketched in the last chapter.
Though they bear the stamp of the same author and period, they
have no inner coherence, though they tend to be grouped around common
thoughts. There may well be a certain chronological progression in them,
for the picture tends to grow darker as we proceed, but it is impossible to
assign a date to most of the oracles, nor can we regard their position in
the book as a necessary guide to their relative order in time. They do
justify the judgment proclaimed in the first three chapters, but give little
aid to answering the unanswered question of ch. 3, viz. how will Israel
respond to God's love?

Where the rendering of the English versions is questionable, and especially where there is corroborating evidence from the ancient versions that
the MT is corrupt, I have in my translation taken liberties with the
Hebrew text. I have avoided major emendations, even where they were
attractive, confining myself mostly to vowel changes and those obvious
scribal errors that are so familiar to the textual critic. There are few realms
where it is harder for the layman to make objective judgments than textual
criticism. Hence I have marked between † . . . † those emendations that
go beyond those of RSV, not that these have always been accepted. They
are briefly commented on in a supplementary note at the end of the
chapter.

The collection of oracles begins understandably enough with a general
condemnation of the people (4:1–4a) in which the prophet acts as pros-
ecutor (v. 1b).

¹*Hear the word of the* LORD, *sons of Israel,*
for the LORD *has a charge against the inhabitants of the land.*
There is no good faith, or loyalty,
or knowledge of God in the land,
²*but cursing, lying, murder, theft, adultery;*
they break into houses, and no place is free of violently shed
blood.

Nature itself must mourn (v. 3), doubtless in the grip of drought, which
was always regarded as a Divine judgment; here, however, as is shown by
the mention of the fish, it is regarded rather as the inevitable reaction or

nature to the sin of man, who should be its lord. Hosea adds in words reminiscent of Amos 5:13, *For all that let none bring a court action or reprove* (v. 4a). It would be waste of time and would bring only trouble on himself.

THE CORRUPTION OF THE PRIESTHOOD

This is followed by a condemnation of those who Hosea considered bore the primary responsibility, viz. the priests (4:4b–11). Though errors in the Massoretic text have half obscured the fact, it is addressed to one priest in particular, probably the high priest of Bethel or Samaria, but he is probably addressed in a representative capacity.

> *My charge is against you, priest.*
> [5]*You will stumble by day,*
> *and the prophet also will stumble with you by night,*
> *and I shall destroy your mother,*
> [6]*for My people is destroyed through lack of knowledge.*
> *Because you have rejected knowledge,*
> *I reject you from being My priest;*
> *since you have forgotten the law[1] of your God,*
> *I shall forget your sons – yes, I.*
> [7]*As they multiplied,*
> *so did their sins against me;*
> *their glory I shall change for shame.*
> [8]*They eat the sin (offering) of My people,*
> *and they set their desire on their iniquity,*
> [9]*and it will be as the priest so the people,*
> *and I shall punish him for his ways and I shall requite him his doings.*
> [10]*When they eat they will not be satisfied,*
> *and when they commit harlotry they will not increase.*
> *Because they have left off to give heed to the* LORD,
> [11]*harlotry and wine and new wine*
> *rob them of their understanding.*

To suggest, as some do, that in contrast with I Ki. 12:31, 32; 13:33 Hosea had earlier accepted the legitimacy of the northern priesthood, but was now rejecting it because of its sins, is to miss the point of the oracle. The reference to the priests of Jeroboam's making in *I Kings* is less to throw scorn on them and more to underline the king's purely self-willed approach to the religious organization of his kingdom. In an isolated story like that of II Ki. 4:42–44 (see p. 51) we find, at least by inference, an individual's rejection of these man-made priests, but otherwise they are passed over in remarkable silence. The prophet's quarrel with the rulers of the North was not on points of ritual but on the fundamental demands

[1] *Torah*, the Divine instruction.

of God. There can be little doubt that God, who is always more concerned with the welfare of the individual than with points of ritual, accepted the sacrifices of the humble and penitent, even though those who functioned as priests had not been authorized by Him.

In addition the ritual linked with the priesthood was for maintaining fellowship with God, not for creating it. Had Hosea announced God's rejection of the priesthood on technical grounds, it would have touched the conscience of none. As it was, the coming destruction would sweep them away because of their sins, and with them both their jackals, the cult prophets, and the people who had been misled by them. If the MT is correct, *your mother* (v. 5) will be the priestly clan; in any case a change of vocalization will give this meaning. There is no contrast intended in this verse between *day* and *night*, priest and prophet. Day and night mean simply all the time. The utter cynicism of the priests is shown in their welcome of the people's sins, because they gave them the more sin-offerings to eat (v. 8). *Hebrews* has made us so familiar with the ritual of the Day of Atonement that we often forget that the normal sin-offering had to be eaten by the sacrificing priest (Lev. 6:26-29).

The harlotry of vv. 10 f. is not mere sexual promiscuity but the sacred prostitution carried on at the sanctuaries. The ostensible reason for it was to promote fertility: fertility of the soil, of domestic animals, of the family. By calling it "harlotry" Hosea makes his disgust and rejection clear, but he stresses also that God's rejection and judgment will be made clear by the increasing sterility of those who practised it.

From the harlotry of sacred prostitution we are led by an extension of the word to the whole semi-Canaanized set-up of northern religion (4:12, 13ab).

> ¹²*My people ask counsel of its tree,*
> *and its branch gives them oracles,*
> *for a spirit of harlotry hasted them astray,*
> *and they have left their God to play the harlot.*
> ¹³*They sacrifice on the mountain-tops*
> *and cause offerings to ascend in smoke on the hills,*
> *under oak, poplar and terebinth,*
> *because their shade is good.*

The parallelism shows that the *branch* (hardly staff) is merely a contemptuous diminutive for the *tree*, which in turn stands for the *Asherah*, the symbol of the female side of deity in this nature worship. It would seem that Hosea is even more shocked that people could think that deity could be expressed by a wooden pole than by their bringing of sex into their concept of Jehovah. It is a thought that is expanded later with biting sarcasm in Isa. 44:9-20. The mention of the shade of the trees is not

E

merely an underlining of the sensuous nature of all this worship.
Reference to passages like Jdg. 9:15; Psa. 91:1, 4; 121:5; Isa. 25:4; 32:2
will show that shade had the ideas of shelter and protection bound up
with it.

This rejection of the popular religion by the prophets was no mere
fanaticism, no striving after an impossible ideal. They knew full well that
men become like the gods they worship, and so it was with Israel. The
degradation of sex in the sanctuary at the alleged command of God led
to the degradation of sex in the home (4:13c, 14). Jeremiah was to see
about a century later that when Josiah swept away the religious sanctions
for sexual abuses they only broke out again the more viciously in purely
secular contexts (Jer. 5:7 f.), thus showing that all along it had been the
expression of depraved human passions. It is a tragically vicious circle, as
Paul made clear in Rom. 1:18–32; the rebellious heart of man leads him
to false worship, and this in turn leads to false living, which in turn
leads either to ever falser worship or to a breakdown of all religion. Only
the grace of God can break this chain of cause and effect. That is why
Hosea says, *For a spirit of harlotry has led them astray.* Here, as not infrequently in the Old Testament, "spirit" is used of an overmastering impulse that may seize a man.

As is so often the case with originally unconnected oracles, a link is found
in a key word, so 4:15, an oracle to Judah, is linked with the preceding
by *play the harlot.* We have too little information on such things to know
whether the roles had actually been reversed with some Judean pilgrims
going to the great northern sanctuaries. With the greater opulence and
pomp prevailing there it cannot be ruled out as impossible. What is certain is that the flare-up of Baalized religion under Ahaz and even more
under Manasseh will have been made possible largely by the religious influences that seeped into Judah from the North. In considering God's
judgment on Israel we must not forget the need to remove a centre of
spiritual infection. *Even though you, Israel, play the harlot, let not Judah become guilty. Go not to Gilgal, go not up to Beth-aven, swear not 'As the* LORD
lives.' Beth-aven, the house of iniquity, is used bitingly by Hosea instead of Beth-el, the house of God. It may be we should read, "swear
not †in Beer-sheba† 'as the LORD lives'." A reference to Jer. 5:2; 4:2
will show the implication of swearing "as the Lord lives" while indulging
in a form of worship abhorrent to God. It is this that is here being condemned.

From 4:17 on we repeatedly find Ephraim used as a name for the northern
kingdom. This can hardly be because Hosea was himself an Ephraimite, an
opinion incapable of proof. Equally it can hardly be an outcome of the
events described in II Ki. 15:29, which left the former tribal territories of
Ephraim and Manasseh as the rump of the northern kingdom. So to explain the use – we need hardly doubt this explanation of Isa. 9:9, 21 –

would be to throw far too many of Hosea's oracles into the last few years we can possibly allow for his activity.

Far more likely would be that we here have evidence of the divided kingdom under Menahem and Pekahiah in Samaria and Pekah in Gilead in the period 752–740 B.C. There can be little doubt that the Biblical evidence must be so interpreted[1] and it would not place an intolerable strain on the dating of the oracles that refer to Ephraim. I prefer, however, to see a spiritual purpose in many cases, the more so as it is improbable that Menahem would have abandoned the proud name of Israel for his kingdom. Already in 3:5 Hosea had indicated that the only future for Israel lay in reconciliation with the Davidic monarchy, and the references to Judah suggest that it is there that God's purposes must be worked out. By referring to the North as Ephraim Hosea reminds Israel that, as we saw in the story of Jeroboam I, it owed its very existence to Ephraim's jealousy of Judah with its God-given institutions of the Jerusalem temple and the Davidic monarchy.

The text of 4:16–19 is particularly difficult, but we may suggest as its meaning,

> *Like a stubborn cow*
> *Israel is stubborn;*
> *can the* LORD *pasture them*
> *like sheep in a broad pasture?*
> *Ephraim is a companion of idols,*
> †*seats himself with a band of drunkards.*†
> *They gave themselves to harlotry,*
> *they loved shame more than their glory.*
> *A wind has wrapped them up in its wings,*
> *and they will be ashamed because of their altars.*

For us it is the mule that is the symbol of stubbornness, but normally, if those who have to deal with mules are to be believed, there is some reasonable motivation for its behaviour. A cow does not often turn stubborn, but if it does, there seems to be no reason at all for it, and so it is the harder to get it to budge. Jehovah was worshipped as the Shepherd of Israel, with all the rich implications of such a title. Hosea asks how He can treat them in that way if their behaviour completely belies that expected of the sheep.

The word translated "wind" (*ruach*) could just as well have been rendered "spirit." Just as Israel had been mastered by his sensuous worship and was unable to free himself from it and the immorality and drunkenness that were its inseparable concomitants, so God would send an irresistible and swift enemy on him that would sweep him into exile. He would

---

[1] Cf. H. J. Cook, *Pekah* in V.T., Vol. XIV (1964), pp. 121 *seq.* and Thiele, *The Mysterious Numbers of the Hebrew Kings*², pp. 118 *seq.* and V.T., Vol. XVI (1966), pp. 83 *seq.*

be ashamed because of his altars, because then at last he would realize
how hollow and useless his religion had been.

Having pictured the tragic results of the priests' failure to teach the
Divine will, Hosea now turns to another sphere of life, that of justice,
where their example and teaching had borne bitter fruit. But in 5:1–5
he links with them those leaders of the people whose special duty it was
to see that justice was done.

> ¹*Hear this, you priests,*
> *and give heed †you elders of the house of Israel.*
> *Hearken you house of the king,*
> *for justice is your duty.*
> *For you have been a snare for Mizpah*
> *and a net spread on Mount Tabor,*
> ²*and a pit dug in Shittim,*
> *but I shall chastise all of you.*
> ³*I know Ephraim,*
> *and Israel is not hid from Me;*
> *for now Ephraim has played the harlot,*
> *and Israel is defiled.*
> ⁴*Their deeds do not permit them*
> *to return to their God,*
> *for the spirit of harlotry is in them,*
> *and they know not the* LORD.
> ⁵*The pride of Israel will bear witness against him;*
> *Ephraim will stumble in his guilt;*
> *Judah also will stumble with them.*[1]

The three places mentioned in vv. 1, 2, viz. Mizpah, Mount Tabor and
Shittim, were almost certainly among the important sanctuaries of the
North. Hosea is affirming that just as false religion led to corruption in the
home so it led also to injustice. Once Jehovah was regarded as a nature god,
His concern with justice was no longer taken seriously. We here meet
Hosea's clear recognition that a call to repentance is of no use. They are so
dominated by "harlotry" that their deeds will not permit them to return
to God. It was not the burden of a guilty conscience that made them fear
the wrath of God until in desperation they went headlong down the way
to destruction, but the sensuous attractiveness of the Canaanized religion
blinded them even on the very edge of the pit. The categoric affirmation
that Judah was walking in the same path was probably due to the fact
declared to us by Isaiah and Micah that particularly the sphere of justice
showed that the South was going in the same way as the North.

[1] The mention of Israel, Ephraim and Judah in the one verse is one of the strongest pieces of
evidence that the first two are not synonyms, at least here.

This section closes with a short oracle (5:6, 7) affirming the complete uselessness of the sacrificial cultus for the position in which Israel found itself. He sees the worshippers coming with whole flocks and herds for the sacrifices, but he assures them that God will not let Himself be found by them because He has withdrawn Himself. The charge that they have borne "alien children" almost certainly links up with the oracles in chs. 1, 2. We must almost certainly accept an emendation in the last clause of v. 7 and render *Now †the destroyer† is eating up their fields.*

FRATRICIDAL STRIFE

There can be very little doubt that Albrecht Alt was correct in seeing in 5:8–6:6 a group of related oracles coming from the period of the Syro–Ephraimite was against Judah (c. 735–732 B.C.).[1] This was the greatest political crisis during Hosea's life, and he is not likely to have long survived it.

The death of Jeroboam II led to the inner collapse that Amos and Hosea had foreseen. His son Zechariah reigned only six months (II Ki. 15:8), but his assassin, Shallum, held his ill-gotten position for only a month before Menahem dealt with him as he had dealt with Zechariah (II Ki. 15:13, 14). His cruelty made him unpopular, and to strengthen his position he became a vassal of Tiglath-pileser III, king of Assyria, in 743 B.C. (II Ki. 15:19, where the Assyrian king is called Pul, his personal name). The nationalists took their revenge; Pekah was able to maintain a rival kingdom in Gilead and after Menahem's death murdered Pekaiah his son, and made himself king of the whole northern area (II Ki. 15:25).

There can be little doubt that this was a deliberate challenge to Assyria, and since an active king like Tiglath-pileser could not be expected to take it lying down, we find Pekah building up an anti-Assyrian coalition with Rezin, king of Damascus, as his chief partner. Probably some of the Philistine cities, and perhaps Edom, joined it also (II Chr. 28:17 f.). Judah was summoned to join the coalition. Jotham seems still to have been alive, but Ahaz was evidently sharing the throne with him. In the crisis he must have taken charge of Judah's foreign policy. He was too clear-sighted to commit national suicide, but when he was attacked by the confederates (II Ki. 16:5; Isa. 7:1 f.) he refused to listen to Isaiah, but preferred to rivet the fetters of vassaldom on Judah by turning to Tiglath-pileser for aid and paying him tribute (II Ki. 16:7).

The effects were immediate and drastic. In 734 Tiglath-pileser dealt with the Philistines. The next year Galilee and Transjordan fell to Assyria. Samaria was saved only by a plot, favoured by the Assyrians, by which Hoshea ben Elah murdered Pekah and became vassal king of Samaria. In 732 Damascus went down to ruin.

All this means that these oracles were spoken in a period in which Judah

---

[1] *Kleine Schriften zur Geschichte des Volkes Israels,* Vol. II, *Hosea 5, 8–6, 6. Ein Krieg und Seine Folgen in Prophetischer Beleuchtung,* pp. 163 seq.

was shaken to the core, lost all its superficial prosperity of the time of Uzziah and ceased to be an independent state, while Israel shrank to the rump vassal state of Samaria, merely waiting until Assyria should have digested its recent conquests and was ready to deal with it.

> ⁸*Blow the war-horn in Gibeah,*
> *the trumpet in Ramah;*
> *give the alarm in Beth-aven (i.e. Bethel),*
> *cause Benjamin to tremble.*
> ⁹*Ephraim shall become a destruction in the day of punishment.*
> *Among the tribes of Israel*
> *I made known trustworthy words.*

As the forces of Israel reeled from the blows of Assyria there came the news that Judah, which had seemed to be at its last gasp, was hitting back from the south. The order of the enemy's advance in v. 8 is clearly from south to north: Gibeah, Ramah, Bethel. The two former lay within Judah (I Ki. 15:17, 22), for the normal frontier ran north of Mizpah and Geba (II Ki. 23:8), Evidently the debatable land of Benjamin had been incorporated into Israel by the apparently victorious confederation. Now, however, the troops of Ahaz were moving north again, thirsting for vengeance.

The closing words of v. 9 suggest that Hosea had attacked both the alliance with Rezin and the attack on Judah. Now the judgment he had foretold was going into effect and it was too late to avert it.

> ¹⁰*The leaders of Judah have behaved*
> *like those that remove landmarks;*
> *upon them will I pour out*
> *My wrath like water.*
> ¹¹*Ephraim is oppressed, crushed in judgment,*
> *because he insisted in going after* †*this enemy*†*.*

Two wrongs never make a right. From this slightly later oracle we gather that Judah not merely won back her lost territory, but went on to add traditional Israelite territory, presumably at least Bethel, to it. Even if the Assyrians tolerated this for the moment it did not last long, and they would have claimed back the area in 723, when Samaria became an Assyrian province. Bethel was indubitably in the Assyrian province of Samaria (II Ki. 17:28) and in the reign of Josiah the traditional frontier was in force (II Ki. 23:8).

It was convenient for Ahaz and his advisers to forget that they were now vassals, and that it was Assyria that had to decide on changes of boundary. It was also easy to forget that Isaiah had foretold the speedy collapse of the confederacy (Isa. 7:4–9) and to think that it was their wisdom that had led to the winning of the last battle. For God, however, they were merely greedy landgrabbers, stabbing Israel in the back when it was down, robbing it of its right. But however unjustifiable Judah's action, Israel had brought its fate upon itself. Strikingly enough, Hosea condemns at this point not Israel's entirely wanton attack on Judah, but its long-continued coquetting with Assyria, mentioned but not by name at the end of v. 11, unless indeed Damascus is intended by "his enemy".

> ¹²*I am as a moth to Ephraim,*
> *and as dry rot to the house of Judah.*
> ¹³*Then Ephraim saw his sickness,*
> *and Judah his wound;*
> *and Ephraim went to Assyria,*
> *and †Judah to the Great King†,*
> *but he cannot heal them*
> *nor cure them of their wounds,*
> ¹⁴*for I am as a lion to Ephraim*
> *and as a young lion to the house of Judah –*
> *I, even I, tear and go My way;*
> *I carry off and none delivers.*

Man has always been moved and impressed, for the moment at least, by great reversals of fortune, whether by the mere fact of death or by the unexpected fall of the great at the height of their power. Shakespeare's lines express it:

> Imperious Cæsar, dead and turned to clay,
> Might stop a hole, to keep the wind away.
> O that that earth which kept the world in awe
> Should patch a wall t' expel the winter's flaw!

or again, Samuel Johnson, writing of Charles XII of Sweden:

> His fall was destined to a barren strand,
> A petty fortress, and a dubious hand;
> He left a name at which the world grew pale,
> To point a moral, or adorn a tale.

The Bible is much more realistic. It knows that the sudden reversals of fortune are rare, and that normally signs of downfall and judgment are there clearly to be seen by all who wish to. For the neighbours of Israel the vanishing of the glories of Jeroboam II would have been as unexpected as for Israel itself. Yet Hosea could say,

> *Strangers have devoured his strength,*
> *and he knows it not:*
> *yea, grey hairs are here and there upon him,*
> *and he knows it not (7:9).*

Sin and judgment sap the strength and glory of a nation little by little. If there really is a sudden collapse it is like that of the house whose timbers have become empty shells, their heart eaten out by the attacks of the termite.

In this oracle, however, Hosea goes farther. He declares that it has been God who has been eating away the strength of Israel and Judah, like moth and dry-rot.[1] It has been more than a merely natural deterioration that might be cured by merely natural means. To avert Divine judgment one must turn to God. They, when their weakness and emptiness were made plain to all, turned in desperation to Tiglath-pileser. Even had he wished to do them good, he could do nothing, for they were the prey of God.

> [15]*I go and return to My place,*
> *until they know themselves guilty and seek My face*
> *and look to Me in their affliction:*
> [1]*"Come, let us return to the* LORD
> *for He has torn, and He will heal us.*
> *He has smitten, and He will bind us up;*
> [2]*after two days He will give us life,*
> *on the third day He will raise us up*
> *that we may live before Him.*
> [3]*Let us know, let us press on to know the* LORD*;*
> *as surely as the dawn comes, He will show Himself;*
> *He will come to us as the rain,*
> *as the spring showers that water the earth."*
> [4]*What am I to do with you Ephraim?*
> *What am I to do with you Judah?*
> *Your loyal love is like a morning cloud,*
> *like dew that vanishes early.*
> [5]*Therefore I hew them by the prophets,*
> *I slay them by the words of My mouth,*
> *and My judgment goes forth as the light.*
> [6]*For loyal love I desire and not sacrifices,*
> *and knowledge of God more than burnt offerings.*

It is not clear whether 6:1-3 is meant to represent the people's reaction to Hosea's message, or whether it is a sad, sarcastic forecast of what may be expected (cf. Jer. 3:21-25). In either case the superficial optimism is painfully evident. They assume that the Divine mercy is at the beck and call of human expressions of repentance. There is no conception that it is possible to go too far, to leave things too late. Above all there is no indication that the lessons of chs. 1-3 had been understood and assimilated.

God has to tell them that what they lack above all is loyalty. Neither goodness (RV) nor love (RSV) is adequate in 6:4. In a stranger instability of behaviour may be excusable, but where there is a firm covenant bond, as

[1] On the basis of Arabic Hirschberg (V.T. Vol. XI (1961), pp. 378 f.) suggests "lion" and "wolf".

between Hosea and Gomer, God and Israel, repeated expressions of repentance cannot take the place of what is expected in the covenant, its love and loyalty. This does not suggest that there is not forgiveness in plenty with God, but that forgiveness is for the lapse from the covenant, hardly for its ignoring until the bitterness of circumstances draw a few perfunctory and stereotyped expressions of regret to the lips.

That we are in the realm of the stereotyped is seen in 6:2. There has been a strong tendency in recent years to explain the terms by the resurrection festival of Tammuz-Adonis, the dying and reviving vegetation god (cf. Ezek. 8:14). All the most recent research, however, seems to have made it clear that the god died only and did not come to life. But even if we cannot explain the words in this way, it does seem almost certain that we are hearing the echo of ritual language. Repentance there is, but a repentance that knows neither the nature nor the will of Jehovah.[1]

One thing, and one thing only, He demands, a loyal, covenant love that will be a reflection of His, and this can be obtained only through a knowledge of God. This knowledge, analogous to but much higher than the mutual knowledge of husband and wife in marriage, can be obtained only through loving obedience and fellowship. It is based on what God has said and done, but that saying and doing must become living realities through trust and loving response. If Israel does not show them, there is nothing God can do except let judgment have its way.

THE TESTIMONY OF HISTORY

The following sections, all of which probably come from an earlier period of Hosea's activity, serve in the book to confirm the great oracle of condemnation. By underlining various evils of the past, whether nearer or more distant, they make it clear that the lack of true loyalty to the covenant was no new feature in Israel's history, but had dogged it throughout.

6:7 – 7:2 is generally interpreted as involving a list of Israelite sanctuaries in which its sin had been specially revealed in one way or another, viz. Gilead, Shechem, Bethel, Samaria. Hence, though the Hebrew makes perfect sense, it is usual to make a change of a letter in v. 7, making it read "in Adam" (so RSV). That there was such a city is shown by Josh. 3:16; it lay at the Jordan ford Ed-Damije. Unfortunately we are completely ignorant of its history and even whether there was a sanctuary of any importance there. We are also in the dark as to what outstanding breach of the covenant, significantly standing first in the list of sins, may have taken place there. We can obtain a perfectly good sense without the emendation, but the "there" does seem to indicate a place – parallelism makes it difficult to interpret it of the places that follow.

If we keep the Hebrew as it is, we can hardly render with RV "like Adam". However much it may be legitimate for systematic theology to

---

[1] For a detailed discussion of the passage cf. R. Martin-Achard, *From Death to Life*, pp. 74 *seq.*

speak of a Divine covenant with Adam in Eden, there is no scriptural warrant for the term; hence it would be better to translate, "But they like mankind have transgressed the covenant," implying that Israel has behaved no better than others in spite of its privileges. In either case we have once again stress on the basic importance of loyalty to the covenant.

With the possible exception of 12:11 (q.v.) we have no other mention of Gilead (v. 8) as a city. If it is correct, we can assume that it was in Trans-Jordan and that there was a sanctuary of some importance in it; otherwise we are in the dark. As the place of the first and second covenant renewals or confirmations in Canaan (Josh. 8:30–35; 24:1, 26–28) Shechem was a place of high sanctity; this was reflected in its being the first capital of the northern kingdom. Now its priests had sunk to being highway robbers, prepared to flout the law at will. Just as Bethel becomes Beth-aven in 4:15; 5:8; 10:5, so here in v. 10 it becomes Beth-yisrael, the house of Israel. God disowned it as being in any sense His house.

On Kings and Kingship

The following oracle, 7:3–7, almost unintelligible in AV and RV, has had its meaning veiled by a number of scribal errors. It is not sufficiently realized that a conscientious scribe, or oral transmitter for that matter, faced by virtual nonsense, will copy or pass it on accurately. Let him, however, be faced with a simple slip, like the inversion of two letters in v. 3, and he will normally without thinking "improve" the text to suit the apparent meaning. This can go on through a series of scribes, the whole becoming less and less clear, until only one or two passages point to the original sense. Those familiar with the modern compositor will know that the same is very often true of him. Here v. 7 makes it clear that it was not the immorality of the rulers, even though it was very real, that Hosea was attacking; that it was not even the rulers themselves who are the point of the oracle, but the men responsible for their destruction and murder. Once this is grasped it is relatively easy to feel one's way back to the original form of the oracle, though certain details must remain doubtful. A probable translation is,

³*In their wickedness they anoint kings*
and leaders in their lies.
⁴*Their heart holds back their anger;*
they are like an oven that is heating,
while the baker ceases to stir it up
from the time the dough is kneaded until it is leavened.
⁵*They make their king sick (i.e. drunk),*
the leaders with the heat of wine;
he has fellowship with scorners (i.e. plotters).
⁶*For like an oven their hearts burn with their intriguing;*
their anger sleeps all night;

in the morning it burns as a flaming fire.
[7]*They all glow as an oven*
and devour their rulers;
all their kings are fallen;
there is none among them that calls upon Me.[1]

There is no doubt that v. 7 is intended to be a general picture of the relationship between the great men of the North and their kings; vv. 4-6 refer especially to one incident, which is not identifiable by us with our lack of knowledge. Is v. 3 a general introduction or does it introduce the particular incident? If it is the latter, we can with Rudolph[2] retain the Heb. *yismeḥu*, they make glad. The former seems more probable; then with most moderns we have to emend to *yimseḥu*, they anoint.

We cannot doubt that the background of this oracle is Hosea's own time. The last six kings of Israel from Zechariah to Hoshea cover a period of only some thirty years and of them only one had a peaceful end. We have only to compare this with the lament of Ethan the Ezrahite (Psa. 89:38-45) and above all with the gasp of pain in Lam. 4:20,

The breath of our nostrils, the anointed of the LORD,
was taken in their pits;
of whom we said, Under his shadow
we shall live among the nations,

to realize how the whole concept of kingship had collapsed in Israel in contrast to Judah. The Davidic monarchy had its grievous faults, but to the very last it was regarded as God's gracious gift and looked back to with longing. It was quite otherwise in Israel. As we saw earlier, God's choice of Jeroboam ben Nebat was as much a judgment on the North as on Judah, and it was not long before the concept of the king as God's anointed ceased to have any real meaning in Israel.

The only plot where drunkenness (v. 5) is explicitly stated to have played a part was Zimri's against Elah, a full century earlier (I Ki. 16:9). We are not able to affirm that Hosea had this in mind, for he may be, and probably is, referring to a contemporary incident, but he saw in it an expression of what had been true for all the northern dynasties. They all began in treachery and plotting, and they all ended in a blood bath. So the terrible end was merely a light on what had been true all along.

We see the people anointing the new king and accepting his ministers and the families that swept into power with him, but all the time with lies and treachery in their hearts. Their loyalty lasts as long as their advantage dictates. Just as the heat of the baker's oven is allowed to moderate until the dough is ready, so their anger is restrained until their time is ripe. Then the

[1] Op. cit., pp. 146 f.
[2] For readers who know Heb. there is a full discussion by S. M. Paul in V.T. Vol. XVIII (1968). pp. 114 *seq.*

treacherous plotters sit at the table of the doomed king plying him with wine until the moment of his assassination.

So blinded had the people become that they did not realize that even though their kings had been of their own making, in destroying them they were destroying God's order (Rom. 13:1). This is brought out in v. 7 by Hosea's placing in parallelism to "kings" the word *shophetim* (this is traditionally translated "judges", but I prefer "rulers" here), the age-old term for the early rulers of Israel raised up by God.

At this point it may be well to ignore the order of the oracles, as they now stand, and look at those other prophecies that involve the monarchy. This will help us to obtain a clearer view of Hosea's message about Israel's kings, and indeed about the legitimacy of the state.

The first oracle to concern us is 8:1–14:

> [1] *The war-horn to your mouth!*
> *One like a vulture (comes) against the house of the* LORD,
> *because they have broken My covenant*
> *and against My instruction they have rebelled.*
> [2] *To Me they cry, "O God,*
> *we know Thee, for we are Israel."*
> [3] *Israel has spurned the good;*
> *let the enemy pursue him.*
> [4] *They have made kings, but not from Me;*
> *they set up lords, but I knew not.*
> *With their silver and their gold they made themselves*
> *images, that they may be cut off.*
> [5] *Rejected is your bull, Samaria!*
> *My anger is kindled against them.*
> *How long will it be before †the children of Israel are pure?*
> [6] *As for it†, a craftsman made it;*
> *it is a no-god,*
> *for it will become splinters,*
> *Samaria's bull.*
> [7] *For they sow the wind*
> *and shall reap the storm-wind;*
> *standing corn without ears –*
> *it will yield no flour!*
> *If it were to yield,*
> *foreigners would swallow it up.*
> [8] *Israel is swallowed up;*
> *now they have become among the nations*
> *like a vessel there is no more use for,*
> [9] *for they have gone to Assyria –*

a lonely wild ass!
Ephraim seeks to buy lovers.
¹⁰*Even if they buy among the nations,*
    now I must gather them in (for judgment);
    they will cease a little
    from †the anointing† of kings and rulers.
¹¹*Because Ephraim has made many altars,*
    they are for him altars of sinning.
¹²*Were I to write for him the myriads of My instructions,*
    they would be regarded as something strange.
¹³*† They love† sacrifices;*
    they sacrifice flesh and eat it –
    the LORD *is not pleased with them.*
    Now He will remember their iniquity
    and punish their sins;
    they shall return to Egypt.
¹⁴*For Israel has forgotten his Maker*
    and has built palaces,
    and Judah has multiplied
    fortified cities;
    but I shall send fire on his cities
    to devour his strongholds.

Just as Hosea in 1:4 reinterpreted Jehu's purging the land of Ahab's descendants and of Baal worshippers, so here he does the beginnings of the northern kingdom. As I argued in ch. II the disruption was really a punishment on the north as well as on Solomon through his son. In the truest sense the Divine choice of Jeroboam was based on his unworthiness. He was, like Jehu (I Ki. 19:17), the instrument of God's judgment on Israel. What applied to Jeroboam applied equally to the dynasties that followed his.

The wrongness of the northern kings is shown by the way they riveted a profoundly false concept of God on their people. Had Jeroboam been a very different man – but would he then have plotted against the Lord's anointed? – he would have trusted God to preserve his throne. In his materialistic outlook Jeroboam needed the guarantee of organized religion.

The glory of the temple in Zion was not the building Solomon had erected but the ark it housed. The ark had been the visible symbol of Jehovah's rule over Israel, so its house was perforce the religious centre of the people, and that Jeroboam could not face. He turned back into the nation's past and chose a symbol that would appeal both to long-buried memories and to the Canaanite elements in the population, namely a variant of the bull that was the chosen symbol of El, the head of the Canaanite pantheon.

Commentaries usually state that the Old Testament, including Hosea,

calls Jeroboam's bull images in mockery *'egel*, i.e. calf. I am not convinced
that they are right. That neither Aaron nor Jeroboam made a calf image is so
obvious that it need not be argued. In heathenism an animal symbol of a
deity was always intended to express some major characteristic of his. What
characteristic of Jehovah would a calf imply? It is questionable whether in
any passage where *'egel* is used we should understand it as "calf" in our
modern sense. In Isa. 11:6 it is linked with *kephir*, the young lion in the first
full flush of adult strength. It seems likely that the image was a bull in its
first maturity, partly to differentiate it from the El symbol, partly to speak
of the God who never grows old, as indeed El seems to have done, abandoning most of his authority to Baal.

It is not certain but highly probable that Omri will have provided the
sanctuary in his new city of Samaria with a bull image; otherwise he would
hardly have regarded it as an adequate rival to Jerusalem. There is no necessary contradiction to this in 10:5, especially if the interpretation of 10:9
offered below is correct.

It is doubtful whether Jeroboam's advisers – we can hardly regard him
as the sole originator of the change – had any special theology behind their
choice, but it did involve a repudiation of the past – witness the rejection of
the Levites (I Ki. 12:31). This in turn made it much more difficult for the
religion of the North to resist the inroads of neighbouring religions.

When we are told with absolute regularity of the kings of Israel, whether
bad or relatively good, that they "walked in all the way of Jeroboam the
son of Nebat, who made Israel to sin", it is merely a reminder of the trap
into which Jeroboam had led the North. He had made the bulls a symbol of
Israel's legitimacy as a separate kingdom; for a successor to destroy them
would have been interpreted as a denial of that legitimacy. That is probably
the reason why the bulls were not attacked by Hosea's predecessors, for
such an attack would have been interpreted as treasonable rather than
religious. Hosea, aware that the kingdom was on the brink of destruction
and that nothing short of a complete repudiation of the past could save it,
attacked both the monarchy and its religious expression as equally contrary
to God's will. Since both were of the flesh fleshly, they led to a fleshly
foreign policy as well.

The comparison in v. 9 with a wild ass – Israel, not Assyria! – is partly for
the sake of a pun (*pere'* with *'ephraim*); but it is also an unnatural wild ass
that wanders by itself. Normally wild asses are found in herds. Israel had
turned to all sides for help and had been left friendless.

There is apparently an advance on the thought of ch. 8 in 10:1–10.

[1] *A luxuriant vine is Israel,*
  which yielded much fruit;
  the more his fruit increased,

the more he multiplied altars;
the greater the prosperity of his land,
the more he made his mazzeboth[1] *attractive.*
[2] *Their heart is divided,*
now they shall suffer as guilty;
He shall break their altars,
devastate their mazzeboth.
[3] *For now they say,*
"No king for us!
For we do not fear the LORD,
and what could the king do for us?"
[4] *Speaking (mere) words,*
swearing empty oaths,
making covenants (with foreign powers) –
and justice sprouts like a poisonous weed
in the furrows of the field!
[5] *For the bulls of Beth-aven*
the inhabitants of Samaria are afraid.
Its people go into mourning for it,
and its heathen priests[2] howl for it,
for its glory has departed from it.
[6] *For it will be brought to Assyria*
as tribute to the Great King
†*in the year*† *that he takes Ephraim;*
Israel will be ashamed of his †*piece of wood*†.
[7] *Samaria will be destroyed;*
its king is like a snapped-off twig on the face of the waters.
[8] *The* bamoth[3] *of Beth-aven will be destroyed,*
the sin of Israel;
thorns and thistles will grown up
on their altars.
They will say to the mountains, "Cover us",
and to the hills, "Fall on us".

[1] The *mazzebah* was an up-ended stone – the traditional rendering "pillar" is far too grandiose. It might be no more than a commemoration stone as in Gen. 28:18, Exod. 24:4, but in the cultic sense in which Hosea uses it here it was a symbol of the male deity, and was accordingly forbidden (Exod. 23:24; Lev. 26:1; Deut. 16:22). This and the *'asherah*, the symbol of the female diety, were sure signs of Canaanite influence on Israel's religion. With growing prosperity the *mazzebah* would be more carefully cut and smoothed, and finally became an image. Obviously the more carefully carved the less easily it could be explained away as a mere commemorative stone.

[2] *Chemarim*, a word never used of legitimate priests. In II Ki. 23:5 RV, RSV translate "idolatrous priests."

[3] *Bamah*, plural *bamoth*, is traditionally but incorrectly translated high places. Its most probable meaning is that given by Albright, "an elevated platform on which cultic objects were placed" (*Archaeology and the Religion of Israel*[3], p. 105). This is no denial that many, though not all, of these sanctuaries were on hill tops. A later development of his views may be found in V.T. Supplement, *Strasbourg 1956, The High Place in Ancient Palestine.*

⁹*From the days of Gibeah you have sinned, Israel.*
There they have remained!
Will not war overtake them in Gibeah
¹⁰*when I come against the wayward nation to chastise them?*
For nations will be gathered against them,
when they are chastised for their double iniquity.

While there are four separate oracles here, they belong together in inner meaning. In vv. 1, 2 we have the almost schizophrenic condition of Israel torn between loyalty to Jehovah and Baal. This showed itself in practice in the frenzied repudiation both of the king and the God he claimed to represent (v. 3). This oracle must come from the last desperate days of Israel after the murder of Pekah (II Ki. 15:29 f.). The condition of things had become so corrupt that justice had become synonymous with injustice; it was a poisonous plant to be shunned (v. 4).

In perhaps his most sarcastic oracle (vv. 5–8) Hosea exposes the strange Alice in Wonderland state of Israel's religion. In heathen religions the images – in this case the bulls – were the outward sign of divine protection, but here the people are concerned about their bulls!

Most moderns follow the LXX in v. 5 and change to the singular "bull". In spite of the grammar I am not convinced. In v. 8 we find the *bamoth* ("high places") of Bethel in the plural. Not only would it be unusual for a place like Bethel to have more than one Canaanite type sanctuary, but II Ki. 23:15 clearly implies the existence of only one. It is not unlikely then that Beth-aven ("the house of wickedness") stands not merely for Bethel but also for the whole official, semi-pagan religious set-up. So Hosea may have used the plural "bulls" in v. 5 in the same way, though his immediate reversion to the singular shows that it was the Bethel one he was thinking about most.

Rudolph may well be correct in taking it as an abstract singular, meaning, more or less, "bull-work". He points out that its glory had departed, and suggests almost certainly correctly, that the gold covering of the wooden core (cf. v. 6) had been removed to make up the heavy tribute money payable to Assyria. If this was the original bull-image made by Jeroboam I, it is most improbable that it was of solid gold.

There was quite evidently something in the history of Gibeah (vv. 9 f.) that Hosea considered fatal for the history of the North. Already in 9:9 we find "the days of Gibeah" mentioned as an example of deepest depravity. We must beware of taking for granted that we can of necessity explain these references; 6:7 ff. is an indication of the opposite. It is, however, striking that we have preserved for us two incidents (the *double iniquity*) in the early history of Israel, where Gibeah played an important part in Israel's revolt against God's will.

The former is given us in Jdg. 19–21, which contains the story of how

Benjamin was almost annihilated in the early days of the judges – Phineas was still alive (20:28). We shrink back at the story of gross lust described in 19:22–25, but it is very questionable whether it was this that Hosea was thinking of. Had it been, it would have left most of his hearers unmoved, for Benjamin had thrown in its lot with Judah at the disruption, and most of its tribal portion fell outside the boundaries of Israel. Hence *Shall not war overtake them in Gibeah?* means throughout the northern kingdom.

In trying to understand the story we must bear in mind the two days of disaster that the other tribes had had to face (20:20–25). Clearly we are meant to understand that the other tribes were far from guiltless and had to experience God's judgment before they might act as His executioners. Benjamin's sin was its solidarity with the men of Gibeah in defying Israel's call for justice to be done. In other words, they were contracting out of the twelve-tribe confederacy of God's people, and probably the other tribes had been thinking along similar lines. But that is precisely what the North, not Benjamin, did in the days of Rehoboam. As we saw earlier they had the legal right to do it. But for all that they were in a majority they were contracting out of God's people. They might call themselves "Israel", but it was Judah with Benjamin and Levi that had the real right to the name. No wonder that Hosea said *There they have remained!* Benjamin reversed their early error, Israel persisted in it.

This does not explain the *double iniquity*. Some commentators quite gratuitously connect the second incident with the story of Micah in Jdg. 17. This is arbitrary, for the only indication of Micah's home is that he lived in Ephraim, not Benjamin. In addition, for the Danites to have passed near Gibeah on their way north would have violated all canons of common sense. There was one period, however, and one period only, when Gibeah enjoyed a modest blaze of glory. It was the home and capital of Saul.

If this is the correct understanding of Hosea's words, it means that he condemned not merely the Israelite kings of the divided monarchy but also the whole Israelite conception of kingship as expressed in Saul. There is some controversy as to whether David represented God's relative best once the people had insisted on His conceding the principle of kingship, or whether God had all along intended a king of the Davidic type. This is probably a mere wrangle about words. The word which in the Old Testament we render judge (*shophet*) was among the Phoenicians their title for king. The fact of rule was never contrary to God's will. But kingship, as it came in under Saul, was not merely the expression of man's desires; it also involved the hereditary system, which bore its evil fruit in the Davidic dynasty as well as in the North. But there was probably a deep contrast between Saul's and David's concept of what being a king meant. The story of Absalom's rebellion and Adonijah's attempt on the throne contains elements hard to understand, and it is very likely that among the men behind them were those who deeply resented David's concept of his position, a concept they expected Solomon to continue, viz. the willingness to accept a restricted sphere of royal power.

A very similar note is struck in 13 : 1–11. For the present we shall consider only vv. 9–11, as the rest of the section is best studied in another context.

> ⁹*I have destroyed you, Israel;*
> *who can help you?*
> ¹⁰*Where is now your king*
> *to save you from all your enemies,*
> *and your rulers,*¹ *those of whom you said,*
> *" Give me a king and lords"?*
> ¹¹*I give you a king in My anger*
> *and take him away in My wrath.*

The tenses used in v. 11 are the "imperfect" in Heb. expressing continuous action which would end only with the collapse of the state. "I gave" (AV) and "I have given" (RV, RSV) are both equally misleading. The truth of Hosea's words may be tested by the fact that of the twenty-two non-Davidic kings from Saul onwards who claimed kingship in Israel fourteen at least met a premature death on the battlefield, or by assassination or accident. It would be hazardous to assume that of the others all met a normal end.

In these verses Hosea is stressing that throughout the history of Israel Jehovah had been its Lord. Those who thought that they lorded it over God's people were in fact merely the instruments of His judgment; He removed them, when they had served their purpose.

This estimate of Israel's national existence, its religion and its kingship will have to concern us further when we come to sum up Hosea's prophecy as a whole. For the moment it will suffice to say that the picture is much darker than many superficial readers of the prophecy grasp.

ISRAEL'S UNFAITHFULNESS

If neither the existence nor the constitution of Israel expressed God's true will, it was to be expected that this would show itself in its foreign policy, and so it was.

For us alliances between nations are such a commonplace of life that we can hardly imagine a nation standing alone, unless indeed, like Switzerland, it makes its refusal to make alliances a virtual moral claim on other nations for help should it be wantonly attacked. I do not imagine that I was the only one to be deeply grieved when on Sunday, 22nd June, 1941, I heard Mr. Winston Churchill declare over the air, "Any man or state who fights on against Nazidom will have our aid. . . . It follows therefore that we shall give whatever help we can to Russia and the Russian people." I was grieved that Britain would be from that time allied to an evil and a godless govern-

¹ Cf. note on 7:7, p. 124.

ment, but I knew also, the world being what it is, that this was inevitable and unavoidable.

It should have been fundamental, however, for Israel that no foreign alliances were possible. The reason was quite simply that in those days the secular state did not exist, and so in practice it was impossible to distinguish between a state and its gods. In an extant treaty of peace between Rameses II of Egypt and Hattusilis the Hittite king it is a thousand of their gods on either side who are the witnesses to and guarantors of it.[1] So even a treaty on equal terms with a neighbouring country would have involved for Israel a recognition of the other country's deities as having reality and equality with Jehovah. To turn to Assyria or Egypt for help implied of necessity that their gods were more effective than the God of Israel. The logical outcome of Ahaz's appeal to Tiglath-pileser III for help (II Ki. 16:7) was his recognition of Assyria's gods by sacrificing on an altar which was probably a copy of Tiglath-pileser's travelling altar (II Ki. 16:10–15). Equally the initial slowness of Josiah's reformation (II Chr. 34:3, 8) is best explained by its involving of necessity rebellion against his Assyrian overlord, the symbols of whose gods were being destroyed. This then explains the bitterness of Hosea's attack on Israel's contemporary foreign policy in 7:8–16. He starts by saying,

> [8]*Ephraim among the peoples!*
> *He mixes himself;*
> *Ephraim is a cake*
> *not turned.*

G. A. Smith followed by ICC, understood this of Israel's commercial relations with the nations around and of the dislocation of internal conditions that followed. His vivid conclusion is worth quoting. "How better describe a half-fed people, a half-cultured society, a half-lived religion, a half-hearted policy, than by a half-baked scone?"[2]

However true Smith's vivid picture of Israel, it is doubtful whether this was uppermost in Hosea's mind. The prophets do not seem to have been particularly concerned with international commerce, probably because Israel indulged in it far less than many scholars assume. But, as earlier chapters have shown us, Israel was involved in international politics at least from the time of Omri and Ahab. Indeed, there would probably have been no "Israel" but for Jeroboam's help from Pharaoh Shishak. It seems that friendship with Assyria had helped to make Jeroboam II great, and it was the desperate alliance between Pekah and Rezin of Damascus that brought down the vengeance of Tiglath-pileser and made the end of Israel certain.

It is obviously true that the thin unturned loaf was "half-baked", but once again this phrase seems to miss the point. Normally the half-baked can with some skill be saved and baked through. Here, however, one side was

[1] ANET, pp. 200 f.   [2] Op. cit., p. 273.

so overbaked and charred that the whole was fit for nothing. While the visible part seemed normal, in fact the whole was ruined. The maturity of Israel had been sapped and squandered by his political efforts, and though he still dreamt his dreams of splendour the signs of old age were already visible (v. 9). For all that, Israel was still proud of its policy (v. 10).

> ¹¹*And Ephraim is like a dove,*
> *simple and without fixed purpose;*
> *to Egypt they called,*
> *to Assyria they went.*

In Eastern proverbs the dove is notorious for its simplicity, largely because of its apparently aimless flight, which repeatedly seems to take it from danger to danger, out of the frying-pan into the fire. It was not as though there had been any fixed purpose in Israel's foreign policy, beyond unwillingness to do God's will. But just as the pigeon-owner takes precautions that his birds do not get lost, so Jehovah was watching over Israel, not to save them but to punish them (v. 12).

The oracle of 7:13-16 seems to be concerned with false religion rather than false foreign policy, but the false religion had come through wrong foreign contacts.

> ¹³*Woe to them, for they have strayed from Me!*
> *Destruction to them, for they have rebelled against me!*
> *I would redeem them,*
> *but they have spoken lies against Me.*
> ¹⁴*They did not cry to Me from their heart,*
> *but they kept howling about their †dwellings†;*
> *for corn and new wine they gashed themselves;*
> *they are in rebellion against Me.*
> ¹⁵*Although I trained and strengthened their arms,*
> *yet they devise evil against Me.*
> ¹⁶*They turn again to †a people that cannot help†*
> *like a treacherous bow.*
> *Their lords will fall by the sword,*
> *because of their broken speech*
> *in the land of Egypt.*

Though originally there was probably no close link with 7:12, this shows the effects of their foreign policy. Both the preoccupation of their prayers and the form of worship (cf. I Ki. 18:28) showed that they were worshipping Baal, even if they called him Jehovah. Even though God had treated and educated them as sons (v. 15), they kept turning to their foreign allies, who could not help them. They became like "a deceitful bow" (cf. Psa. 78:57). Once they had marched out of Egypt with a high hand; now for the few fugitives who would save their lives there would be only mockery at their unintelligible speech from the people they had once humbled.

THE PROPHET'S REJECTION

Just as Amos had stood at the great New Year feast at Bethel and pronounced God's word of judgment, so the time came for Hosea to stand on this same occasion, possibly in the same place.[1] Amos had received a good hearing, even if at the last he was driven away, but now men were tired of prophets, and so there is only this short oracle (9:1–6) that we can link with the occasion.

In the Mosaic law-giving, though harvest rejoicing had its due place, Tabernacles stressed the historic liberation of Israel as more important. In Israel's Canaanized religion it had been forgotten or allowed to drop into the background.

[1]*Rejoice not, Israel;*
exult not like the peoples,
for you have played the harlot (and forsaken) your God.
You have loved the harlot's hire
on every threshing floor.

The loud rejoicing of the festival merely grated on Hosea's ears. It was precisely of the same nature as the festival rejoicing he could have heard by crossing the frontiers into Philistia, Phoenicia or Syria. It was a rejoicing purely in the kindly fruits of the earth without a thought of the salvation which gave them their real meaning and value. The mention of the harlot's hire needed no explanation for those who heard him. Unrestrained eating and drinking kindled bodily passions, and for many the carousal ended in the arms of a strange woman, helping forward the fertility of the year to come, as they believed, by abandoning themselves to their sexual passions. The outcome would be God's judgment on the things they rejoiced in and misused.

[2]*Threshing floor and wine-vat will not feed them,*
and the new wine will fail them.
[3]*They will not stay in the land of the LORD,*
but Ephraim will return to Egypt,
or in Assyria they will eat polluted food.
[4]*They will not pour out libations of wine to the LORD;*
and they will not be able to bring their sacrifices to Him.
Like mourner's bread will be their bread;
all who eat it will be polluted.
For their bread will be for themselves alone;
it will not come into the LORD's house.

[1] For comments on 8:1–14 see pp. 124 ff.

[5]*What will you do on the festival day,*
and on the day of the LORD's *pilgrim feast?*
[6]*For behold they are on the point of going to Assyria;*
Egypt will gather them,
Memphis will bury them.
Weeds will grow over[1] *their precious articles of silver;*
thorns will grow in their tents.

It is not the impossibility of sacrifice in exile that is being stressed in v. 4 but that before that day came the land would yield such inadequate crops that there would be nothing left for God. We have no details of this early dispersion in Egypt, but we can understand why it arose. Once Ahaz had become the vassal of Assyria, fugitives would not have felt safe in Judah. It may be that the peculiar "Jewish" military colony at Elephantine at the south frontier of Egypt with its corrupt religion was in fact, as some have maintained,[2] begun by fugitives after the fall of Samaria.

The oracle of 9:7–9 is probably fairly closely linked with the foregoing one, for it will almost certainly have caused a burst of popular anger. It is one of the very difficult oracles in Hosea which seems to make little sense as it stands, cf. RV.

I have essentially followed Rudolph.

[7]*The days of visitation have come;*
the days of retribution have come:
Israel will know it.
(They say) "The prophet is foolish,
the spirit-filled man is mad."
† *The fullness of your guilt*
(is matched by) the greatness of your enmity†:
[8]†*Ephraim opens his mouth wide,*
the people of my God against the prophet†;
fowler's snares are on all his ways/
enmity (even) in the house of his God.
[9]*They have deeply corrupted themselves*
as in the days of Gibeah.
He will remember their iniquity,
He will punish their sins.

Just as Amos was scornfully rejected by Amaziah as a "seer", so Hosea was dismissed as foolish and mad. But where Amos was apparently allowed to go in peace they sought some ground to kill Hosea. As later with Jeremiah, men spied on him and tried to trap him and trip him up. It is doubtful whether we have changed much with the passing centuries. The main

---

[1] Literally "will possess".
[2] e.g. Oesterley in Oesterley and Robinson, *A History of Israel*, Vol. II. pp. 160 ff.

difference is that today we are apt to accuse the prophet of being "unsound", though the general principle remains the same.

ORIGINAL SIN

It is often stated that the Old Testament knows nothing of original sin. If this is interpreted to mean that the doctrine is nowhere expressed as a universal human fact, this may be accepted without demur. But there are not a few passages, of which 9:10–14 in Hosea is a notable example, which point irresistibly towards the doctrine as we find it in the New Testament.

Men revolt against the concept that God visits the sins of the fathers upon the children unto the third and fourth generation – under Old Testament circumstances the whole family group was likely to be living together when the grey-haired hater of God went to his reward – but in their soberer moments they acknowledge that the Bible seems to be borne out by very much in life. They find it still harder to accept that there is a mysterious something in man, not of the individual's creating, though often of his strengthening, that mysteriously poisons and distorts his best hours and motives.

We gain the impression that Hosea was concerned, more than other prophets except Ezekiel, with the mystery of Israel's continued and continuous rejection of God's will. Perhaps it was the mystery of Gomer's unfaithfulness that first turned his thoughts to the problem. We find him referring to the sins of Jezreel, Achan, Gibeah and Gilgal (9:15) as still working out their tragic consequences, but we see this most clearly in his reference to Baal-peor.

If ever there had been the possibility of a completely new beginning it was at the Exodus. So unexpected, so unique was Israel's position that God says:

Like grapes in the wilderness I found Israel, and He found intense delight in her; *like the first fruit on the fig tree in its first season, I saw your fathers.* But, alas, *they came to Baal-peor and consecrated themselves to Baal.*[1]

We, when we think of the failure of Israel in the wilderness, put our stress on the golden bull and then on Kadesh-barnea. Hosea knew that there was some excuse for the generation of the Exodus, for they carried into the wilderness all the heritage of slavery and humiliation in Egypt. But forty years later this generation, all but Joshua and Caleb, and Moses, who was under sentence of death, had passed away. Even those who could faintly remember Egypt carried no psychological scars from it. However hard their life had been, they had been surrounded from their birth by the care and love of God. They had no tradition of unfaithfulness to poison their future. But scarce had they left the wilderness and God had opened the way for the possession of Palestine by the complete defeat of Sihon and Og (Num. 21), than they turned their back on their God (Num. 25). They were

[1] AV. RV "shame" (*boshet*), a scribal replacement for Baal.

carried away by sheer lust, which blinded them to the fact that the women who inveigled them did it to bring glory to their god, the god of Moab, the Baal of Peor. On the one hand this lifted the veil from the abyss of the human soul. We should look and fear. On the other hand Hosea saw clearly that here was one of those fountains of corruption that had poisoned his people throughout their history.

Sex in the animal is a blind instinct, but man knows that it gives him the mysterious power of creation. Here God allows him to exercise the Divine prerogative; that is why it is constantly stressed that children are a gift of God. The New Testament has taught us that God has given us much that we must put before sex, yet sex is the supreme *natural* gift God has given man. To defile it is to scorn God's special gift. We need not be surprised therefore at the bitterness of Hosea's words.

> ¹⁰*Like grapes in the wilderness*
> *I found Israel,*
> *like the first fruit on the fig tree in its first season*
> *I saw your fathers.*
> *They came to Baal-peor*
> *and consecrated themselves to Baal;*
> *they became abominable*[1] *like the one they loved.*
> ¹¹*Ephraim – his glory flies away like a bird.*
> *No more birth! No more pregnancy! No more conception!*
> ¹²*Even if they bring up their sons,*
> *I shall bereave them that none be left,*
> *for woe is them also,*
> *for they are †their flesh†,*
> ¹³*Ephraim, †which I foresaw*
> *as a young palm, planted in a meadow†,*
> *the same Ephraim must lead out*
> *his sons to the slaughterer.*
> ¹⁴*Give them, O Lord – what wilt Thou give?*
> *give them a womb bereft of children*
> *and dry breasts.*

If the misuse of the fruits of the earth was to bring famine (9:1–6), how much more surely should the misuse of sex bring childlessness. Hosea's own deep disgust is shown by his passionate prayer.

It is a pity that we cannot recapture more of Hosea's outlook today. Christianized Europe has tended to swing between an unbiblical and God-dishonouring rejection of sex, either by an undue exaltation of celibacy or by regarding it as something dirty to be hidden away as far as possible, and on the other hand treating it as something little above the feelings of hunger and thirst, to be satisfied almost as soon as its urge is felt. We must learn to

---

[1] Literally "abominations".

regard it as one of God's supreme gifts to man, at all times to be brought into subjection to the will of Christ. It is no chance that the vast mass of human misery takes its rise in the home. Not only will the child bear the marks lastingly in his soul, when his parents have not been in fullest God-given harmony, but most adult neuroses and psychoses are linked in some way with the failure to find a God-honouring answer to the problems of sex.

In spite of v. 16 it is unlikely that the short oracle 9:15-17 is part of the one on Baal-peor. Since we do not know what the sin committed at Gilgal may have been – we do not even know which sanctuary of that name is being referred to – we cannot interpret it with any certainty, except to see in it one more picture of the grievous spiritual state of Israel.

ADDITIONAL NOTES ON THE TEXT

4:15, "In Beer-sheba" could easily have dropped owing to the similarity between *sheba* and the Heb. word "to swear".

4:17 f., "Seats himself with a band of drunkards." MT, as AV, RV bear witness, does not make much sense. At the same time no emendation commands general assent.

5:1, "You elders of the house of Israel." The oracle is clearly addressed to the leaders of the people. The word for "elders" has dropped out through similarity with its setting.

5:7, "The destroyer." The emendation follows Weiser (*Das Buch der Zwölf Kleinen Propheten*). The MT makes perfect sense with "a month", but there is no trace in Hosea of a prophecy of such imminent destruction.

5:11, "His enemy." Neither MT nor LXX are possible. The emendation adopted presupposes the dropping of one consonant in MT.

5:13, "The Great King." The Heb. consonants of King Jareb are *mlk yrb*. If we divide them *mlky rb*, we have "the Great King", the official title of the king of Assyria.

7:14, "Their dwellings." There is a change of one consonant from "beds" or "couches".

7:16, "A people that cannot help." The emendation, which follows Rudolph, is easier and more likely than "Baal" of RSV.

8:5, 6, "... the children of Israel are pure? As for it ..." MT of "For from Israel is even this" (RV) has been divided between the two verses. Another emendation is "What has Israel to do with it?", i.e. the bull image (Rudolph).

8:10, "The anointing." The change of one letter is involved.

8:13, "They love." The Heb. word is found only here. LXX and Syriac seem to support the meaning given.

9:7, The main change depends on a different division of the consonants.

9:8. This is known as one of the textually most difficult verses in *Hosea*. Those who know Heb. and Gk. are referred to the discussion by Dobbie in V.T., Vol. V (1955), pp. 199-203. I reproduce Rudolph's rendering, which must remain hypothetical. It does not involve many changes. The chief assumes that two consonants have dropped by haplography; for the rest it is a matter of vowels and punctuation.

9:12, "Their flesh." This represents a different division of the basic consonants.

9:13, MT represented by AV, RV, is clearly meaningless. The rendering is based in part on LXX. The translation "palm" is vouched for by Arabic.

10:6, "In the year." No change in the Heb. consonants is involved. "His piece of wood." This comes merely from a different interpretation of the Heb.

CHAPTER XIII

ISRAEL'S DOWNFALL AND EXILE

FROM CH. 10 ONWARDS, WITH THE POSSIBLE EXCEPTION OF ch. 14 (*q.v.*), we gain the impression that the prophet had lost the last spark of hope – not that there had ever been much – and so he looked forward merely to destruction and exile.[1]

FALSE REPENTANCE AND FALSE TRUST

In 10:11 Hosea looks back to the early days of Israel:

> [11]*Ephraim was a trained heifer*
> *that delighted in threshing,*
> *but it was I who put a yoke on her fair neck.*
> *I yoked Ephraim*
> *to plough* †*this field*†*;*
> *Jacob harrowed.*
> [12]*Sow for yourselves as is right;*
> *reap the fruit of loyal love;*
> *break up your virgin soil.*
> *It is time to seek the* LORD
> *that He may come and rain salvation on you.*
> [13]*You have ploughed evil,*
> *iniquity you have reaped,*
> *so you will eat the fruit of lies.*

If this rendering is true to Hosea's thought he was looking back to those very early days in Israel's history, when the service of God seemed light. Once it has learnt what is expected of it, it is a pleasure for the unmuzzled heifer to tread out the grain (Deut. 25:4). Once the Conquest had been carried through the implications of the law grew heavier. Not only had life to conform to the standards set by God – *Sow for yourselves as is right*, which seems to be truer to the Heb. than "sow righteousness", and gains some support from Isa. 28:23–29, where the farmer's wisdom is seen as God's gift – if they were to reap the fruit of God's covenant love, but it would also be entirely different from that lived by those they killed, or dispossessed and drove out. This is obscured by the standard English rendering "break up your fallow ground". Fallow ground is soil that has gone out of use or is being allowed to rest for a season or two. But, as in Jer. 4:3, land

[1] For comments on 10:1–10 see pp. 126–130.

that has never been tilled is intended. God's will is not merely higher than man's natural walk; it is completely other. He wished Israel to show a quality of life in Canaan of a kind not to be found elsewhere.

When the prophet spoke there was still time, but only just, to seek the Lord before they reaped the full harvest of what they had sown. *The fruit of lies* is disappointment and disaster. When he speaks of God raining salvation on them, Hosea was not holding up the hope of sudden salvation, but the beginning of a process that would lead to salvation and would follow on repentance. As the whole context implies, he was stressing the long course of retraining that would have to follow it (cf. 3:3). In the Christian life too the joy of salvation is often so stressed that young converts are oblivious to the steady discipline that must follow it. Hence in the Church too there is often all too little breaking up of virgin soil and sowing of righteousness.

With some hesitation I have omitted "Judah" in v. 11. Unlike so many of the references to the southern kingdom in Hosea, there seems to be no special admonition which is being addressed to the south. In addition it is not even required for parallelism, this being supplied by "Jacob".[1]

In spite of the traditional Hebrew punctuation in v. 13, it does not seem possible to make *ki* ("because" or "for") explain Israel's reaping of what it had sown and eating the fruit of lies. RSV recognizes this but has not been prepared to draw the natural conclusion and start a new section. We should take these verses as a completely separate oracle. A closer study of the Heb. will show ample evidence for this, and in any case vv. 11–13a are complete in themselves.

> [13]*Because you have trusted in your own way,*
>   *in the multitude of your heroes,*
> [14]*therefore the tumult of war will rise against your people,*
>   *and all your fortresses will be devastated,*
>   *even as Shalman devastated Beth-arbel*
>   *in the day of battle;*
>   *mothers were dashed to pieces on top of their sons.*
> [15]*Even so shall I do to you, house of Israel,*
>   *because of your great wickedness;*
>   *as quickly as the dawn*
>   *the king of Israel disappears.*

This rendering is in some respects more conservative, i.e. nearer the MT, than the RSV.

Since there seem to be no other such abbreviations of the names of Assyrian kings, the identification of Shalman with Shalmaneser III, to whom Jehu paid tribute, or Shalmaneser V, who besieged Samaria, though it was left to his successor Sargon to capture it, must be considered very

[1] See additional Note on the text at the end of the chapter.

doubtful. On the whole moderns are inclined to see in him Shalmanu, a contemporary Moabite king, cf. NBD *ad loc.* Beth-arbel will have been a town in Gilead. No convincing identification of it has yet been made.

The dictum – which is attributed on inadequate evidence to Oliver Cromwell – "Trust in God and keep your powder dry" has often been derided. Especially the Christian perfectionist has seen in it a supremely subtle form of unbelief. But such in fact seems to be the general outlook of the Old Testament. It is taken for granted there that Israel will take and use the normal weapons of defence available to them, but trust in warriors and weapons is always condemned in strong terms.

Much Christian pacifism is vitiated because it is not really based on trust in God; rather it reveals a pathetic belief that the weapons of non-violence have an almost magic force if only they are resolutely used. In these matters the individual Christian is bound to seek his Lord's will, but once he puts his trust in a method rather than in his Lord he will find that the means he uses to defend himself will also bring about his ruin.[1]

Obviously the particular principle here enunciated has its more general application. More and more in our affluent age the churches of the West are seeing in money a substitute for spirituality. We are expected to make use of the normal things of this life in the service of God. This applies to all forms of riches, which we are never called on to despise (Lk. 16:1–13). But it is the end of all true spirituality once we begin to put our trust in these things.

The Love of God as Father of His People

As in 10:11, so here in 11:1 God looks back to the beginnings of His people.

> [1]*When Israel was but young I loved him*
> *and out of Egypt did I call My son.*
> [2]*The more I called them*
> *the more they went from Me –*
> *they kept on slaying offerings for the Baalim,*
> *making sacrifices smoke to idols.*
> [3]*But it was I who taught Ephraim to walk,*
> *taking them up in My arms,*
> *but they did not know that I healed them.*
> [4]*With humane cords I drew them,*
> *with loving ropes;*
> *I treated them*
> *as one that lifts up the yoke upon their jaws,*
> *and I bent down to him and fed him.*

---

[1] It should be clear that there is no reference here to those who think that it is better to lose one's life than to take the life of another.

⁵*He returns to the land of Egypt,*
and it is the Assyrian that is his king,
because they refused to repent.[1]
⁶*The sword will whirl in his cities*
and will destroy †to the full†,
†and they will eat what they have prepared for themselves†.
⁷*My people †will give itself pains† to turn to Me,*
and to Me will they cry †because of the yoke†,
which they cannot lift by their united power.
⁸*How can I give you up, Ephraim,*
how deliver you up, Israel?
How can I make you as Admah,
how treat you as Zeboim?
My heart has changed within me;
all My compassion grows warm and tender.
⁹*Shall I not carry out My fierce anger?*
Shall I not return to destroy Ephraim?
for I am a Mighty One[2] *and not man,*
Holy in your midst.
Shall I not come to destroy?
¹⁰*After the* LORD *they will go.*
He will roar like a lion;
When He roars there will come trembling
His sons from the west;
¹¹*they will come trembling like birds from Egypt*
and like doves from the land of Assyria,
and I shall cause them to dwell in their homes –
oracle of the LORD.

Though the tendency of expositors is to take these eleven verses as a unit – the Heb. quite correctly makes the chapter division after v. 11 – it is very doubtful whether this is the case. In vv. 10 f. we have the eschatological resolution of the tension expressed in the main oracle, but we may be allowed to doubt whether it was from the first part of it. Then it is hard to believe that vv. 4–7 do not belong elsewhere. The picture in v. 4 looks back rather to a passage like 10 : 11, for it is speaking of the people as oxen, not as God's son. Though He has had to lead or drag them, the cords He has used are rather such as would be used for men than for beasts, and His ropes have had a loving purpose. Though He had to place a yoke on them, He always saw to it that it did not rub their jaws, and He was careful that they had their food in due season.

It is equally hard to believe that vv. 5–7 are a continuation of either v. 3

[1] Literally "turn" or "return".
[2] The Heb. is *El*, not *Elohim*, which seems to stress God's might.

or 4. In my translation I have contented myself in following Rudolph, for the Heb. of these verses refuses to create a coherent whole; we have little or no help from the versions, and no scholar has produced emendations which have been accepted with any enthusiasm. It may very well be true, as suggested by T. H. Robinson, that we have here some broken fragments of oracles that can never be restored.

AV, RV render in v. 5 "he shall not return into the land of Egypt", but this is a direct contradiction of 8:13. The negative belongs in changed form to the end of the preceding verse. Quite evidently a fair number of Israelites in their despair sought refuge in Egypt before the Assyrian destruction could be carried through. It is quite possible that some at least of that strange community at Elephantine on an island in the Nile near the modern Aswan consisted of the descendants of Israelite rather than Judean refugees.[1]

The remainder of this chapter forms one of the most beautiful passages in Hosea. We need not find the slightest difficulty in Israel's being called Jehovah's son and not His wife. In a book of so many brief and normally unconnected oracles, with their wealth of metaphors and pictorial imagery, it is worse than pedantic to see a contradiction. In addition the picture of Israel as Jehovah's son is much older than Hosea (cf. Exod. 4:22 f.) and was probably always more popular than that of the wife.

We may, however, with some probability go farther. At this stage of the book we cannot avoid the feeling that we are in the eventide of Hosea's activity, with the long shadows of Assyria falling over doomed Samaria. Earlier I expressed my very strong doubt whether Gomer, Hosea's faithless wife, ever responded to his love. Certainly we have not found the least suggestion in any oracle that this had been the case. If that is so, we should try to visualize Hosea's home in which his love was strenuously rejected and in all probability mocked. Under such circumstances he will have come to realize that however suitable a picture marriage may be of God's covenant with His people it cannot of itself convey the concept of the life and character that God seeks in His people.

Though true marriage demands loyalty and love it can never mean the swallowing up of the character of the one in that of the other. Rather the two fuse in harmony, as each is subject to the same Lord and God. So while Gomer's marriage could speak to the people of the love and loyalty that God expected from His people, He had to find a supplementary picture as well. This was admirably suggested by that of father and son. Especially in the Semitic world it was taken for granted that the son would show the characteristics of his father and be the doer of his will as no servant could ever be. Doubtless fathers were as often disappointed as they are now, but at least this remained the standard to be expected.

Hosea uses this picture very circumspectly, for all too often in heathen

[1] Cf. p. 134.

circles the fatherhood of a god was understood in the crudest materialistic way, as we know especially from the stories of the Greek heroes. Hence in v. 1 there is no suggestion of God's creation of Israel. Alas, however, the contrast between the toddler and the grown man grew ever more marked. Whatever one does or does not expect from a son, he should know his father's character and nature. But Israel throughout its religious history insisted on confounding Jehovah with the Baalim, the nature gods worshipped by their heathen neighbours.

It is far from easy to interpret vv. 8 f. with certainty. The most popular exegesis suggests that God's love is so great that it will overcome His righteous anger and so He will at least not exact the full penalty. This is an obviously attractive interpretation for the modern man, but it is questionable whether it has any place in Scripture, especially in the Old Testament. In addition, so to understand Hosea is to introduce an intolerable tension into his message, a contradiction which finds no solution.

Clearly enough Hosea portrays a conflict within God Himself, between His wrath over evil done and His love which looks back to the beginnings of Israel's history. But this conflict finds its solution, as in ch. 3, in an essentially eschatological event, i.e. the restoration of Israel from exile and its reunion with Judah. I feel compelled, therefore, to follow T. H. Robinson, among others, in his exegesis and translate v. 9 as a series of questions. That is surely the force of the stress on the might and holiness of God. Man, especially where his son is involved, may show himself weak and change. He may show favour, even if favour is not deserved and there is no turning from the old paths. The translation "for I am God and not man" hardly does full justice to the Hebrew. The use of *El*, which can hardly be explained by the needs of the metre, rather than of *Elohim,* surely suggests that it is a particular attribute of God that is being stressed, viz. His strength and might in contradiction to man's weakness and instability. This seems to be borne out by the addition of holy. God's ways are not man's ways, however much man might like them to be, and God's thoughts are not man's. Because God can see the end from the beginning, because the centuries of man's sinning, suffering and travail are as but a few moments in His presence, He is not bound to these actions which man loves so much, but which only postpone a solution to the future.[1]

So then God would come to destroy what was left of the glory of His people, but He would destroy in love. The outcome of that love is seen in vv. 10 f. – it is of no practical importance whether we regard them as an integral part of the preceding or merely as a suitable ending. Some time – when matters not – the roaring of God will be heard. As in Amos 1:2, the

---

[1] Rudolph stresses vv. 10 f. and on the basis of them justifies the usual translation of v. 9. I feel he underestimates the whole concept of exile, equated with Sheol and death in 13:14. It seems unlikely that his hearers would see in an eschatological restoration from exile a mitigation of God's anger.

lion's roar of God speaks of His rising in judgment, but now it is not against Israel but against the nations of the world. Once again it matters not when or against whom. When God arises to judgment, those who have held and enslaved Israel have no power left.

On swift wing like the bird His people are gathered to Him. The choice of the dove and the *tsippor*, which though a general term seems to be used more especially of smaller birds, stresses the insignificance of those who return. On the other hand, their trembling stresses that we are in the realm of grace. This return is not the fruit of good works; the remnant to be spared and resettled cannot forget that, though they are dealing with the one who has called Himself Husband and Father of Israel, He is also the righteous judge both of them and of all men

Here then in this oracle we have possibly the finest presentation in the Old Testament of the tension between the love and justice of God. An answer is not given, for the time was not yet ripe for that, but the prophet did see clearly that whatever answer the future might hold it would not compromise either of these attributes of God, who is the Mighty One and Holy.

JACOB AND HIS DESCENDANTS

In the Hebrew 11:12 stands as the first verse of Hos. 12. It is in fact closely connected with 12:1, and, while there is no direct link with what follows, the general agreement of thought justifies the position of this short oracle (11:12; 12:1). The second half of 11:12 is very difficult, and we do not really know whether Judah is being praised or condemned. I have simply followed the general lines of RSV in my rendering

> ¹²*Ephraim has surrounded Me with lying,*
> *and the house of Israel with deceit;*
> *but Judah is still known by God*
> *and is faithful to the Most Holy One.*
> ¹*Ephraim herds the wind*
> *and chases the east wind all day long;*
> *imposture and violence multiply.*
> *At one moment they make a covenant with Assyria,*
> *at another they bring oil to Egypt.*

The deceit that Israel is here particularly charged with is political (cf. 5:13, 7:11, 8:9). Not only was Israel unfaithful to Jehovah by his political entanglements, but he was unfaithful in his unfaithfulness. The imperfects in 12:1b justify my translation. There was continual shilly-shallying between the two great powers, Assyria and Egypt. In one of his most striking metaphors Hosea compares such doubly deceitful policy with a shepherd who would seek to pursue the winds or chase the east wind to add it to his flock, which scatters in all directions. D. J. McCarthy has pointed out that oil was

F

a generally recognized element in the making of a covenant.[1]

It is likely that 12:2–14 consisted of at least three independent prophecies (vv. 2–6, 7–9, 10–14), but they have been bonded together by the double mention of Jacob.

> [2] *The LORD has an indictment against Judah*
> *to punish Jacob[2] according to his ways*
> *and to requite him according to his deeds.*
> [3] *In the womb he had hold on his brother's heel,*
> *in his maturity he strove with God.*
> [4] *He strove with the angel and prevailed;*
> *weeping he implored him.[3]*
> *At Bethel He would meet us*
> *and there He would speak with us.*
> [5] *But Yahweh, the God of hosts,*
> *Yahweh is His name!*
> [6] *But as for you, by the help of your God, repent!*
> *Keep loyal love and justice*
> *and hope always in your God.*

In v. 2 almost all moderns (but not RSV!) substitute Israel for Judah. Though the change is superficially almost obvious, it does seem to miss the real meaning of the oracle. Is Jacob here being praised or blamed? Surely the latter. As I see it, Judah who is not really under consideration, is mentioned instead of Israel, to make it clear that this is not one of Israel's peculiar sins. It was shared by Judah and existed before the break-up of Solomon's kingdom.

It is not clear whether *in the womb he had hold on his brother's heel* merely stresses Jacob's self-assertiveness, or whether we should render "he supplanted his brother", or "he overtook his brother". I feel the first is the more likely, but it is not very important; the real stress lies on the striving with God, which cannot be justified. Jacob felt he had to have his own way, if not by strength, then in his weakness. Israel (*Yisra'el*) means "God strives". Though He had to cripple Jacob to do it, God triumphed. But many have thought of the name as meaning "He that strives with God". This is no name of honour, though clearly many in Israel so understood it. Note that while he strove with God he wept and implored his brother. How human! They stressed that one of the immediate results was that God met with Jacob at Bethel, thereby confirming His earlier promise to him (Gen. 35:1–7). What on God's part was an act of sheer grace they evidently

---

[1] V.T., Vol. XIV (1964), pp. 215–21.

[2] There has been much study of these Jacob passages recently, cf. V.T., Vol. X (1960), pp. 272 *seq.*; Vol. XIII (1963), pp. 245 *seq.*; Vol. XVI (1966), pp. 53 *seq.*, pp. 137 *seq.* and literature there mentioned.

[3] "Him" is more likely to refer to Esau than to God.

interpreted as the result of Jacob's assertiveness. From that followed for them the certainty that the same blessing was theirs as descendants of Jacob: *At Bethel He would meet us and there He would speak with us* (no change in the Hebrew is involved in this rendering).

Most of Israel's sin and falling-short can be led back to the conviction, which is equally prevalent in the Church, that election, revelation and covenant in some way and measure put God under our control, and so there are things He must do for us. Though there was almost certainly an element of bribery in the popular concept of sacrifice condemned by Hosea and the other eighth-century prophets, the cultus was certainly in addition thought of as a reminder to God of His covenant *obligations*.

Hosea's only answer to the completely false concept of God that had poisoned the people ever since the time of Jacob was a reminder of whom Jacob had striven with. *But Yahweh the God of hosts, Yahweh is His name!* How foolish, how presumptuous! If God in the utmost weakness of manhood could triumph over all the hate of men and the forces of evil on the cross, how can puny man hope to *extort* anything from Him? Repentance and obedience are the only possibilities left for Ephraim. In v. 6 we have a foreshadowing of Mic. 6:8.

Next, in vv. 7–9, follows yet another exposure of Israel's sin, this time revealed by his completely false set of values. If our concept of God is entirely wrong our values are bound to be wrong too.

> [7]*A Canaanite!*[1] *In his hands are false scales;*
> *he loves to exploit.*
> [8]*And Ephraim says, "But I have grown rich;*
> *I have gained wealth for myself.*
> *All the fruit of my labours has caused nothing*
> *that could be reckoned to me as iniquity."*
> [9]*But I am the* LORD *your God*
> *from the land of Egypt;*
> *I shall make you live once again in tents*
> *as in the days of the appointed feast.*

When we speak of the Phoenicians we are merely using the Greek name for the Canaanites. This identity is very often overlooked because we use the name normally only for those Canaanites who inhabited the narrow strip of coast along the foothills of the Lebanon range. Geographical necessity forced them to become a primarily commercial people, and so Canaanite is used a number of times in the Old Testament with the meaning of merchant or trader. Here Hosea uses it to stress that the wealth of which Israel was so proud had been obtained at the cost of lowering the nation to the level of the people they had been commanded by God to drive out and exterminate.

[1] i.e. trader.

Even today we have not freed ourselves from the idea that material prosperity is of necessity a sign of God's blessing. Like Israel, we tend to judge our relationship with God by the number of what we are pleased to call His blessings to which we can lay claim. No amount of prosperity can undo the destruction of character by a life lived in the light of false ideals and methods. V. 9 seems to take up 2:14 again. The booths of tabernacles, for presumably this is intended by "the appointed feast", were intended to remind Israel of the humility of its glorious beginning. Now back it would have to go to the wilderness experience of exile, there to learn a true set of values.

Finally, in vv. 10–14 the faithfulness and grace of God are stressed in contrast with the people's ingratitude.

> ¹⁰*I have repeatedly spoken by the prophets;*
> *it was I who multiplied vision*
> *and through the prophets presented Myself.*
> ¹¹*But when †they revealed† iniquity,*
> *they were considered worthless*
> *In Gilgal they sacrifice to †demons†,*
> *so their altars will be like heaps of stones*
> *on the furrows of the field.*
> ¹²*Jacob fled to the fields of Aram,*
> *and Israel did slave service for a wife,*
> *and for a wife he guarded (sheep).*
> ¹³*And by a prophet the* LORD *brought up Israel from Egypt,*
> *and by a prophet was he guarded.*
> ¹⁴*Ephraim has provoked (Him) most bitterly,*
> *so his bloodguilt will He leave upon him,*
> *and his reproach his* LORD *will return to him.*

We should not forget that Amos has earlier declared that the prophets were an outstanding evidence of God's grace to Israel (Amos 2:11), and this is echoed here by Hosea. They were the evidence of God's continuing care over His people.

If MT is correct with its mention of Gilead, cf. 6:8, then two sanctuaries, one either side of the Jordan, are taken as representative. More likely only Gilgal is mentioned, possibly because the oracle was given there. In any case we have a deliberate assonance, Gilgal being taken up by *gallim* (heaps of stones), just as *sedim* (demons) is by *sadai* (field).

Then the true greatness of Jacob is brought out. It was not in his striving with God, but in his humble and trusting service with Laban, his scheming uncle, in Aram. Hosea's words were sure to have called to his hearers' minds the opening of the great confessional thanksgiving, "An Aramean ready to perish was my father" (Deut. 26:5). And just as Israel's ancestor was a shepherd, so Moses, the greatest of the prophets, learnt to be a shepherd.

Our standard translations strangely ignore the verbal parallel between the end of v. 12 and of v. 13. As Asaph expressed it, "Thou didst lead Thy people like a flock by the hand of Moses and Aaron" (Psa. 77:20).

Faced with the grace of God, Israel insisted on emulating his ancestor by resistance and provocation and not by humble trust, so his fate was sure.

Rudolph sees in this oracle a further condemnation of Jacob and hence places vv. 12 f. before vv. 10 f. While the necessity for his flight to Aram arose out of his own self-centred conduct and lack of faith, the flight itself and his conduct in Padan Aram are never criticized anywhere else, so the contention is not likely to be correct.

THE END OF EPHRAIM

Though a number of different oracles can be recognized in ch. 13, it forms a coherent whole.

> ¹ *Whenever Ephraim spoke, men trembled;*
> *he was a leader in Israel.*
> *Then he incurred guilt through Baal – and died.*
> ² *And now they go on sinning,*
> *making for themselves molten images,*
> *idols according to their understanding,*
> *all of them craftsman's work.*
> *They are saying, "Sacrifice to these";*
> *men kiss bulls.*
> ³ *Therefore they shall be as an early morning cloud*
> *and as dew that goes away early,*
> *as chaff swirling up from the threshing floor,*
> *as smoke through a lattice.*

Though in v. 2 the text is undoubtedly corrupted beyond certain mending, the general meaning is clear enough. Except for a time towards the end of the period of the Judges, when they had suffered very heavy losses, first at the hands of the Gileadites under Jephthah and then in the two defeats at Eben-ezer (I Sam. 4:3, 10), Ephraim was indubitably the strongest and most influential tribe in Israel. Even Solomon, when he divided up the country for administrative purposes, seems to have respected the borders of Ephraim (I Ki. 4:8). Neither the Hebrew tense nor the context will allow us to understand *then he incurred guilt through Baal* of the insidious Baalization of Jehovah worship which had been active in Israel from the conquest on. Some definite action at a given moment in time is indicated. The only one that seems to suit is Jeroboam's making of his golden bulls. Hosea knew that they were no accident; the manner of the disruption of the kingdom led inescapably to the open corruption of religion. Cut off from the true monarchy and with his sanctuaries defiled, Ephraim died. It is true that there were still outward signs of life, but let us look at the reality: man-made images hailed as "God"; men denying their high calling to the image and likeness of God by honouring bull-images. Where human wisdom and understanding are so debased, national existence becomes as the early morning cloud and the dew, as the chaff cloud swirling over the threshing-floor or the smoke curling out of the ventilation hole – one moment there and another gone.

> ⁴*I have been Yahweh your God*
> *from the land of Egypt,*
> *and you know no God besides Me;*
> *besides Me there is no Saviour.*
> ⁵*It was I who shepherded you in the wilderness,*
> *in a land of fever heat.*
> ⁶*The better they fed and the more satisfied they were,*
> *the more their heart was lifted up;*
> *therefore they forgot Me.*
> ⁷*So I shall be to them as a lion;*
> *as a leopard by the way I shall lurk.*
> ⁸*I shall encounter them as a she-bear robbed of her young;*
> *I shall tear open their breasts,*
> *and there †the dogs will devour† them;*
> *the wild beasts will tear them in bits.*
> ⁹*I have destroyed you, Israel,*
> *who can help you?*
> ¹⁰*Where is now your king,*
> *that he may save you from all your enemies,*
> *and your rulers, those of whom you said,*
> *"Give me a king and lords"?*
> ¹¹*I give you a king in My anger*
> *and take him away in My wrath.*

Here too we find an echo of Amos. He had shocked his hearers by saying, "You only have I known of all the families of the earth: therefore I will visit upon you all your iniquities" (Amos 3:2). Hosea expresses this thought in even more drastic form.

Whatever the systematic theologian may wish us to believe, there is no real abstract knowledge of God. We know Him only in the measure He has revealed Himself, and this revelation becomes a reality only in the measure that the Holy Spirit makes it part of our experience. It is the experience of all of us that a truth that had been mentally grasped for years may suddenly become a transforming power through the work of the Spirit. It is the difference between knowing about God and knowing Him. Truth unresponded to means spiritual destruction. Material suffering, though it may seem to involve a contradiction of the revealed character of God, is often a supreme expression of His love. We are all apt deliberately to forget the teaching of Heb. 12:3–11. The ever-present Gentile dislike of the Jew frequently finds an expression in saying that the sufferings of the Jews show how bad they must be. That is true – just as bad as the Gentiles! But they also show how greatly God must love them.

There is hardly need to stress the dangers of prosperity. There is not much good to be said for "crisis Christians", but there are few of us who do not relax our zeal, vigilance and prayer when all seems to be set fair. The great Socialist fallacy is that sin and vice are the result of outward circumstances; once they become perfect, so we are told, man will be perfect, too.

We studied vv. 9–11 earlier (cf. p. 130). For the present context it is only necessary to note that Hosea maintains that God used precisely that clement in Israel, viz. the monarchy, to destroy Israel, which Israel hoped would make it in some measure independent of God.

> [12] *Ephraim's iniquity is collected,*
>   *his sin laid up in store.*
> [13] *The pangs of childbirth come upon him –*
>   *he is an unwise son;*
>   *for this is no time*
>   *for standing in the mouth of the womb.*
> [14] *Shall I ransom them from the power of Sheol?*
>   *Shall I redeem them from death?*
>   *Where are your plagues, death?*
>   *Where is your destruction, grave?*
>   *Repentance is hid from My eyes.*
> [15] *Though he flourish as †a reed plant†,*
>   *the east wind, the LORD's wind, will come,*
>   *coming up from the wilderness,*
>   *and his spring will be parched.*
>   *He will strip the treasury*
>   *of all its precious things.*
> [16] *Samaria must bear her guilt,*
>   *for she has rebelled against her God.*
>   *They will fall by the sword;*
>   *their babes will be dashed to pieces*
>   *and their pregnant women ripped up.*

The apparently very mixed metaphor of v. 13 suggests that just as a baby may refuse at the last moment to leave the womb, so at the last critical chance given it Israel refuses to turn to God. Assuming that the conjectural translation adopted by RSV is correct, we are asked to recognize that Israel's few remaining signs of prosperity were like those of a green reed in a swampy patch of ground (a pun on Ephraim is involved), but almost as soon as the desert wind, the *chamsin* or *shaarav*, begins to blow the swamp dries up and the reed is withered. Is there, however, in spite of all this a last whisper of hope in the passage?

In dealing with 11:9 I followed T. H. Robinson in translating, "Shall I not carry out My fierce anger? shall I not return to destroy Ephraim?" – for Hosea never gives any grounds for doubting that God will execute His judgment, however great His love, unless, of course, judgment is averted by repentance. Here, however, in v. 14 the position is different, for if hope is being held out it is of deliverance by resurrection from national death. This would be no contradiction of the certainty of judgment, but an affirmation of it.

We must accept it as a fact that we are faced with a major problem of interpretation, where the text helps us not at all. We must let ourselves be guided by our subjective estimate of the message as a whole. Instead of the translation offered above, we may, so far as the Hebrew is concerned, render, "I will ransom them from the power of Sheol: I will redeem them from death." The rest of the verse is no help in deciding. There is virtually universal agreement that we must leave the AV rendering and, in agreement with LXX and Paul (I Cor. 15:55), translate, "O death, where are thy plagues? O grave, where is thy destruction?" (RV).[1] But this can equally mean that God is deriding the power of death, or that He is summoning it to do its work. The final clause, *Repentance is hid from My eyes* (many render with uncertain propriety "resentment" or "compassion"), may mean that God will not see Ephraim's repentance, even if it comes, or that God Himself will not think of changing His mind. On the other hand, it could mean that the promise of salvation from death is immutable. There is no consensus of exposition to guide one. On the side of hope may be placed the ancient versions, AV, RV, Cheyne (Cam. B), T. H. Robinson, Weiser, G. A. F. Knight (T. Com.); on the side of doom, RSV, Harper (ICC), G. A. Smith, Horton (Cen. B.), Moffatt, P. R. Ackroyd (Peake), Martin-Achard, Rudolph, J. B. Phillips; Hadjiantoniu in NBC is clearly undecided.

Most reluctantly I feel compelled to agree that there is no hope being expressed here. The door of mercy stands open for Israel as long as Israel exists, as indeed the next chapter assures us. But once the gates of Sheol close on the nation it is for later voices to say whether there is hope or not. It is the same problem as faces the Christian when he considers the fate of the individual. He may find one and another passage in Scripture which make him believe that there may yet be hope for the sinner beyond the grave. But there is no passage which permits him to preach that there is, for were he to do so he might destroy the last glimmer of hope for repentance in this life. So surely it was also with Hosea, even though God might,

---

[1] Paul's use of this verse in the context of Christian resurrection is no indication of how it should be understood in the context of Israel's sin.

through the very ambiguity of the oracle, hold out hope once Samaria had fallen.

THE FINAL APPEAL

Ch. 14 could come from any period of Hosea's activity. Its position at the end of the book is most suitable, although it was probably spoken considerably earlier in his prophetic ministry. There is absolutely no merit in the suggestion that it comes from a later hand, and there is no shred of proof for it.

After the categorical affirmation that Israel must go down to Sheol (13:14) and the pregnant picture of Samaria's destruction (13:15, 16), we are given this beautiful picture of the outstretched hands of the everlasting mercy. It reminds us of our Lord's words, "How often would I have gathered you . . . but you would not."

We first hear the plea of the prophet as he speaks in God's stead, *Turn, Israel, to the* LORD *your God, for you have stumbled through your iniquity*. How truly Faber sang:

There is no place where earth's sorrows
  Are more felt than up in heaven;
There is no place where earth's failings
  Have such kindly judgment given.

Here is Israel, broken and on the verge of ruin, going into exile or already there; yet God's word comes, *You have stumbled*. We are reminded of Paul's words, "Did they stumble that they might fall? God forbid" (Rom. 11:11). What to man is sin abounding (compare popular judgments on the Jew) is to God a stumbling. It is a stumbling through their iniquity, their crookedness of character. The man crooked in body finds it hard to avoid stumbling; for the crooked in soul it is even more difficult. Though God may send Israel from his land, He does not send him from His presence. He has only to turn to find Him there with outstretched hands (cf. Isa. 65:2).

There will always be room for new books on the Atonement for no theologian has yet been able to bring all the factors involved into true Scriptural balance. One point that is so often overlooked is that the reconciliation God has wrought in Christ (II Cor. 5:19) is not only operative for all men (Rom. 5:18 f.), though men may refuse it, but that in fact the work of the cross was effective backwards as well as forwards. This is exemplified especially in the history of Israel. There is never suggestion made that the repenting man and the repenting nation would not find acceptance with God. If any asked how this could be, the answer was that the ineffective sacrifices received efficiency from the sacrifice to which they looked forward.

> 2 *Take with you words*
> *and turn to the* LORD.
> *Say to Him,* †"*Our God*†,
> *completely take away iniquity,*
> *that we may receive good*
> *and offer as recompense*
> †*the fruit*† *of our lips.*
> 3 *We will not look to Assyria to save us,*
> *nor will we ride on horses,*
> *nor will we say any more 'Our God',*
> *to the work of our hands;*
> *for in Thee the orphan finds compassion.*"

Israel is to compare himself to an orphan, because while strictly speaking *yatom* means precisely what orphan means to us, in its Biblical usage it obviously implies also a lack of relations who could act as protectors.[1] The orphan boy taken under the roof of a wealthy and powerful uncle and given the standing of a son of the house would not have been called a *yatom*. Israel implies that every protection has gone. Human protectors (Assyria), human means of protection (war-horses) and man-made religion (the work of our own hands) have vanished.

When Phillips renders "And we will ride no more on Egypt's horses" he is merely making explicit what is assumed to be the meaning by some commentaries. He is, however, probably wrong. The time was long past when Egypt held a special place as a supplier of horses (cf. II Ki. 18:23). Since cavalry had not really been developed by this time, horses probably stand for the horse-drawn chariots which played such an important part in ancient warfare. Hosea here stands in the same tradition as Psa. 51:16, 17. Not sacrifice, but prayer from the repentant heart is called for. Passages such as these do not refer merely the fact that sin and guilt offerings did not avail for deliberate and persistent sin (Num. 15:30 f.). "It is impossible that the blood of bulls and goats should take away sins" (Heb. 10:4) is not a New Testament discovery.

> 4 *I shall heal their apostasy;*
> *I shall love them of My own free will,*
> *now that My anger has turned from them.*
> 5 *I shall be as the dew to Israel,*
> *that he may blossom as the lily*
> *and may strike his roots (deep) as Lebanon.*
> 6 *His shoots will spread out;*
> *his splendour will be as the olive tree,*
> *and his fragrance like that of Lebanon.*

[1] This applies equally to the Old Testament use of "widow".

The prayer of penitence is answered by God Himself. While He promises to heal the results of their apostasy, He makes it clear that it is an act of sheer grace. The "freely" of the English versions does not make it clear enough that it is through an act of God's free will, unforced by an outward confession of sin, whether or not it represents an inward reality. We may not interpret this as meaning that God's grace is dependent on whether He is angry with us or not. C. H. Dodd has said very well, "While there is a tension, not wholly resolved, between the wrath and the mercy of God, it would be fair to say that in speaking of wrath and judgment the prophets and psalmists have their minds mainly on events, actual or expected, conceived as the inevitable results of sin; and when they speak of mercy they are thinking mainly of the personal relation between God and His people. Wrath is the effect of human sin: mercy is not the effect of human goodness, but is inherent in the character of God."[1]

It is important to note that God's promise seems to be a qualified one. *I shall be as the dew to Israel* is commonly misunderstood, partly through ignorance of the climate of Palestine, partly through forgetfulness of the situation of those to whom it was spoken. Generally it is taken to refer to that gracious refreshment that God's children are wont to experience in times of special stress and strain. In Palestine in any but an abnormal year the amount of rain between mid-April and the beginning of October is nil or negligible. Unless irrigation is used, all the main agricultural work, except harvesting, has to be carried out in the months of rain. During the dry period, however, when all seems parched and burnt up, the evening brings with it the west wind, the sea wind, and this carries inland low clouds of night mist (rather than the dew of the English versions). This gives sufficient moisture to fill out the melons, grapes and other "summer fruit".

The full restoration of Israel would have to await, metaphorically speaking, the coming of the rains, the day when the children of Israel would seek David their king (3:5). But even in the furnace of judgment and exile they would know refreshment from God. How far this may have been true of the exiles from the north we do not know. We have no record of a prophet's being raised up among them or of any spiritual revival. Certainly when the time came for Judah to go into exile, first to Babylonia and then in ever widening circles into the world, he repeatedly experienced seasons of refreshing from the Lord.

The emendation in RSV of poplar instead of Lebanon (v. 5) is quite unnecessary. The simplest explanation is that it is a reference to the cedars and other large trees of Lebanon.

RSV irons out the difficulties in vv. 7, 8 by skilful emendation; we may doubt, however, whether it is correct. In spite of Rudolph's protests against its improbability, v. 8 probably contains a dialogue between Ephraim and God. This is in part supported by some of the early versions (see ICC *ad loc.*)

[1] *The Epistle of Paul to the Romans*, pp. 49 f.

and has been defended recently by S. L. Brown in WC and J. Mauchline in Int. B. The following may be accepted as an approximate rendering:

> [7]*They will dwell again in His shadow;*
> *they will live again and increase;*
> *they will flourish like the vine,*
> *and be fragrant like the wine of Lebanon.*
> [8]*Ephraim (speaks), "What have I to do any more with idols?"*
> *"It is I who have responded to him and will look after him."*
> *"I am like an evergreen cypress!"*
> *"From Me comes your fruit."*

It seems that Israel is fascinated with his new glory, which is not to fade away. But he is reminded by God that it is the fruit of the new life that matters, not its outward glory.

The words of Hosea ben Beeri are ended, for there can be little doubt that some editor or scribe added 14:9 when the judgment had come upon Israel. We may take it that God in His mercy spared him the sight of the fulfilment of his words, and that he went down to the grave before the full weight of God's judgment fell on his people. The words of judgment were fulfilled to the letter, but what of the gracious promises of restoration? Before we try to answer this we should look at some further prophetic oracles concerning the North.

ADDITIONAL NOTES ON THE TEST

10:11, "His field". The MT "Judah" can hardly be said to fit the context and leaves the picture of Ephraim unfinished. The conjecture comes from Rudolph; see comment on p. 140.

11:6, "To the full." No consonantal alteration is involved. "And they will eat what they have prepared for themselves." This is based partly on LXX and Syr. ("they will eat") partly on the supposition of a scribal error due to mishearing – copying from dictation was undoubtedly practised at an earlier date.

11:7, A reference to ICC will give some idea of the variety of emendations proposed for a very difficult text. "Will give itself pains": Rudolph assumes a case of haplography for one letter. "Because of the yoke" is based on most of the old versions.

12:11, "They revealed." A change of one letter is involved. "To demons." Again only the change of one letter is really involved, for the absence of "to" in MT can easily be explained by haplography. Jerome obviously had it, for Vulg. has "to bulls", a rendering that might be accepted were it not another word than that used by Hosea for the bull images.

13:8, "The dogs will devour." The emendation follows partly LXX, partly Duhm. Again no great change is called for.

13:15, "A reed plant." This generally accepted emendation involves the dropping of one consonant, though this is not supported by the old versions.

14:2, "Our God." The metre seems to demand something of the sort; it involves the assumption that the second of two very similar words was accidentally dropped. "The fruit"; so LXX, Syr. It may be that we should render, "Instead of bulls the fruit of our lips."

CHAPTER XIV

THE GRACE OF GOD AND THE HARDNESS OF MAN

THERE ARE CERTAIN PROPHECIES INVOLVING THE NORTH which can best be ignored in our survey.

No more terrible picture of the last days of the Northern kingdom can be found than in Isa. 9:8–10:4; 5:24–30, but we have the impression that this is an oracle about Israel rather than to it. The same applies to Mic. 1:2–9. It was necessary for the self-confident in Judah to know that neither chance nor natural law were in operation in the North but God's will and judgments. Isa. 28:1–4 is once again an oracle against Israel, but it has come down to us in its application against the rulers of Jerusalem. We have no grounds, therefore, for affirming the vv. 5 f. were necessarily a promise to Israel. Indeed, they are almost certainly an independent oracle intended as a contrast to man's self-confidence.

There can be no reasonable doubt that once Samaria fell and its leaders had gone into exile the prophets in the South took up the name Israel, which the North had arrogated to itself, and applied it to the South as the only visible representative of the people of God. The one major exception to this will be mentioned later.

The one message of hope that Isaiah holds out to the North is in 9:1. Here the promise is that since judgment first fell on Galilee, so the Messianic light should first illumine it. We know how Matthew saw this promise being fulfilled (4:14 ff.). We need not doubt that many who heard the early preaching of Christ were descendants of those who had not been carried into exile by Tiglath-pileser III (II Ki. 15:29). No more than in Samaria was the whole population removed.

The position is quite different, when we come to Jeremiah. A little over a century after Samaria's downfall, after Josiah's reformation had been carried through in Judah, it would seem that Jeremiah began a ministry in those northern provinces that Josiah had been able to bring under his control, as Assyria in its turn slid down into the pit of extinction (II Chr. 34:6, 7). He preached to the remnants of old Israel left there and possibly through them to the exiles. The idea, still sometimes met, that the Assyrians had swept the north clean of its original Israelite inhabitants, can find no justification either in the general Assyrian customs of the time or in the express details of the capture of Samaria.

Older writers could not do justice to the hints scattered in Jeremiah's prophecies, for until the advance of knowledge about the ancient Near

East created by modern archaeology it was only a few who guessed that there were any considerable number of Israelites left in northern Palestine after the Assyrian deportations. It was not grasped that normally only the cream of the population was deported, and that the mixed immigrants brought in by Assyria (II Ki. 17:24; Ezr. 4:2) were a reluctant ruling *élite* over an Israelite majority.

True enough the Bible itself gave ample hints of the true state of affairs (e.g. Jer. 41:5; II Ki. 23:17; II Chr. 30:10, 11; 35:18), but there were few willing to give full weight to them. As far as rabbinic evidence went, more weight was laid on their calling the Samaritans "Cutheans" than on their virtual recognition of their Israelite origin, for they acknowledged that they were entitled to join in Jewish worship provided they accepted the southern approach to the Torah.

When archaeology revealed that Assyrian deportations were concerned only, or mainly, with the ruling classes, and that Sargon had actually removed only 27,270 or 27,290 after the capture of Samaria,[1] the true facts became clear, though there are still those ultra-conservatives who do not want to accept them. But liberal scholarship, which by this time was firmly in the saddle, was slow to apply this new knowledge. This was partly because a recognition that the Samaritans were in fact, and not only in their claims, genuine inheritors of the traditions of the North carries with it far-reaching consequences for many critical theories. There was further the factor that the prophecies of chs. 30, 31 were entirely, or for the most part, denied to Jeremiah, and therefore the mention of the house of Israel, Samaria and Ephraim in them was not felt to be of any special interest.

In Britain one of the first to point to the true facts of the case was A. C. Welch,[2] but his deductions were too extreme, and so there was a reaction away from them without a satisfactory answer being given to the problem he had raised. As far as Jeremiah was concerned, he maintained, and in this he has been partially followed by Pfeiffer,[3] that the oracles of 2:1–4:2 were addressed with only few exceptions to the North, i.e. that Jeremiah began his ministry by turning to the descendants of those with whom Hosea had pleaded in vain.

Elsewhere[4] I have argued against this view, but I recognize that 3:6–13 is indubitably a prophecy addressed to the North and not to Judah:

> [6]The LORD said unto me in the days of Josiah the king: "Have you seen what Apostasy Israel did? She went on every high hill and under every green tree and played the harlot there. [7]I thought, "After she has done all this, she will turn to Me," but she did not turn, and Treachery, her sister Judah, saw it. [8]She saw also that because of her adultery I sent away

---

[1] The figures vary in different inscriptions cf. ANET, pp. 284 f., DOTT. pp. 58 ff.
[2] Especially in *Jeremiah – His Time and His Work* (1928) and *Post-Exilic Judaism* (1931).
[3] *Introduction to the Old Testament*[2], pp. 493, 502.
[4] E.Q. Vol. XXX (1959), No. 4, p. 205, and Vol. XXXII (1960), No. 2, p. 111.

Apostasy Israel and gave her her writing of divorce. Treachery Judah, her sister, was not frightened but went and played the harlot as well. ⁹Harlotry came so easy to her that she polluted the land, playing the harlot with stone and tree. ¹⁰ In spite of all this Treachery, her sister Judah, did not return to Me with her whole heart, but only in pretence – oracle of the LORD."

¹¹And the LORD said to me: "Apostasy Israel has shown herself less guilty than Treachery Judah. ¹² Go and cry these words to the North and say: 'Repent, Apostasy Israel! – oracle of the LORD – No longer with angry face will I look on you, for loving and faithful am I – oracle of the LORD – I will not be angry for ever. ¹³Only recognize your guilt, that you rebelled against the LORD your God and squandered your love on strangers under every green tree, but did not obey My voice – oracle of the LORD'."

The message here is not that Israel may be forgiven because Judah has sinned worse, but that since Judah still exists, in spite of its greater sin, Israel might still hope for pardon. There is no suggestion that this is an oracle only nominally addressed to Israel in order to stir Judah to the enormity of its sin. Equally there is nothing to give the impression that it was sent to the Israelite exiles on the borders of the expiring Assyrian empire. No appeal can be made to *shubu* (v. 12), rendered "return" in RV, RSV. Its primary meaning is "turn", and then in contexts like this it means "repent". The oracle is primarily a promise of the renewal of God's grace, not of return from exile and the restoration of statehood.

It is the most natural inference, therefore, that as Josiah gradually extended his political power northwards over Samaria and at least eastern Galilee (II Ki. 23:15–20; II Chr. 34:6, 7) – religious interference implies political control – Jeremiah will have followed, bringing the gracious call to true repentance. There is nothing surprising in our having only inferential evidence for this ministry. The bulk of Jeremiah's oracles recorded for us form what was essentially the enlarged roll of Jer. 36:32, the object of which was the calling of Judah to repent. In this promises of grace to Israel would play no part, and the oracle in 3:6–13 owes its present position to its indirect condemnation of Judah.

Quite other is the position with the "Book of Comfort", as chs. 30, 31 are commonly called. This was originally an independent document in which isolated oracles have been arranged in an order which gives a fairly continuous message. The mention of "Israel and Judah" in 30:3, 4 underlines the importance of the North in this section, but since the introduction may have been added by the prophet at a later date it is no guide as to the original purpose of the book.

When we study the individual oracles of which the book is composed we find some of them were indubitably addressed to the North, and many of the others would suit the North as well as or better than Judah. Only the barest outline of the facts can be given.

Though 30:5–11 is sufficiently vague to be applicable to both kingdoms, the placing of Jacob in parallel to Israel strongly suggests that the oracle was addressed to the North. "David their king is reminiscent of Hos. 3:5. If, as here seems the more reasonable course, we follow LXX in 30:17, "You whom the hunters called an outcast, 'Our quarry! No one cares for her'" (Moffatt), and regard "Zion" in Hebrew as a scribal error – the change is small – 30:12–17 is also seen as an oracle to Israel.

The obscure promise in 30:21, which can hardly be Messianic, and which so carefully avoids the mention of a king, would suit the conditions of the North, which for over a century had been under the immediate rule of the foreigners who had been brought in by the Assyrian kings. In any case no special applicability to Judah has ever been suggested, so once again we may infer that 30:18–22 was addressed to Israel. The promise of 30:23–31:1 is too general for any inferences to be drawn, but it should be noted that it expressly includes the northern tribes (31:1).

It is useless to question that 31:2–6 is a promise of restoration to the North; the mention of Zion (31:6) only underlines (as did 30:9) that Israel's only hope lay in the acceptance of the Davidic king of God's choice and of the God-appointed sanctuary. 31:7–9 is also expressly addressed to Israel. The comparison in "the chief of the nations" (31:7) is between Israel and the nations, but it is not one that could have given any special pleasure to a patriotic Judean.

Unless on mainly subjective and apparently inadequate grounds we omit 31:14 as a later gloss, as do many commentators, we shall be safe in seeing a Judean oracle in 31:10–14, for it is virtually impossible to see Jeremiah suggesting the restoration of the northern priesthood in any form. There is, however, nothing in the promise that suggests the exclusion of the North from it.

Rachel's grave lay on the border between Benjamin and Ephraim at Zelzah, north of Ramah (I Sam. 10:2).[1] In spite of the views of Rudolph and Weiser, the most recent German commentators on the book, it seems unlikely that Jeremiah is depicting Rachel lamenting and weeping over the deportation of the northern exiles after the fall of Samaria. We must surely take as the basis of our interpretation of 31:15–17 the leading of the Benjamite captives northwards along the road past Rachel's tomb after the fall

---

[1] Quite apart from the clear statement that Zelzah was on the border of Benjamin, a site for Rachel's grave near Bethlehem would make nonsense of Saul's route. Even the statement in Gen. 35:19 is not without difficulties. If we allow Mic. 4:8 to interpret "the tower of Eder" (Gen. 35:21), it is part of or near Jerusalem, i.e. Jacob had not yet reached Jerusalem, to say nothing of Bethlehem, at the time of Rachel's death. It should not be forgotten that the name Ephrath or Ephrathah, is used of more than one place, cf. Psa. 132:6, I Chr. 2:24, 50. We must choose between a variant tradition as to the place of Rachel's burial or regard "which is Bethlehem" (Gen. 35:19) as a late scribal gloss.

G

of Jerusalem – a way that Jeremiah went in part (40:1) – for this seemed the end of Rachel's children indeed. If this is so, the oracle belongs to the southern section of the "Book of Comfort".

The next two oracles (31:18–20; 31:21, 22) clearly refer to the North, and 31:23–30 is equally clearly Judean. In the light of what follows we should specially note that Jeremiah seems to have added *the house of Israel and* (31:27) in the final form of the prophecy and so adapted a promise of restoration to Judah for the wider and predominantly northern setting of the "Book of Comfort".

The reverse seems to have happened, as we shall see, in the great promise of the new covenant (31:31–34), and so what was originally a promise to Israel has been widened to include Judah as well. The book ends with an oracle which is almost certainly Israelite (31:35–37) and another (31:38–40) which is indubitably Judean.

It is hard to avoid the conclusion that the "Book of Comfort" appeared in two editions, as did the scroll of judgment (36:2, 32). In its original form it will have been addressed to the North alone, but after the fall of Jerusalem it will have been expanded to cover the South as well. Judah could not be included in the promises until the judgment of God had gone into effect.

There are no grounds at all for suggesting that Jeremiah ever went to the far-distant exiles to give them God's word. Even on his long journeys to the Euphrates (13:1–7), if indeed we are intended to take them literally, he will still have been hundreds of miles distant from them. Nor is there any evidence that the prophecies might have been sent to them. An actual ministry by Jeremiah in Samaritan territory is far more likely, and it is significant that the verses that speak most clearly of returning exiles refer to them in the third person.

If we may argue from the analogy of the scroll of judgment, the writing of the "Book of Comfort", in contrast with the verbal utterance of the oracles, was made necessary by circumstances, and these are not far to seek. The defeat and death of Josiah at Megiddo in 609 B.C. brought with it the loss to Judah of all its territory outside its traditional boundaries. Pharaoh Neco's representatives in Samaria would have looked on a wandering Judean prophet with deep suspicion, thinking that his aim was political rather than religious. So all Jeremiah could do was to remind his former hearers by writing of the promises they had heard from him. Such a dating of the "Book of Comfort" will also allow us to place the composition of the promise of the new covenant, the climax of the book, in the early years of Jehoiakim, a time which other considerations seem to make imperative.[1]

THE NEW COVENANT

The prophetic oracle never seems to be averse to repetition, whenever this serves a purpose; so we are immediately struck by the fact that in

[1] I have dealt with these chapters more fully in E.Q. Vol. XXXVI (1964), Nos. 1, 2, 4.

31:31 the promise is made to *the house of Israel and the house of Judah* but in v. 33 only to *the house of Israel*, a term used exclusively of the northern tribes. Had Jeremiah been aiming at inclusiveness, there were a number of suitable terms to hand, e.g. Israel, all the families of Israel, all the seed of Israel. In the context we gain the impression that the promise was at the first deliberately confined to the North and then later extended to Judah, when circumstances made this desirable, viz. after the destruction of Jerusalem. This Jeremiah did by inserting *and the house of Judah* in v. 31, while the non-insertion in v. 33 permits us to recognize the original form and destination of the promise. The somewhat lengthy investigation of these chapters was intended to show that such an inference is not artificial but consonant with the general tenor of the "Book of Comfort".

This exegesis suggests – it could have been inferred from certain general principles – that the promise of a new covenant was not one of those time-less prophecies that could have been spoken at any time after the making of the first. It had to wait until the first had been, at least outwardly, dissolved by exile and the disappearance of national existence ("the bill of divorce-ment" of 3:8). It would seem, therefore, that J. Jocz, writing in New Testa-ment terms, oversimplifies when he says "The covenant at Sinai is therefore inoperative *de facto*, though *de jure* it is still in existence. . . . The 'new' covenant is therefore *not* a different covenant, but the original covenant established once and for all."[1]

There were certain major differences between God's treatment of Israel and Judah in their experience of exile; in fact they are so great that we are justified in regarding them as essentially of a different type. The major Judean deportation took place before the downfall of the state, and both Jeremiah (ch. 24) and Ezekiel (11:14–21) stress that it was an act of grace rather than of judgment on God's part. The exiles were relatively the best part of the nation, apart from exceptional individuals like Jeremiah, and they were removed that God's wrath might rage unchecked among the remainder. Nothing like this is suggested of the North, but rather the contrary. In addition the Judean deportees were settled in a comparatively limited area in Babylonia in contrast with the scattering of those from Israel (II Ki. 17:6). Even though it may have been his ultimate aim, which was never carried out, Nebuchadnezzar never placed them as a ruling class in an alien population, something which in the case of the Israelite exiles must have led to speedy assimilation. More important still is that, by accident or policy, Nebuchadnezzar left Judah an empty land, so that, once royal assent had been given by Cyrus, there was no major obstacle to a return. Had the descendants of the Israelite exiles returned they would have found their ancestral acres occupied by foreigners, who, although they came to regard themselves as Ephraimites, would have bitterly resisted any claim to them.

It seems clear, then, that though the same gracious promise was given to

[1] *A Theology of Election*, p. 117.

both Israel and Judah the fulfilment was to be the goal of different developments, i.e. it is not merely a question of the way in which the two groups responded to God's will. For present purposes it is sufficient to note this fact and to confine ourselves to Israel.

One of the features of the "Book of Comfort" is its lack of detailed condemnation, something that applies to 3:6–13 as well (this oracle may well have formed part of the first edition of this book). Such condemnation was not needed, for the Divine judgment that had rested on Israel for over a century was sufficiently eloquent. Jeremiah pleaded with them that this judgment should be accepted in penitence, so that the Divine favour might begin to work. It would seem that it was the repentance of those left in the land that would open the way for the exiles to return.

In its context the new covenant promise stands against a background very like that of the old covenant. Already Hosea had spoken of Israel's being allured into the wilderness (2:14) cf. p. 108. In the "Book of Comfort" the deliverance from Egypt is paralleled by return from exile and destruction of enemies (30:7, 8, 16). The promise of Exod. 19:4–6 finds its echo in the thrice-repeated "I will be their God, and they shall be My people" (30:22; 31:1, 33).

God's deliverance of Israel from Egypt preceded the covenant. The Exodus was the outcome of God's electing love and loyalty to the promises made to the patriarchs. The presupposition of the first covenant was "You have seen what I did to the Egyptians, and how I bore you on eagles' wings and brought you to Myself." So too the new covenant is not based on the old but on God's election of Israel and His deliverance of Israel from new servitude.

Hosea in his loyalty to his disloyal wife saw a picture of God's far greater loyalty to a much more disloyal Israel, and refused to acknowledge that God would ever give her up. History, as interpreted by Jeremiah, showed that the time did come when God gave Israel her bill of divorcement by destroying the northern kingdom and sending its leaders into exile, but His election love and loyalty to His promises did not cease. The covenant vanished, but the love and loyalty remained. I do not think it possible to maintain that the covenant with the northern tribes was *de jure* still in existence. If it was not for the North, we may well ask whether it really was for the South either. Much of our misunderstanding of the significance of the inter-testamental period springs from a too facile assumption about the continuance of the old covenant.

Jeremiah repeatedly uses Israel as a title for Judah, for the South was the only visible and viable evidence for the continuance of God's purposes in His people. Precisely, however, in the "Book of Comfort" he makes it clear that his use of Israel for the southern kingdom did not imply that God had cast off the North.

So far then as the northern tribes, who had arrogated the title of Israel to themselves, were concerned the covenant had ceased both *de facto* and *de jure*, but it was not the covenant that was important but the character of God that lay behind it. This character would re-create a covenant relationship once the indispensable prerequisite of repentance existed.

Because the covenant is the expression of the already existing election love of God and reveals it, there is no need for a new law – *torah*, or revelation of God's will. What was new was the application of it, inwardly and not outwardly, and this implied a new power as well. That is why with the first covenant willingness to accept it was sufficient (Exod. 19:8; 24:3), but with the second there must be the recognition of failure and impotence.

The reason given for a new covenant is simple, *forasmuch as they brake My covenant* (31:32, RV, mg). It has become fashionable to stress the one-sidedness of the Divine covenants. True enough, they are initiated and their terms fixed by Divine grace. In certain cases, e.g. the covenant with Noah (Gen. 9:8–17), there is no condition expressed or implied, but where there is a condition its breach is no light thing. It is forgivable, and is in fact forgiven, if there is repentance, but that forgiveness does not automatically restore the covenant. No amount of covenant renewal ceremonies in Israel could in fact renew the broken covenant, for that depended on God, not man.

Jeremiah is the prophet who stresses this more than any other. We have the question in 3:1 "You have played the harlot with many lovers; and would you return to Me?" Then there is the exhortation in 4:3 "Break up your virgin soil, and sow not among thorns," which implies a completely new beginning (see comments on Hos. 10:12).[1] Here, in the "Book of Comfort", Jeremiah says clearly: *forasmuch as they brake My covenant, so I had to lord it over them.*[2] In other words, the whole history of Israel from the golden calf on was lived out under the sign of a broken covenant. All God's dealings with Israel were in grace, even when that grace expressed itself in judgment, but for all that He was acting as a despotic ruler (a Baal), for this was the only way to handle them once the covenant had been broken. This helps us to understand why the history of Israel can largely be summed up in a series of irreversible acts expressive of sin and failure. With the promise of complete forgiveness the element of irreversibility vanishes, for complete forgiveness includes the removal of consequences.

Ezekiel too had his vision of the national resurrection of "the whole house of Israel" (37:11) – which here surely means both Judah and Israel – and of

---

[1] A fuller treatment will be found in E.Q., Vol. XXXII (1960), No. 2, pp. 109 ff., No. 4, pp. 217 f.

[2] *ve- 'anoki ba'alti bam*: the verb *ba'al* means literally to possess or rule over. It is used eleven times in contexts involving marriage, but in none of these is it followed by *be*. Since there is now general agreement that "for I am your master" (Jer. 3:14, RSV.) is the correct rendering of *ki 'anoki ba'alti bakem* it is impossible to justify a refusal to follow the same idiom in 31:32. It also saves us from having to assume a textual variant behind the LXX, for its rendering (cf. Heb. 8:9) is probably only a paraphrase of the rendering I have offered here.

the union of the two sundered brothers (37:15–28). Here, however, even more clearly than in Jeremiah, we are dealing with an eschatological event, with something that will not happen until God's prefect purposes go into fulfilment. There is no suggestion of a return before then, or apart from Judah.

GOD'S TRIUMPH IN ISRAEL

When we ask the question "Will God triumph in Israel?" we can only answer "Did Hosea triumph with Gomer?" He did all that human love could do, but it does not follow that he necessarily succeeded, much as our sentimentality would dearly like to believe that he did. Unless we argue from the rather questionable theological concept of "irresistible grace", from the doubtful postulate that because God had promised He was bound to carry out whether Israel repented or not, we cannot infer from Hosea that God of necessity triumphed in Israel except through a remnant.

It is a matter of historic fact that the only descendants of Israel we can identify with certainty – we have no space here for the many speculations that have occupied the minds of men[1] – are the Samaritans. They are the result of the intermarriage of the foreign settlers brought by Sargon (II Ki. 17:24), Esarhaddon (Ezr. 4:2) and Ashur-bani-pal (Ezr. 4:10) with the old Israelites. Once the amalgamation was carried through they never ceased to call themselves Ephraimites, and the rabbis have never really questioned the claim. The differences between them and the Jews are summed up in the Talmudic passage: "When will we accept them? When they deny belief in Mount Gerizim and confess Jerusalem and the resurrection of the dead." In other words they refused to recognize the hand of God in the return of Judah from exile, and they have kept "the envy of Ephraim" alive even down to our day, when they have become a rapidly dwindling remnant.

To begin with, that which Isaiah was to say to Judah (now bearing the title of Israel without challenge) was bound to be true also of the northern tribes, "A remnant shall repent, the remnant of Jacob, unto the mighty God. For though your people, O Israel, be as the sand of the sea (only) a remnant shall repent. Destruction is decreed, overflowing with righteousness" (Isa. 10:21 f.). It may very well be that, in the face of the North's stubborn refusal to accept God's will, God's purposes had to be finally fulfilled through the trickle of those who from time to time joined themselves to Judah under the monarchy (II Chr. 11:13–16, 15:9, 30:11, 35:18) and those few who will have joined themselves to the returning exiles in the time of Cyrus. We should not make light of the already mentioned differences between God's treatment of the Judean exiles and those from the North. Particularly significant is Hosea's and Jeremiah's silence about the length of the exile.

---

[1] What the representatives of these views are apt to forget is that, while we are grateful to the secular arts and sciences for any light they may throw on passages of Scripture, ultimately it is Scripture that decides its own interpretation. Neither in the Bible nor in the known background to the New Testament is there any support for these theories.

We accept implicitly the statement that "all Israel shall be saved" (Rom. 11:26), but we do not forget that "they are not all Israel who are of Israel" (Rom. 9:6).[1] If God accomplishes His purposes with a remnant from Judah, will it not be even more so with political Israel? It is fascinating how some – I have no idea what proportion – of those who hold firmly to the restoration of a political Israel have been driven by their own logic. The old traditional interpretation of Rom. 11:26 excluded the Jew except in so far as he had become a member of the Church, which was equated with Israel. Some supporters of the theory of a national Israel are maintaining that every person saved by Christ must ultimately be able to trace his descent from one of the twelve tribes.

It is far better to see in Hosea's oracles a glimpse into the mysteries of salvation caused by God's love and man's hardness of heart, mysteries that are only partially illumined even in the New Testament. It was surely a later scribe pondering on the mystery of God's love and man's refusal, of God's loyalty and man's disloyalty, of God's offer of privilege and man's refusal to pay its price, who added as an epilogue to the book: "Who is wise, let him understand these things; who is discerning, let him know them. For the ways of the Lord are right, and the righteous walk in them, but rebels stumble therein.'

[1] For a fuller study see my *The Mystery of Israel*.

BOOKS FOR FURTHER READING

This is neither a student's nor a specialist's reading list. It is merely an outline guide to those who want to read further. In most cases the books themselves will make suggestions for a wider literature. Where two works on the same theme are mentioned, the former is simpler. Those marked ★ are known to be out of print.

E. J. Young, *An Introduction to the Old Testament* (Tyndale Press).
H. L. Ellison, *Men Spake from God: Studies in the Hebrew Prophets* (Paternoster Press).
J. Bright, *A History of Israel* (SCM Press).
J. Skinner, *I & II Kings* (Cen. B.).★
J. Gray, *I & II Kings* (SCM Press).
R. F. Horton, *The Minor Prophets*, Vol. I. (Cent. B.).★
G. A. Smith, *The Book of the Twelve Prophets*, Vol. I (Hodder & Stoughton).★
J. Marsh, *Amos and Micah* (T.Com.).
S. R. Driver, *Joel and Amos* (Cam.B.).★
G. A. Knight, *Hosea* (T.Com.).
S. L. Brown, *The Book of Hosea* (WC).
W. R. Harper, *Amos and Hosea* (ICC).

INDEX

SCRIPTURE REFERENCES

(For brevity a shorter reference may be listed under a longer one)